ARGUMENTATION AND DEBATE

THE MACMILLAN COMPANY
NEW YORK · CHICAGO
DALLAS · ATLANTA · SAN FRANCISCO
LONDON · MANILA

IN CANADA
BRETT-MACMILLAN LTD.
GALT, ONTARIO

ARGUMENTATION
& DEBATE
Techniques of a Free Society

JAMES H. McBURNEY, *Professor of Public Speaking and Dean of the School of Speech, Northwestern University*

JAMES M. O'NEILL, *Professor of Speech and Chairman of the Department of Speech, Brooklyn College*

GLEN E. MILLS, *Associate Professor of Public Speaking and Director of Forensics, Northwestern University*

A Revision of *The Working Principles of Argument* by James M. O'Neill and James H. McBurney

New York · THE MACMILLAN COMPANY

PREFACE

This book is designed primarily for use in college and university courses in argumentation and debate and for all students interested in debating. Argumentation and debate are presented as techniques of a free society, as methods of bringing reasoned discourse to bear on personal and social problems for purposes of decision and action. Attention is given to school debating as an effective means of developing competence in advocacy.

Argumentation and debate is an old subject in the schools and colleges. It has been taught for many centuries, and the exercises in dialectic, disputation, and debate associated with it have engaged countless students. In this volume we have attempted to restate the best classical doctrine in the light of interpretations by many critics, both old and new. Throughout the book we have kept in mind the contemporary scene and the needs and interests of modern students as we understand them. We have also attempted to clarify some of the more vexed questions of principle and theory which persist in the literature of the subject to this day.

Much of the effective deliberation in our society is carried on through argumentation and debate. This has always been the case in a free society and always will be. We see no irreconcilable conflict between cooperative group procedures such as discussion or conference and argumentation and debate. If problems requiring group determination do not yield to discussion, if differences of opinion persist after our best efforts to achieve a consensus, debate is the only logical recourse in countless practical situations. Every member of a free society will profit by an understanding of argumentation and debate, and most persons who assume roles of leadership will find it indispensable if they are to discharge their responsibilities competently.

Competence in argumentation and debate includes the ability to see and state the issues in a controversy, to separate the relevant and significant from the unimportant, to appraise and use evidence and argument, to assess the logical responsibilities of an advocate, to recognize and expose sophisms and fallacies, to present a case and defend it, and to compose language in oral situations under the pressures of time and controversy. Such skills make high demands on any speaker or writer, but they pay important dividends in personal and social competence.

Skill in argumentation and debate is best developed by applying the principles of argument in oral and written exercises followed by competent criticism. We have included such exercises at the end of each chapter. These may easily be adapted and extended as circumstances require. Chapter XIX is designed especially for students who are interested in the problems of school and college debating.

This book is an extensive revision of *The Working Principles of Argument* by O'Neill and McBurney, first published in 1932. The primary responsibilities of authorship in the present volume are as follows: Mr. McBurney, Chapters II, VI, VIII, IX, X, and XVIII; Mr. O'Neill, Chapters I, IV, VII, XIV, and XVII; Mr. Mills, Chapters III, V, XI, XII, XIII, XV, XVI, and XIX.

CONTENTS

Chapter I · THE STUDY OF
ARGUMENTATION AND DEBATE

Argumentation is probably best defined as the art or activity by which one person, through the use of reasoned discourse, seeks to get other persons to believe or to do what he wants them to believe or to do. Argumentation uses language, discourse. It may be, of course, written language or speech. Whenever either in writing or in speech we seek to get other people to believe or to perform as we want them to, by the use of language which has a thread of reasoning running through it, we are using argumentation. Language may, of course, be used in purely emotional suggestion without using a line of reasoning to attempt to influence another person to believe or act. An example of this activity would be a situation in which A, knowing that B is listening in another room, sings a song or tells a story to C in the expectation that as B hears the song or the story it will arouse emotions in B which will influence him to conduct himself in the way desired by A. Such a use of language will fall outside the area of activity known as argumentation.

When we say that argumentation may have as its purpose either belief or action, we may be challenged by some people who say that, since either belief or action resulting from argument is a response to the stimuli of the arguer, and since all response necessarily involves action of some kind, either hidden or overt, it shows that we have one objective, namely, action, instead of either belief or action. This position results from the failure to make a sufficient distinction between overt behavior and the hidden action which is involved to greater or less degree when the hearer simply agrees privately to himself that the speaker is right. In other words, simple intellectual agreement which is not carried out in overt action should be distinguished from the action which results when the hearer does what the speaker wants him to do (such as contributing money, signing a petition, voting in the affirmative). Regardless of the psychological similarity of the action which is intellectual assent and the action which is open public performance of the act desired, it is clear that the rhetorical problem of the speaker or writer who is aiming at intellectual assent is very different from the rhetorical problem of the speaker or writer who is aiming at influencing conduct. For this reason it is held to be wise to distinguish in argumentation between belief and action as objectives.

Debate consists of opposing arguments on a given proposition between a supporting affirmative and an opposing negative. Debate may be carried on either in writing or in speech. One may be competent in written argument and, to a less degree in certain situations, in spoken argument without being competent in oral debate. When one sits in his study and writes an argument in favor of either side of a proposition, he need not be skillful in all the aspects of analysis, investigation, evidence, the forms of argument, fallacies, refutation, and the emotional control of himself and others, which are of primary importance in all spoken debate and of great, though of somewhat less importance, in written debate.

There is, however, another and quite separate way in which an understanding of argumentation and debate is highly beneficial to any member of a free society, even though he may never wish to practice either activity in order to influence other people. Every member of a free society is being subjected, some more and some less, to arguments that are aimed at him. Whether or not we are practitioners of argumentation and debate, we are all more or less constantly on the receiving end of this process of stimulus and response. It is almost impossible for any person who lives in a free society to avoid being in a position in which he has to react to argumentation. For his own protection, in order that he may evaluate with some degree of capability the written and spoken arguments to which we are all constantly exposed, every person should understand the technique of argument and be able to distinguish good argument from bad.

Controversies big and little arise inevitably and constantly among individuals, groups, and nations. Mankind throughout its history has known and used only two ultimate methods of settling the inevitable controversies which are a part of living. These two methods always and basically are either to *fight it out* and decide the controversy by force, giving the victory necessarily to the side with the stronger muscles, the heavier clubs, the abler armies, or the bigger bombs, or else to *talk it out* and decide it in private conversation, in court, in legislature, or in international conference, giving victory necessarily to the party with the more acceptable (either logically or emotionally) evidence, argument, appeal. In other words, the only ultimate choice is between bullets and arguments— force and reason.

Our American society is, and always has been, from Colonial times to the present, and probably will be throughout the foreseeable future, a society made up of an aggregation of minorities. We all belong to one or several American minorities. There is in America no homogeneous majority in racial background, religious affiliation, political philosophy, economic interests, or geographical loyalty. In such a society those who preach that we must avoid controversy are simply burying their timid heads in imaginary sand. Those who say we must live in peace and harmony and that therefore we must not engage in controversy and debate are saying substantially that we must cease to live an active, full, responsible life in a free society. Those who seek such peace and harmony as can be obtained only in the absence of differences of opinion and the controversies which inevitably arise from them, are incapable of either the satisfactions or the responsibilities of freedom. Such people, of course, will profit little from studying argumentation and debate. In our society they can probably find that complete freedom from responsibility, from thinking and acting, only in the shelter of some such social institution as the graveyard or the jail.

There are some among us at the present time (there seemed to be more of them fifteen or twenty years ago) who take the position that advocacy, argument, debate are outmoded activities, no longer of value in our brave new world where the only proper objectives are peace and harmony. This unrealistic attitude (which must arise from failure to observe the world around them, to follow the activity of human society as recorded day by day in the newspapers, spoken on the radio, and reported from the conferences, legislatures, courts, and other agencies through which society performs its various functions) has led them to try to substitute for argumentation and debate one of the most valuable forms of one of the most useful types of speech activity, namely, discussion. They

say that speakers should substitute the particular function of discussion which aims at *finding out what people want,* ascertaining
consensus, for *trying to make people want what the speakers think
they ought to want.* The truth is that consensus *per se* has neither
merit nor morality. Both the social wisdom and the ethical validity
of any consensus depends, like any other human decisions, upon
the nature of the consensus. If the consensus results from "the
pooling of ignorance," or the sacrifice of moral or political principles, or the overevaluation of "peace in our time," or other spe-
cious rewards, the consensus is always an evil thing. If, on the
other hand, the consensus results from a distribution and understanding of accurate information, from sound reasoning, from an
acceptance of valid principles and decent objectives, the consensus is a fine thing. Whether any discussion ends by serving a
decent and legitimate purpose depends inevitably upon the decency
and legitimacy of the purpose and the validity of the process by
which it is achieved. However, this is a long way from saying that
in a world like ours there is no place for advocacy and debate.

This book is prepared in the expectation that it will be helpful to
those who are alive to the realities of the rewards and satisfactions,
and the responsibilities, of a full and active life in a free society.
It is prepared in the further conviction that unless our society can
somehow develop citizens who are aware of, and able to promote
and defend, the rewards and satisfactions of a free society through
the effective use of advocacy and debate, we shall inevitably cease
to be a free society. Our successors will then have only a society in
which their lives are controlled by orders, directives, decisions, by
such big or little dictators, native or foreign, as may decide to take
over the control of the lives of those who miserably inhabit what
was once the free, though somewhat incompetent, society of the
United States of America.

Frequently as he reads this book, the student should keep in
mind the differences between debating in actual life situations,
such as legislature, court, or campaign, and the situations in school
or contest debates. Obviously the basic principles of debating are
identical in both situations. The debater in the legislature is trying
to get a vote on the merits of the proposition; the debater in the
courtroom is trying to get a vote on the sufficiency or insufficiency

of the plaintiff's or prosecution's (the affirmative's) case. In the school or contest debate, where the contestant is practicing and learning, in order to achieve ability in debating, the debater, if the contest is judged, is trying to get an affirmative vote in regard to his ability as a debater as compared to his opponent. However, if the contest is competently judged, the judge will estimate the debater's ability on the basis of how well his debating exemplifies, uses, observes the sound principles and techniques of debating in actual life.

In addition to these important differences between actual debates and contest debates, the student should bear in mind that there are certain procedural differences among other types of debate. In parliamentary or legislative debate, the debater is subject to the rules of the assembly and the laws under which the assembly is organized, and he has the advantages of any privileges which the laws or rules may give to him as a member of the assembly. For instance, under normal circumstances, a senator debating on the floor of the United States Senate can talk indefinitely and cannot be sued in court for any remarks he may make in the Senate debate. In many assemblies, however, he has limitations as to the frequency with which he can speak or the length of time for which he can hold the floor. The point is that in parliamentary debate the member of the assembly has all the limitations and all the privileges that are expressed in the rules.

In campaign debating, the debater is almost always on his own. He can probably talk for as long as he can hold the attention of the audience or the audience will stay and listen to him. However, such freedom may be interfered with by some aggressive chairman or other person or group of persons by demonstration, persuasion, or force. Almost any speaker, of course, is subject to the laws of slander, and may be sued if he violates the laws in remarks he makes on the public platform.

In courtroom debating, the lawyers are subject to rather rigid control by the presiding judge, and they are limited by the laws of evidence and principles of sound courtroom procedure usually accepted in the courts in regard to what they may or may not say.

In the informal debating of the street corner, the fireside, and the dinner table, debaters are obviously rather free except for the limitations of good taste, politeness, and the forbearance of their listeners. The debater preparing for a debate in any of these situations should be very careful to consider in advance what his probable privileges and limitations are and to stay within them without breaking the laws, demanding improper privileges for himself, or violating the ordinary rules of acceptable behavior.

Exercises

1. Discuss the following statement in relation to the point of view developed in this chapter: "The essential need is the improvement of the methods and conditions of debate, discussion, and persuasion. That is *the* need of the public."—John Dewey, *The Public and Its Problems*, p. 208.
2. Discuss the ways in which a speech designed to secure belief might be expected to differ from one designed to get action.
3. Write a two-hundred word essay setting out what you believe to be proper objectives in the study of argumentation and debate. Read the Preface to this book and Chapter i before writing the paper. Compare these papers in class.

Chapter II · THE RESPONSIBILITIES OF THE ADVOCATE

I. INQUIRY AND PROOF

There is a useful distinction between inquiry and proof which helps to explain the province of argumentation and debate and provides a basis for assessing the responsibilities of the advocate. Richard Whately made this distinction over a century ago in these words:

> ... Reasoning may be considered as applicable to two purposes ... the *ascertainment* of the truth by investigation (inquiry) and the *establishment* of it to the satisfaction of *another* (proof) ... The process of *investigation* must be supposed completed, and certain conclusions arrived at by that process, before the advocate undertakes to *prove* the justness of those conclusions. And in doing this, the advocate will not always find it expedient to adhere to the same course of reasoning by which his own discoveries were originally made; other arguments may occur to him afterwards, more clear, or more concise, or better adapted to the understanding of those he addresses.
> ... If a man begins (as is too plainly a frequent mode of proceedings) by hastily adopting, or strongly leaning to, some opinion which suits his inclination, or which is sanctioned by some authority that he blindly venerates, and then studies with the utmost diligence, not as an Investigator of Truth, but as an Advocate labouring to prove his point, his talents and his researches, whatever effect they may produce in making converts to his notions, will avail nothing in enlightening his own judgment, and securing him from error.[1]

The offices of the investigator and the advocate may be performed by the same person or by different persons, but it is important to distinguish between them. The advocate begins with a proposition to which he is committed as a result of inquiry, or any

[1] Richard Whately, *Elements of Rhetoric*, Seventh Edition (London: John W. Parker, West Strand, 1846) pp. 5–6.

other circumstances which may commend the proposition to him, and attempts to persuade others to accept it. We are concerned here with his rights and responsibilities as a member of a free society in the performance of this task.

II. RESPONSIBILITY FOR THE PROPOSITION

As we shall see in Chapter III, the propositions which advocates defend and attack may be of their own choice (a result of their own inquiry and investigation), or they may be dictated by circumstances which limit this choice in very practical ways. Anyone who deliberately attempts to influence the belief and action of others in directions which he knows (or thinks he knows) to be false and unwise, if he has a completely free choice in the matter, is quite obviously in a difficult moral situation. Such advocacy is basically dishonest and every effort consistent with the tenets of a free society should be made to expose such impostors. Fortunately, *free* public discussion and debate have within them the means of separating the true from the false and the honest from the dishonest in such ways as to protect society. Much of what is said in this book is written to explain how this can and should be accomplished.

We would be completely unrealistic, however, if we failed to recognize that the advocate does not always have a free choice in selecting the proposition. Many institutions in a free society which make use of argumentation and debate exist for the precise purpose of determining truth, wisdom, and justice. Our courts are such institutions, and they will serve as an example here. Lawyers appear before our courts as professional advocates. In this capacity, their choice of propositions is limited by the circumstances of their clients. To be sure, they do not have to take a case, but our whole system of jurisprudence is based on the assumption that a man is innocent until he is proved guilty in a duly constituted court. He has a right to a trial and the right to expect that a competent advocate will undertake his defense. If we adjudge such an advocate morally reprehensible for taking the case, we are, in effect, judging the accused before the trial takes place.

Actually, there are many circumstances which may commit

honest advocates to propositions—*circumstances which at least limit freedom of choice.* These may be circumstances of employment (as in the case of a salesman or public relations counsel), circumstances of representation (as in the case of a man who represents a constituency), and circumstances of prior commitment (where promises have been made). These cases are illustrative of many factors which may limit the choice of an advocate in the propositions he elects to defend and attack, and they may or may not justify his decisions. It should be clear, however, that the decision to defend a proposition is in many circumstances a complex moral decision which cannot be considered morally reprehensible without knowing the factors which limit or dictate the choice.

III. RESPONSIBILITY FOR THE CONDUCT OF THE ARGUMENT

Once a cause has been undertaken, the advocate has a responsibility to present *the best possible case for his proposition within the limits of the facts as he knows them or believes them to be.* He should not deliberately do less nor does he have any moral right to attempt more. No man has a moral right to lie, cheat, or intentionally distort, much less a responsibility to do so. What is more, the practice of argumentation and debate in a free society is one of the better ways of exposing lying, cheating, and distortion in ways which are not designed to make life pleasant for those who resort to such practices.

The primary purpose of the advocate is to secure belief (or action) through proof. By "belief" we mean conviction—the acceptance of a proposition on intellectual grounds or grounds which are thought to be logically adequate. It implies voluntary acceptance of a statement of fact, value, or policy on the assumption that this statement is true, just, or wise. The person who "believes" may or may not be correct in his conviction, but he thinks he is, and for reasons which appear to him to be adequate.

One way of influencing belief is through proof. By "proof" we mean a logical demonstration which establishes the truth, justice, or wisdom of a proposition or the *probability* that the proposition is true, just, and wise. Unfortunately, perhaps, the correlation between belief and proof is not a perfect one. In other words, people do not always believe what has been proved and they most certainly believe many things which have not been proved. We are not unaware of the psychological factors which influence belief—emotions, desires, tastes, and the like; nor do we underestimate the powerful influence of faith. These factors can and often should be brought to the aid of proof in attempting to influence belief and action. Actually, they are inescapable in matters of human conduct.

The study and practice of argumentation and debate involve four basic assumptions which merit careful consideration.

A. Propositions can be proved. First, it is assumed that propositions *can* be proved, that evidence and argument can be adduced in support of a thesis which establish it as a true, just, or wise position. At least, it is assumed that demonstrations can be presented which show a proposition is more likely to be true than untrue, more likely to be just than unjust, and more likely to be wise than unwise. Only the confirmed skeptic would deny this assumption.

B. Truth, justice and wisdom are more powerful than their opposites. It is further assumed that a proposition shown to embody truth, justice, or wisdom is more likely to prevail than one which is false, unjust, or unwise. Other things being equal, a sound proposition has a better chance for acceptance because it offers greater possibilities for support and defense. As Aristotle put it more than 2,000 years ago, " . . . truth and justice are by nature more powerful than their opposites; so that, when decisions are not made as they should be, the speakers with the right on their side have only themselves to thank for the outcome."[2]

C. Rational decisions are preferred. Thirdly, it is assumed that rational behavior is to be preferred to irrational behavior. In other words, it is desirable that men give their assent to propositions on rational grounds. Rational commitments are more likely to be sound and they are pragmatically more significant because they are understandable. A man who believes something for good reason,

---

[2] Aristotle's *Rhetoric* I. 1.

and knows why he believes it, is in a better position than one who accepts blindly.

D. Emotional reactions are more easily enlisted in intellectually defensible causes. Finally, it is assumed that man's sympathies, tastes, faiths, desires, and intuitions are more natural allies of truth, justice, and wisdom than they are of the false, the unjust, and the unwise. The advocate who proves his point is in a better position to enlist the emotions of his listeners in his cause than one who does not. Rational behavior and emotional impulses are more likely to pull together than to pull apart. Even if more people can "feel" truly than can "think" accurately, there appears to be an inherent desire for truth, justice, and decency.

These basic assumptions not only lay the groundwork for what we believe to be a sound philosophy in argumentation and debate, but they also constitute a credo for the advocate—sound working principles for the speaker who seeks to influence the belief and action of others.

IV. PROBABILITIES

From the standpoint of acceptance, a proposition may be regarded as *possible, plausible, probable,* or *certainly true*. These same terms may be used to characterize the support or the demonstration which the advocate offers in behalf of a proposition.

To show that a proposition is possible, at best gives it the status of a hypothesis which one is willing to entertain as a possibility. When a man says, "That is possible," he does not mean to say that he accepts nor that he is disposed to accept. He says only, "That may be true."

Plausibility moves a step beyond possibility. The plausible proposition is one which appears likely. But discreet individuals will not ordinarily commit themselves on grounds of plausibility. They want more proof and are entitled to it. A quick, superficial analysis may lead one to give enough credence to a thesis to say it is plausible—"it appears to be true," or "it is worth looking into"—but it cannot as yet be depended upon as a basis for conviction or action.

When an advocate shows that a proposition is *probable*, he has shown that it is more likely to be true than untrue. He has shown it to be the most "likely" description, interpretation, or position among those available. It is the best "bet." It is true beyond a reasonable doubt. The establishment of such probabilities is the primary purpose of argumentation and debate. Under most circumstances a speaker cannot do more or be expected to do more. Sensible people govern their lives by probabilities. Indeed, in most areas in which argumentation and debate play any significant role, it cannot be otherwise.

It is a nice question to ask whether any proposition can be regarded as certainly true or whether any demonstration can achieve absolute and final certainty. Many modern scientists appear to support relativism in all areas of thought. Fortunately, this profound philosophical question does not have to be settled to clarify the role of argumentation and debate. No one will deny that the advocate should seek the best possible demonstration for his proposition. In some cases, such demonstrations will approach "practical" certainty. Propositions which lend themselves to such demonstrations are not the usual questions for public discussion and debate, however, because their very certainty removes them from the realm of debatable questions.

Classical writers in this field point out that argumentation and debate have their greatest usefulness in the fields of "ethics and politics." In more modern terminology this is to say that questions amenable to argumentation and debate are usually those of value and policy involving social, political, and economic issues. Actually, all personal and public questions of a controversial nature, where people can and do differ in their opinions, lend themselves to debate. For many centuries debate has been the principal policy-determining method in such situations. As we shall see in the next chapter, many questions of fact must also be adjudicated by debate, as for example in a court of law.

In terms of this analysis, it may be said that argumentation and debate operate in the realm of probabilities. The purpose of the advocate is to present a case in support of a proposition which demonstrates it to be true beyond reasonable doubt, or that the proposition is more probably true than false. In other words, he seeks to show that the probabilities are in favor of the proposition, cause, thesis, or position which he is advocating.

V. PRESUMPTIONS

The best way to describe the logical responsibilities of the advocate is in terms of presumptions, burden of proof, and burden of rebuttal. Richard Whately presents one of the most competent treatments of this subject in the literature:

> It is a point of great importance to decide in each case, at the outset, in your own mind, and clearly to point out to the hearer, as occasion may serve, on which side the *Presumption* lies, and to which belongs the (onus probandi) *Burden of Proof*. For though it may be expedient to bring forward more proofs than can be fairly *demanded* of you, it is always desirable, when this is the case, that it should be *known*, and that the strength of the cause should be estimated accordingly.
>
> According to the most correct usage of the term, a "Presumption" in favour of any supposition means, not (as has been sometimes erroneously imagined) a preponderance of probability in its favour, but, such a *preoccupation* of the ground, as implies that it must stand good till some sufficient reason is adduced against it; in short, that the *Burden of Proof* lies on the side of him who would dispute it.[3]

The crux of Whately's explanation of presumptions is in the phrase "a preoccupation of the ground." The presumption is always with "things as they are." It may be defined as the *advantage* which lies with the party who is *defending* things as they are or as they are commonly accepted or believed to be. As Whately very properly points out, this "advantage" does not mean that the position of the defense is any stronger or more probable than that of the party who opposes this position. It is the function of the debate to assess the probabilities for purposes of decision. The "advantage" of the presumption is limited to such benefits as accrue to the party who is "in possession of the ground," who is defending the status quo or "an opinion commonly held." The nature of this advantage can be illustrated by a body of troops who occupy a fortress which the opposing troops must take if they are to win their objective. The advantage has nothing to do with the merits of the cause for which the troops are fighting and nothing to do with the relative strength of the opposing parties. The advantage is in the fact that one of the parties to the action is "in

[3] *Op. cit.*, p. 112.

possession" and presumably will remain in possession until a decisive attack is made by the opposition.

Some of the more common presumptions encountered are the presumption in favor of existing institutions, the presumption of innocence, the presumption in favor of possession, and the presumptions in favor of traditions, customs, habits, mores, creeds, doctrines, and laws now in use or generally accepted.

With this explanation in mind, it is not difficult to see the great practical importance of knowing where the presumption lies in any situation which calls for argument. If the presumption is in your favor, you may fairly demand that your opponent show cause for reply before you advance any argument; and if you do choose to go forward with the argument even though the responsibility is not yours, it is decidedly in your interests to do so with full knowledge of this fact and with adequate explanation to all interested parties. On the other hand, if the presumption is against you, you have the obligation of initiating the argument and presenting a case for your position. If you fail to do this, your opponent may maintain his silence with impunity.

VI. THE BURDEN OF PROOF

The burden of proof is defined as "the risk of the proposition," the burden upon that party to the controversy who will lose if nothing is done. It is the burden of making good his claim which rests upon the one who starts an action, who demands a change from the existing situation. In terms of *presumptions,* the burden of proof may be defined as the responsibility which rests upon that party to the controversy who has the presumption against him. He is the dissatisfied party, the party who is opposing the status quo or an existing institution, custom, law, or creed. The responsibilities of the party with the burden of proof are identical with those of the party who has the presumption against him. He must present what we shall later explain as a "prima facie case" before he has any claim to a reply from the man who has the presumption in his favor in the argument.

As in the case of presumptions, it is a matter of considerable practical importance to understand the burden of proof and know where it lies in any controversy. The sides in an argument and their responsibilities are determined by the burden of proof. The *affirmative* should be understood as the party or side with the burden of proof and the *negative* as the party or side with the presumption in its favor. Wherever there is debating which pays proper attention to logical sequence and economy of time, the case of the affirmative (opposing the present and advocating the new) is always advanced before the defense of the negative.

There are three vexed questions in argumentation concerning the burden of proof which need clarification: (1) How do changing situations and conditions affect the burden of proof? (2) How does a counter-proposition affect the burden of proof? And (3) does the burden of proof ever shift in a debate? To illustrate the first of these problems, suppose it is proposed that Illinois adopt a state income tax. Since Illinois does not now have a state income tax, the burden of proof lies with the party who proposes it. If Illinois were to adopt an income tax at a later date, the burden of proof would then rest on the party who proposed its abolition. Changing conditions do affect the burden of proof in ways which are perfectly consistent with our definition of the burden of proof. This burden always rests with the party which opposes whatever may be the status quo at the time of the debate in the jurisdiction in which the change is proposed.

Whenever the answer of the negative takes the form of a "counter-proposition" (in law an "affirmative defense"), it seeks to defeat the affirmative proposal by offering another proposal which counters that of the affirmative. In this case, the negative, of course, becomes essentially an affirmative and has the burden of proof *on the new proposition.* For example, if in a first-degree murder case the answer of the defense is not that the accused did not kill the deceased, but that the accused was insane at the time, this constitutes a counter-proposition. For the time being the question at issue is not, "*Resolved,* That A is guilty of murder in the first degree," but, "*Resolved,* That A is (or was at the time in question) insane." On this proposition the original defense becomes the affirmative. The accused is presumed to be sane until the contrary is established. The original prosecution becomes the negative, and seeks to prevent the establishment of the fact of insanity. Here, clearly, there is no shifting of *the* burden of proof. There is a new proposition with a burden of proof of its own, and this burden is on the new affirmative and never shifts.

It is frequently said that the burden of proof can shift from one side to the other in a debate. As we have defined the burden of proof here—and this is the only proper definition in general argumentation—the burden of proof *never* shifts! The man who has "the risk of the proposition" at the beginning of the argument holds it throughout the argument. To be sure, there devolves upon his opponent (the negative) a responsibility to reply when he (the affirmative) has presented a prima facie case, but this does not mean that the burden of proof has shifted. The final adjudication of any argument will be made in the light of the original affirmative case, the rejoinder by the negative, and such replies and counter-replies as may be made by both sides. *All* of these arguments must be assessed in terms of the responsibilities imposed by the burden of proof and the success of the affirmative in discharging this burden in relation to the success of the negative in defending the presumption in its favor. To say that the burden of proof shifts after each reply serves only to confuse the final accounting.

VII. THE BURDEN OF REBUTTAL

The burden of proof (understood as "the risk of the proposition") does *not* shift, but the responsibility of "going forward with the argument" may and usually does change sides in a debate. As we have seen, the negative has a responsibility to reply after the affirmative has presented a prima facie case, and the negative rejoinder may call for an answer from the affirmative. Unless there are prearranged agreements as to the number of replies and counter-replies, these may be limited only by the endurance of the protagonists or the settlement of the question. We shall refer to this responsibility of "going forward with the argument" as the burden of rebuttal. Unlike the burden of proof, it may shift many times in a debate—just as many times as the parties to a controversy advance arguments of sufficient merit to demand a reply.

Exercises

1. Discuss the following statements. Are they true or false? Why?
    a. A lawyer has no moral right to defend a guilty man.
    b. Since you have not proved your proposition, it should not be accepted.
    c. A man who loses an argument has only himself to thank for the outcome.
    d. The man with the presumption on his side in an argument is defending a sound proposition.
2. Discuss the following statement: "Fortunately, *free* public discussion and debate have within them the means of separating the true from the false and the honest from the dishonest in such ways as to protect society."
3. How are presumptions determined in argumentation and debate? Why is a man presumed to be innocent until he is proved guilty?
4. Where do the presumptions lie on the following propositions? Why?
    a. Honesty is the best policy.
    b. The President should be elected for a single six-year term.
    c. John Doe is a thief.
    d. Let's go to the movie tonight.
    e. The world is round.
5. Discuss the following statements. Are they true or false? Why?
    a. The burden of proof never shifts in debate.
    b. The burden of rebuttal never shifts in debate.
    c. The burden of proof rests with the party who has the presumption against him.
    d. The burden of proof shifts to the negative when the negative proposes a counter-proposition.

Chapter III · THE PROPOSITION

I. THE NATURE OF PROPOSITIONS

A. The proposition defined. The word "proposition" is used in several fields of knowledge, as well as in colloquial speech, and its meanings are consequently varied: linguistically, a proposition is a declarative sentence; psychologically, it is any judgment expressed in words; logically, it is a statement that is capable of being either true or false; rhetorically, as in argumentation, it is a judgment expressed in a declarative sentence which the listener or reader is asked to accept. The last meaning will be used in this book.

This judgment is stated in a declarative sentence consisting of two terms and a copula. The subject of the sentence is one term, the verb is the copula or connecting link, and the object of the verb or some other predicative expression is the other term. A judgment so stated is a proposition. The following propositions are divided into their three parts:

First Term	Copula	Second Term
Dictatorships	are	undemocratic.
Public utilities	should	be regulated.
Honesty	is	the best policy.

B. The proposition distinguished from other statements. A proposition is the indispensable basis of fruitful argumentative communication. It must be stated, or at least understood, as a complete sentence. The titles of discourses which are primarily narrative, descriptive, or expository need not be stated in sentence form, nor are they propositions: "My Experiences as a Football Player" suggests a narrative; "How To Play Guard" befits an exposition; and "Drama and Color in the Stadium" is appropriate for a description. A proposition for argumentative discourse must state, or be understood as, a sentence, such as, "Intercollegiate Football Should Be

18

Abolished." These distinctions do not deny the frequent use of all four forms of discourse in a primarily argumentative composition.

C. Forms in which propositions are stated. Subjects for debate in parliamentary assemblies are expressed as motions, resolutions, or bills. In less formal situations the matter in dispute is often expressed as a statement of opinion, as a question, or as a single term. Lengthy propositions of educational debate may be shortened for publicity purposes into terse questions. It is erroneous to assume there is no proposition simply because the subject is not formally phrased. However, all parties concerned in an argument should at least understand a complete sentence which poses the controversy.

The forms of statement are illustrated in the following table:

MOTION— Mr. Chairman, I move that the question be laid on the table.

RESOLUTION— *Resolved,* That capital punishment should be abolished.

BILL— Be it enacted by the Senate and House of Representatives of the United States of America in Congress assembled, That . . .

STATEMENT
OF OPINION— Bridge is more fun than poker.

QUESTION— Should Railroads Be Publicly Owned?

SINGLE TERM— Public Ownership of Railroads.

II. THE FUNCTIONS OF A PROPOSITION

A. To express a conclusion from study and reflection. A proposition is often (perhaps usually) a conclusion from study, reflection, inquiry, investigation, or discussion. In this capacity it should accurately express the conviction of the person or persons making the inquiry. It should represent their conclusion, their attitude toward the problem, the position on which they take their stand.

B. To express the meaning and intent of an advocate. In all circumstances, the proposition should express the meaning and intent of the advocate. This is true irrespective of the source of the proposition and the speaker's convictions with respect to it. Any man who makes a motion or proposition has the *privilege* of phrasing the proposition and the *responsibility* of making his meaning and intent clear. So long as he uses language accurately, he is within his rights in interpreting the proposition as he sees fit. A negative has no right to tell the affirmative what the affirmative means by its own proposition so long as the affirmative interpretation is a reasonable and linguistically accurate interpretation of the language in which it has chosen to express its meaning and intent.

The reasonableness and accuracy of this language can be established by using reliable definitions. The methods of definition for this purpose include: (1) classification, which means placing a term in a logical class of which it is a member and then differentiating it from other members of that class, as in genus, species, and differentia; (2) gradation, or a modification of classification which takes into account the principle of continuous variation as opposed to fixed, arbitrary classes; (3) negation, or defining by pointing out what is *not* meant; (4) illustration or example, which means the citing of a specific case; (5) context, or the placing of the term in meaningful surroundings which show the verbal or nonverbal (real-life) situation or thing to which the term refers; (6) quotation of synonyms found in dictionaries and other reference works; (7) etymology, or reference to origin or derivation of the term.

If the affirmative fails to make its meaning clear or chooses to place strained and unreasonable interpretations on the terms of the proposition, the negative has a right to object. The discussion of the meaning of terms which often occurs in a debate should not be stigmatized as "quibbling" when a serious effort is being made to determine the intent of the affirmative and whether or not the affirmative interpretation is a legitimate interpretation of the proposition. "Quibbling" means a confusing or distorting misuse of words and ideas to evade the point or the truth. No intelligent debate can take place until the meaning of the advocate is clear.

C. To serve as the basis of the argument. Regardless of how formally or informally a proposition is stated, it should be the basis of every argument. An intelligent argumentative discourse cannot take place in the absence of such a statement. Thus a speaker or writer should phrase the proposition for his own use, even though he does not express it to his public.

When an individual is presenting one side of an argument, a

well-phrased proposition is necessary if he is to analyze and organize his material adequately. Such a statement also assists listeners or readers in following the argument, because they are enabled to see the end in view and can relate individual arguments to that end or proposition. However, in dealing with a hostile audience, a speaker should determine whether it is wise to state his proposition at the outset.

In case two or more persons speak and both sides are presented, a well-phrased proposition serves to keep the controversy within proper bounds. At times the statement of a proposition can even prevent pointless and futile argument. From the standpoint of the audience, it is a part of critical listening to attempt to identify the proposition, even if the disputants do not state it.

D. To name the affirmative and the negative. There are two sides to every argument, the affirmative which favors the proposition and the negative which opposes it.

The fact that several positions may be taken on a proposition does not mean that there are more than two sides. One may affirm or deny for many different reasons. For instance, an advocate might oppose compulsory health insurance because it would allegedly undermine private medicine, or he might take the position that the extension of voluntary plans of health insurance is preferable. The taking of either of these positions would place one on the negative side.

E. To state the desired audience reaction. Since an advocate seeks to influence attitudes and actions, his proposition should state the desired reaction. It should tell the audience what they are being asked to buy, join, view with alarm, etc. One pragmatic test of the advocate's success is the willingness or unwillingness of the listeners to react as the proposition directs. Persuasive communication is unlikely if speakers and their audiences do not have a common notion of what is to be favored or opposed. Thus a proposition should not merely mention compulsory arbitration, for instance, but should call for its adoption or rejection in a definite context.

F. To place the presumption and the burden of proof. We have previously discussed the key concepts of presumption and burden of proof as they relate to matters of probability. One function of a correctly worded proposition is the placing of the burden of proof on the affirmative and the granting of the benefit of presumption to the negative. Thus the burden of proof falls upon the supporters of a well-worded motion, the State in a criminal trial, the plaintiff in a civil action, and the affirmative in a school debate on a properly worded proposition. The opposing side in each case has the initial benefit of presumption.

However, if the proposition is improperly worded, the side which nominally affirms it may escape the burden of proof. In order to understand this, it is necessary to distinguish between the nominal affirmative and the actual affirmative. The nominal (bearing the name of) affirmative is the side which affirms (says "yes" to) the proposition. The actual affirmative is always the side which has the burden of proof and thus remains unsatisfied if no action is taken.

> WRONG: Congress should enact a federal income tax.
> RIGHT: Congress should reduce the federal income tax 10 per cent in all brackets.

Since we have a federal income tax, the nominal affirmative (saying "yes") in the "wrong" proposition will be satisfied if no change is made, and is therefore the actual negative. On the same proposition the nominal negative (saying "no") is the actual affirmative, because it will be dissatisfied if nothing is done. The "right" proposition is worded so that the nominal and the actual affirmatives are the same, and the nominal and the actual negatives likewise coincide. Thus a properly phrased proposition always places the burden of proof on the affirmative and gives the benefit of presumption to the negative.

III. A CLASSIFICATION OF PROPOSITIONS

A. **Propositions of fact.** These express simple factual judgments. They state or imply the question: Is this true? Thus, in a criminal action, the State may charge that a certain person is guilty of first-degree murder; the defense may deny that he committed the alleged act, or deny that the act is first-degree murder. In either event, a question of fact is raised. Other examples follow:

*The United States could be induced to surrender sovereignty
completely to an international government.*
Labor unions seek to control American industry.
*Democracy, in the sense of social-political-economic equality of
opportunity, does not exist in the United States.*
*The election of the President by direct vote would impair states'
rights.*

B. Propositions of value. These express evaluative judgments concerning the goodness or badness, desirability or undesirability of some person, institution, or conception, without recommending any policy or action. The following are examples:

The strike is an ethically legitimate weapon of organized labor.
Military training is beneficial to most young men.
Chain stores are detrimental to the American public.

C. Propositions of policy. These propose a new policy or a change of policy, and call for some specific action. A proposition of policy raises the question: Should this be done? Here are some examples:

Jurisdictional strikes should be outlawed by federal statute.
*The tenure of the President of the United States should be limited
by law to eight years.*
Intercollegiate football should be abolished.

The meaning of "should" in propositions of policy is often disputed in school debates. The consensus of experts is that "should" implies "could" but obviously not "would." Assuming the establishment of a cause of action (need), we may say that a plan "should" be adopted if it is sound, just, and in other ways the best of the available remedies.

The foregoing sequence of fact, value, and policy propositions is based upon developmental complexity. The first depends entirely upon the establishment of fact for proof. The second depends not only upon facts but also upon standards of judgment. The third involves facts and values, but it extends into considerations of expediency, practicality, and action. In general, propositions of policy and value are better for debate than are those of fact, because factual matters such as dates of events, population data, authorship, and the like are more properly matters of investigation than of argument.

IV. SELECTING THE PROPOSITION

Generally speaking, there are three circumstances under which propositions become the subjects for argumentation and debate.

A. In a problem-solving situation. When any group, however large or small, is confronted with a problem which must be resolved and in which disagreement persists, debate is the logical recourse. In such cases, motions are made and debated. These motions are propositions and are subject to all the requirements and conditions of propositions discussed in this chapter.

B. When the proposition is given to the advocate. The selection of a subject, or the proposition emerging from it, is often not a matter of independent choice. When an advertising agency or a lawyer is engaged by a client, the proposition and the side are imposed by circumstances. Similarly, when a student "goes out for debate," his proposition or propositions are seldom of his choice. Also, if one becomes a defendant in a legal action, the proposition and his side on it are determined without his being consulted. In case the general subject, but not the specific proposition, is imposed, one should carefully study the situation and phrase the proposition accordingly.

C. When a deliberate choice is made. There are many occasions on which the speaker is given the privilege of selecting what he is going to talk about. Under these circumstances, there are four general criteria which may help to direct his choice.

1. **Can the proposition be argued profitably?** It may be harmful as well as futile to argue propositions which cannot be handled rationally, *i.e.*, without emotional tirades. Furthermore, it is unwise to select trivial matters or those of sheer speculation which are not worthy of the best efforts of the participants. A substantial proposition of fact, value, or policy is preferable, either for purposes of instruction or policy formation.

2. **Is the proposition adapted to the advocate?** The speaker or writer ought to choose his subject and proposition from those fields in which his study and experience enable him to say something of interest and profit to others. He will then express himself with greater conviction, and his audience will be more likely to respect his judgment.

3. **Is the proposition adaptable to the audience?** The proposition should be of interest to the audience, or of such nature that the speaker can make it so. Although one ought not to cater basely to an audience, he is obliged to select propositions and treatments thereof which have some potentialities in terms of interest, understanding, and conviction or persuasion.

4. **Is the proposition adapted to the occasion?** This criterion of appropriateness applies to the selection of subjects for all kinds of speeches and writings. There is no special doctrine for argumentative discourse. The suitability of subjects in terms of time and place is presumed to be common knowledge among readers of this book.

In case a deliberate choice is made by persons other than the advocate himself, additional criteria are sometimes used. Committee members who are asked to suggest subjects for use in the national referendum of the state high-school debate leagues are advised to bear these criteria in mind:

1. Is the subject of nation-wide interest?
2. Is a discussion of the subject in the public interest?
3. Is the proposition to be worded from the subject likely to be removed from the realm of debate by being solved or exhausted during the debate season?
4. Are adequate research materials available, or can they be made available?
5. Is the subject interesting to young people?
6. Will audiences be interested in it?
7. Can a suitable proposition be phrased on this subject?

V. PHRASING THE PROPOSITION

A. Importance of careful phrasing. Since all debate takes place on propositions, either expressed or implied, the phraseology of the proposition is a matter of importance. A resolution, bill, or motion which is poorly phrased is likely not only to result in confusion, but also it probably will fail to serve the four functions which propositions should serve.

B. Some principles of phrasing. In the first place, the proposition should state specifically what the affirmative wants, never what the affirmative does not want. Thus a widely-used proposition calling for the abolition of the jury system is defective in that it fails to specify the scheme which the affirmative prefers. The possible substitutions include a single judge, a board of judges, a commission, etc. Equally objectionable propositions are those which call for the abolishment of the direct primary election or an unspecified change in our method of handling juvenile delinquents. These examples show what can happen if the wording of the resolution fails to state specifically what the affirmative wants.

In the second place, the language of the proposition should be simple and free of ambiguous and question-begging terms. By simple language we mean a degree of plainness which is consistent with accuracy of statement. An ambiguous term is one that may be legitimately interpreted to have either of two different meanings, while a question-begging term is one which slants the proposition in favor of one side. The difficulty which such terms may create is obvious. Consider this proposition suggested by the Cambridge University team for the American tour in 1947: *"In the opinion of this House the extreme emphasis on science and technology in modern education is destroying the foundations of Western Civilization."* The word "extreme" is question-begging because it assumes what it should be the affirmative's burden to prove. To correct this fault, the word "present" was substituted for "extreme." An instance of ambiguity may be seen in the proposal: *The State should abolish child labor.* What does "child labor" mean, and does "State" mean the Federal Government or one of the forty-eight states thereof? A recent national proposition for college debates contained an expression, "direct share," which was more than ambiguous; it was vague: *That labor should be given a direct share in the management of industry.*

In the third place, the wording of the proposition must place the burden of proof on the affirmative. In discussing the functions of the proposition, we have defined burden of proof and presumption, and have shown why the nominal and actual affirmative must coincide. In propositions improperly worded with respect to this matter, there will be confusion as to the two sides and their responsibilities. In a school debate, for example, it is customary for the affirmative to open and close the debate. If the proposition is phrased in such a way as to place the burden of proof on the negative, the team opening the debate (nominal affirmative, but actual negative) will find itself in the position of having to defend the *status quo* which has not yet been attacked, and the nominal negative (in this case, the actual affirmative) will be denied its right to close the debate.

The allocation of the burden of proof may be seen in two wordings of the proposal to take some action regarding capital punishment. In Michigan, which does not employ the death penalty, we can debate the proposition that it be adopted; in Illinois, which employs this penalty, that it be abolished. In both cases the burden of proof is properly placed, because the party saying "yes" to the proposition has the risk of nonpersuasion. The problems posed by the national proposition for high schools in 1950 illustrate the importance of this principle. Nominal affirmatives were obliged to call for the rejection of the welfare state, even though it was not the *status quo*.

A fourth requirement is that the desired audience reaction should be stated in a single, declarative sentence. This should be a concise, accurate statement of the belief which the audience is asked to accept, or the specific action which is called for.

A fifth possible requirement is that the proposition be single, that is, embody only one central idea. This is akin to the fourth requirement, but it goes further to stipulate that the single sentence must have only one main idea. Otherwise, one might resolve that the term of office of Congressmen be extended to four years and that the Congressional districts be remapped.

Some critics of current practices in the wording of propositions for nation-wide use suggest a sixth requirement; namely, that a statement of context be framed to supplement the announced proposition. It is argued that this would reduce uncertainty or argument about the interpretation. Such a statement should whenever possible be avoided by exercising great care in phrasing the proposition or by making reference to a specific bill, book, or other document.

Finally, it is proposed that the interest of contest debaters and their audiences would be enhanced by modifying the proposition during the season in order to adapt to local conditions or to fit new circumstances. A familiar parallel can be drawn between this procedure and that of amending a motion, a bill, or resolution during the process of deliberation. This may well be done whenever agreements can be reached easily in regard to changes.

Exercises

1. On each of the following subjects, phrase a proposition of fact, a proposition of value, and a proposition of policy:
   a. Labor-management relations.
   b. Capital punishment.
   c. College athletics.
   d. Military training.
2. State the propositions involved in three selected samples of argument, such as editorials, articles, speeches, or advertisements. Classify each as fact, value, or policy.
3. Criticize these propositions:
   a. The paving on Main Street should be improved.
   b. The jury system should be abolished and a judge or board of judges substituted for the jury in all trial courts.
   c. One term of office of the President should be four years.
   d. Our unjust immigration quotas should be revised.
   e. The powers of state governors should be extended.
   f. The welfare state is detrimental to the best interests of the American people.
   g. Labor unions deserve the confidence of the American people.
4. Prepare a short expository talk or paper in which you explain how you chose a controversial subject, phrased a proposition about it, tested it according to functions and the first five rules of phrasing, classified it, and prepared a context for it, or avoided the necessity for doing so.
5. Phrase four propositions of policy which you would like to use for short argumentative speeches in class. Be prepared to submit these propositions to the class for criticism and suggestions.
6. Prepare and present a five-minute affirmative or negative speech on the proposition you choose from the list of four submitted in Exercise 5.

Chapter **IV** · ANALYZING THE
PROPOSITION: THE ISSUES

I. THE THEORY OF THE ISSUES

A. Issues defined. The issues are the inherently vital points, contentions, or subpropositions, affirmed by the affirmative and denied by the negative, upon the establishment of which depends the establishment of the main proposition. They are the ultimate, irreducible, essential matters of fact or of principle (law) upon which the conclusion of the question hinges. They are not simply "important main points" or "points on which there is a clash of opinion." They are the crucial points, each one of which the affirmative must *establish* (unless it is admitted by the negative) in order to establish the proposition.

The issues in any proposition are inherent in the essential meaning of the proposition itself. Many English sentences, even some which can be used as propositions in argumentation or debate, are capable of more than one legitimate meaning. It is the first duty of every advocate (whether he is writing an individual speech or editorial or engaging in an oral debate with an opponent) to decide early in his preparation what the proposition means to him. He should then plan to make that meaning clear to readers or hearers near the start of his writing or his speech.

It should be realized that this problem of meaning frequently has different implications for the affirmative and the negative. For instance, when in a debate a proposition is capable of two *legitimate* interpretations, it is clearly the privilege of the affirmative to choose which is the meaning to be debated. It is the affirmative that speaks in the proposition. The proposition belongs to it, expresses its position. The negative may not tell the affirmative what the affirmative means by any legitimate use of language. As soon as possible, of course, this meaning should be made known to the negative. The negative ought to have an opportunity to prepare to oppose the actual position which it is going to have to oppose, and the negative has to oppose the affirmative position.

Having determined an inherent and legitimate meaning of the proposition, the next thing to be realized is that *the issues are to be discovered in the meaning of the proposition.* Finding the issues in a proposition is essentially parallel to finding the elements in a chemical compound. If one has a chemical compound to analyze he cannot very well decide in advance that he is going to find three elements or six elements or two elements. If he is a competent chemist, he will so analyze the compound as to find the number of elements that are there. And if he is dealing with a chemical element instead of a compound, he won't attempt to break the element into separate elements for convenience. In other words, we must realize that if we work competently in analysis we find the number of issues that are inherent in the proposition, whether this be one or half a dozen.

Frequently the issues in a proposition are evident as soon as one finds an authoritative definition of a keyword in the proposition. A good example of that is the elements of the charge of burglary. The same would be true of any criminal charge. When one is accused of first-degree murder, trespass, or grand larceny, there are just as many issues as there are *essential* elements in the criminal charge specified. Especially in propositions of fact which lie clearly within the limits of highly specialized fields (such as law, medicine, government, engineering) one should realize that there are many terms which will be found to have highly specialized, professional meanings. In all such cases the burden of analysis is pretty well carried when one learns the exact meaning of the words used.

When an understanding of the words used and a bit of preliminary research give the exact meaning that one has to attack or defend in argument, one ought to be able to state the issues *tentatively* and then proceed with his investigation on the basis of the tentative list of issues. As the work of investigation brings more understanding, the phrasing of the issues may be improved. This possibility should be held in mind until all of our work of investigation and organization has been completed.

B. Examples from law and general argument. These will help to make clear the exact nature of issues—which are essentially the same in law courts and elsewhere.

1. In law. Let us say, for example, that A is accused of the crime of burglary at common law. This crime has five essential elements, (1) breaking and (2) entering (3) a dwelling (4) at night (5) with felonious intent. There are five possible or "potential" issues here. The State (affirmative) must prove all that are not admitted. They are all *vital*. If the defense (negative) prevents the affirmative from establishing any single one beyond reasonable doubt, the case of the affirmative fails. Then the defendant is not guilty of *burglary*. He may be guilty of a number of other things, but that is another story. The defendant may admit that he broke and entered a dwelling at night, but may deny that it was done with felonious intent—may say he did it to put out a fire. The affirmative has established (or gained an admission of) four of the five necessary points, but the whole case falls. No affirmative case can stand after the loss of a single issue. Any point which the affirmative can fail on and still establish the case *cannot be an issue,* though it may be very important. Importance is not enough—each issue is *vital* in the strictest sense of that word, in the sense in which every *vital* organ is necessary to the life of a dog. When only one *vital* organ is destroyed the dog is dead.

2. In general discussion. Here the situation is essentially the same. A good type of proposition with which to illustrate analysis is, *Resolved, That the X Manufacturing Company should adopt the Y system of production and distribution.* Let us assume that the X Manufacturing Company exists for the purpose of making money for its stockholders, and that there is no question of the legality, labor problems, or public morality involved. It follows that the only real question at issue is whether or not it will be profitable to change to the Y system. Let us assume further that the proponents of the Y system are ready to argue that under this system the X Company will (1) buy cheaper raw material, (2) save a great deal of money in advertising, (3) save further large sums in the payment for royalties and patents, and (4) greatly increase sales. Let us suppose that the affirmative inevitably goes into the debate with argument and evidence on each of these four points and the negative goes into the debate with argument and evidence against each of these four points. Do we have four issues? The answer is no. There is only one issue. And that issue will ultimately be resolved by striking a balance and adding up probable profits and probable losses and seeing whether, on the whole, financial advantage or disadvantage is indicated by the change. If the affirmative succeeds in carrying three of these points, and the negative one, it does not mean that the affirmative wins the debate. Suppose the affirmative convinces the board of directors that they will have additional profits of a million a year on raw material, another million on advertising, and another million on sales, but the negative succeeds in convincing the board of directors that they will have a loss of six million a year on royalties and patents. The balance is in favor of the negative by three million dollars. It is not a case of the affirmative's winning by three points to one, any more than in the classic burglary case a man is guilty of burglary when the prosecution is convincing on four of the five essential elements of burglary. The accused is innocent of the charge of burglary if he is innocent of any one of the five essential elements of burglary.

A type of proposition which might be confused with the one just discussed is the following, *Resolved, That the town of A should adopt a new water system taking water from Lake B.* Let us assume that the town of A is, at the present time, using water from wells. What are the issues? Is this a case in which we just strike a balance in comparing the good and the bad points of the well-water system and the lake-water system? The answer is no. This is a very different kind of proposition, because here the subordinate questions one has to ask are different in kind. They are not all of the same kind, namely profit and loss. Obviously the first issue is: *Is the present well-water system unsatisfactory?* It is a very common type of proposition in which the affirmative first has to demonstrate (or gain an admission of its contention) that the present system is vitally unsatisfactory. Having established (or received the admission) that the well-water system is indefensible and must be abandoned, does it follow that the city must use the water of Lake B? Clearly not. First, the people of city A ought to know that if they go to the expense of a new water system from Lake B, they will (1) have water enough; (2) that the water they get will be fit to use; and (3) that they will get it at a price they can afford to pay. In other words, after the affirmative has established the position that the well-water system must be abandoned, it has still to establish three vital contentions concerning the water in Lake B: *i.e.*, that it is satisfactory in *quantity, quality,* and *price or accessibility.* So in this case we have four issues and not one.

C. The issues and the kinds of propositions. Before one attempts to analyze any proposition one should have in mind clearly whether the proposition dealt with is a proposition of policy, fact, or value. If it is a proposition of fact, the exact nature of the fact, the kind of fact it is, must be recognized or discovered before going any further. Criminal charges are always essentially propositions of fact. Sometimes they get treated as propositions of policy, and the jury decides that it would be good policy not to convict the accused of the crime mentioned, rather than the question of fact, *Did he commit the crime specified?* If such a charge is to be treated (as it is supposed to be) as a strict question of fact, the issues will probably be discovered by learning the exact, official definition of the crime charged. In many propositions of fact, the nature of the fact, *how many essential elements always have to be present in order to have the fact present,* will determine the number of the issues.

Finding the issues in propositions of value is in a way somewhat more difficult, and likely to remain in a tentative stage somewhat longer, than finding them in propositions of fact. This follows from the very nature of value judgments. In propositions of fact, we are pretty much in the realm of the wholly objective. In propositions of policy we are in a realm in which the objective and the subjective tend to get inextricably mixed. In propositions of value we are likely to be in a realm in which decisions are very largely subjective.

If your proposition deals with a moral judgment you obviously have to satisfy the moral code of those who are to vote. If your proposition deals with an esthetic judgment, you have to satisfy the esthetic code of your judges. There can be no judgment on whether a certain act, program, or practice is morally justifiable, economically sound, or esthetically good *in the absence of moral, economic, or esthetic standards of judgment.* The standards accepted by those who are to judge your argument are almost inevitably going to control the decision you will get. You had better know what they are. If you think you have better standards than the judges, your first obligation is to convert the judges to your standards. Unless you can do this, you will have to accept judgment on theirs.

When you attempt to prove to anyone that Carl Sandburg is a great poet, it is important for you not only to know what you think constitutes great poetry and to know Mr. Sandburg's poetry; it is also important for you to know what *those who are to judge* consider to be the essentials of great poetry. Until you know that, you are not ready to try to prove to them that Mr. Sandburg's compositions possess those essentials. So in a debate concerning whether or not the M Company performs a fine social service in our community, you need to know not only what the M Company does and how they do it, but you need to know *what those who are to judge your arguments* consider to be the proper standards by which social service must be evaluated. All this is not to say that propositions of value cannot be properly analyzed, that it is unnecessary to try to find the issues in a proposition of value.

Often the economic, moral, or social code of those who are to judge is well known or easily ascertained either by inquiry or deduction from known facts. However, if your jury or board or legislature happens to be composed of moral vagabonds (those who have no individual codes of morality, but who seek to substitute for individual codes a vague guess, or even accurate information as to *what the public accepts*) you have no opportunity to get a *moral judgment*. You have really no genuine proposition of value before you. What you have to do, in such circumstances, whether you like it or not, is to debate the *question of fact* whether or not the public involved believes in or accepts the action concerning which you sought a moral judgment.

A valid public opinion on a moral question can arise only in a public the members of which have individually valid private moral opinions, just as a valid public opinion on an economic question can arise only in a public the individual members of which have valid, private, economic opinions. The attempt to say that private judgments should arise from, or yield to, public judgments in problems of truth or ethics is simply an attempt to substitute the classic fallacy of arguing in a circle for the codes of moral conduct and the standards of truth which underlie civilization and separate mankind from wild animals. Such a position necessarily says in essence that a particular action is good because the majority of the public believe it is good, and the private individuals who make up the public opinion vote that it is good because they had been made to believe that public opinion supports them in that position. In other words, the private opinion is derived from the public opinion which is derived from the private opinion, and the whole process has nothing to do with morality or truth. It has to do only with political power. Such a philosophy can easily justify Buchenwald, the wholesale extermination of Jews, or any other group. It can easily justify the Communists' liquidation or enslavement of all who differ with them on any question. It has nothing to do with the human process of reasoning and persuasion, and it is of no value to either an individual or to a society concerned with morality and truth.

In such a situation ignorance and vice have equal standing—equal voting power—with truth and virtue. Perhaps a better way of putting it is to say that "truth" and "virtue" become meaningless words. Then whatever the public supports is "right," not because it meets valid tests of either truth or ethics, but because it has "might" (majority vote) on its side. It easily follows that anyone who refuses to abide by the decision of the majority (however obtained), anyone who chooses to follow his own conscience, his private opinions of truth and justice and morality, is readily labeled a bad citizen. Then he can be punished in any way that seems "right," from petty persecution to the gas chamber or the firing squad. This is of the essence of Fascist, Nazi, and Communist philosophy, and is the antithesis of all philosophies of democracy and individual integrity and responsibility.

Analyzing propositions of policy is likely to involve a combination of the problems of analyzing the other two types. The *nature of the objective facts* must be ascertained, and the *standards of judgment* to be used must be understood, before we are ready to discover and phrase the issues.

The nature of the primary facts being *what they are* in our problem (water works, the high-school situation, the mayoralty election) what will the affirmative have to prove (or get admitted) in order to get the voters (who are to judge), using *their* standards of judgment (the only ones they have to use), to vote for the proposition? This complex question, we think, fairly represents the complexity encountered in the analysis of many propositions of policy. A proposition of policy *may be* relatively simple. The advocate needs to know which it is before he attempts to phrase the issues.

A proposition of policy frequently is a proposition with *a single issue*. This is not necessarily true, as we have shown in the water works proposition discussed. However, propositions of policy which deal with such matters as the election of a president or governor frequently cannot be broken up into a number of issues. There can be many talking points, but in most such cases the issue will probably be, *Will it be good for the country or the state or the city to elect Mr. X?* A thorough understanding of this whole situation—both the objective facts and the subjective values involved—is the only safe basis for analysis.

D. Kinds of issues. Since various kinds of issues are frequently mentioned in argument, it may be well to consider the uses of the word with its appropriate modifiers.

1. Potential issues. These are the issues that are inherent in the proposition, the possible issues each one of which the affirmative must either prove affirmatively or gain an admission of from the negative (or the judge, jury, or audience) in order to establish its case. In law the term for these is usually the *primary issues*, which are usually declared and set forth in the pleadings before the real argument begins. In law also one finds the term "subordinate issue" used to refer to a point in controversy which would probably be called a "point in partition" in general argument. Examples might be the question of the time at which a clock stopped, or whether a door was ajar, or whether the accused wore a certain pair of tennis shoes. The whole case might depend on the decision of such a point, but it could be only an accidental circumstance. It could not be a vital consideration *inherent in the proposition*.

The potential issues are always the same in the same proposition; they exist independently of the wills of the debaters. They are to be discovered, not invented or chosen. They are always the same for the affirmative and the negative, always the same for every affirmative and every negative on any given proposition. Of course if propositions vary in any way the issues may also vary. *Resolved, That the commission form of government should be adopted in Chicago,* is not *necessarily* the same proposition you would have if you substituted Dayton or New Orleans for Chicago.

2. Admitted issues. Any "potential issues" which the negative will admit may, for convenience, be called "admitted issues." These, of course, drop out of the controversy. Admitted matter obviously cannot be an actual issue. The issues are the inherently vital points that are controverted by the negative. In general argumentation what might be an issue if it were denied, falls back into the class of "admitted matter" when it is admitted, and ceases to be of importance in the discussion.

For instance: If in a given action, possession in A and entry by B are the points on which the proposition must rest, and one is admitted, then the other constitutes the sole issue *in that contest.* So if the basic vital points in a proposal for the adoption of a certain scheme of taxation are (1) the elimination of present evils, (2) the raising of sufficient revenue, and (3) the working of justice to all classes (that is, not bringing in new evils)—if these are the potential issues and the negative admits (1), then the actual issues are (2) and (3). If the negative admits (1) and (2), then the actual issue is (3).

3. Actual issues. These are, then, simply the issues you have left after you subtract the admitted issues from the potential issues. It should be borne in mind that the burden on the affirmative is that of proving all the potential issues which the negative declines to admit. The affirmative has no authority to demand the admission of any particular issues. The negative may admit whatever it wishes to admit and the affirmative must be prepared to prove the rest. It is well for an affirmative in preparing to meet a negative whose detailed proof is not known in advance, to make a tentative guess as to what the negative probably will admit and try to find out as early as possible whether the guess is right. The well-prepared affirmative, however, will go into the debate with the necessary evidence and argument to do whatever it can do to substantiate the affirmative side of any potential issue on which the negative offers an effective challenge.

4. Stock issues. Issues that can be applied to a particular class of propositions are "stock issues." It seems obviously impossible to get stock issues that will apply to all different kinds of questions. This follows from the very nature of issues. But in regard to a large class of propositions, common in every free society and much used in contest or school debate, a certain formula may be used as a *start* in analysis. We refer to *propositions of policy having to do with changes in necessarily continuing systems,* as taxation, education, railways, water, light and power utilities, sanitation, etc. Here are programs that cannot be dropped. Here are enterprises that *are to be kept going* on some basis or other. In such questions we may well start an analysis on the basis of two "stock issues." The phraseology may differ; the points are essentially the same. Various wordings of each are given:

1. Is the present unsatisfactory? Are there fatal evils in the existing situation? Is there a cause for action? Is there a disease? Do we need a change? etc.

2. Is the proposed action an improvement? Will it cure the evils? Is this the action we should take? Is this the proper remedy? Is the proposed change the right one?

New systems will not be adopted while the present is satisfactory, nor unless the proposed scheme looks like a satisfactory remedy or improvement. So the man with a new scheme for doing something that is to continue to be done on *some* scheme, must always show somehow or other (or get it admitted) that there is something wrong and that his scheme will make it right.

Why, then, are these not really the exact issues in all such cases? For two reasons it is unsafe to accept them as such. *First,* because analysis may show a *more specific wording* for these general questions, and this will aid in many ways. *Second,* and principally, because on accurate analysis it may be found that one of these questions, especially number two, will break up into, say, three questions, *each of which* must be proved by the affirmative. The proposition dealing with the change in the water works discussed above, is an example of this type of case.

Notice, however, that it is not sufficient to be able to break up a big question into three or four small ones; *each small one must be absolutely vital, or it is no issue.* For instance, it is impossible to get *four* issues in the manufacturing case discussed above. There is only one issue, and four important points in partition.

E. The necessity of knowing the issues. The importance of this cannot be overestimated. Argument on any question implies some difference of opinion, it means that there are certain ideas affirmed by one side and denied by the other. The proposition is merely an expression of this clash of opinion, and an understanding of its meaning depends entirely upon a comprehension of the points of conflict. If the writer or speaker would prove his proposition, he must prove these critical points. Moreover, the value of his materials depends upon their relation to these points; any evidence that gives a direct and substantial support to these vital contentions is valuable; whatever does not bear directly on these basic positions is, at best, of secondary importance. If an advocate makes a mistake in finding these critical points on which the discussion must be based, he may well waste his time in proving some point that will not help him after it is proved, or he may be surprised in debate by attack on some vital point which he is not ready to defend. This danger is realized and guarded against in the courts of law. They demand that the issues shall be clearly stated in the pleadings before a trial begins, and that every piece of evidence, whether of fact or of law, shall have a direct and evident bearing on some one of these issues, anything that cannot conform to this test being declared irrelevent and being excluded from consideration. Then again, a speaker or writer who does not know the issues will probably *confuse his readers or hearers* by giving them a false, distorted view of his case. If a debater does not comprehend just what are the few vital points of his case, around which all the lesser facts must be grouped, his proof will almost certainly lack the unity and coherence that are indispensable for clearness and force in presentation.

F. Proposition and issues. We have seen in the preceding chapter that in order to have intelligent argumentation, we must first have a proposition. The proper formulating of the proposition insures that we have one single question that can be argued *pro* and *con* directly and so brought to a definite conclusion. This proposition thus makes clear the general position which the advocate must argue for or against. But he is not yet ready to select the evidence or the arguments with which to support his contention. He has merely found the field of battle. Before he can open the fight, or even arrange his forces, he must examine the ground he has chosen, and find out its points of vantage and of weakness. The proposition discloses the task that must in the end be accomplished, but it does not show what are the steps necessary in the accomplishment, or just what method may be most effective. The proposition gives a single question for discussion; but even in any such single question there are innumerable arguments, points, masses of evidence, that may be brought forward. All these arguments and all this evidence cannot be used; it is not all of equal value; some of it will have such a direct and powerful bearing on the question that it must have great weight; but much of it will have such an indefinite and remote bearing that to use it at all would be a waste of time. Clearly, then, the next thing for the debater to do is to get some standards by reference to which he can determine the value of these materials. A century and a half ago, John Ward, in his *Systems of Oratory,* said: "But in all disputes it is of the greatest consequence to observe where the stress of the controversy lies. For, without attending to this, persons may cavil about different matters, without understanding each other or deciding anything." In any discussion the "stress of the controversy" inevitably falls upon the proving or disproving of a few points, which are the center and soul of the question: only as those who have the burden of proof win in the struggle over these points can they win the whole contest. In order, therefore, to know what evidence to use, the advocate on either side must first find out just what are the points that the affirmative *must* establish by the evidence and the argument based on it, in order to establish *the proposition*. These points are the issues.

G. Issues and burden of proof. It is well to consider the relation of the theory of issues to various aspects of the theory of burden of proof, in order that their complete harmony may be clear and all misunderstanding avoided.

1. **The issues, and the affirmative and negative.** The affirmative has no *choice* in regard to issues—every "potential issue" which the negative chooses to fight on, must be established. The negative, on the other hand, may choose among the potential issues which ones to admit and which to oppose. In law this choice must be made known to the affirmative in the course of the pleading, so

that a suit never starts without all parties knowing the issues and agreeing as to what the issues are. In general discussion this situation should be approximated as closely as possible. Before a debate starts, or early in the debate, a direct clash should be brought about on vital points that are left after all admissions have been made. The affirmative, of course, has the burden of proof on *each* issue. Establishing usually means "beyond a reasonable doubt" or by "preponderating evidence," so the negative in trying to block a case seeks to raise reasonable doubts on as many issues as possible, and usually does not risk everything on fewer issues than are absolutely necessary. One man may doubt on one issue and one on another, so it is well to fight on as many as offer a good chance, unless one can be absolutely sure of winning on fewer. Suppose the water works case mentioned above was to be decided by a city council of twenty men. If the negative were ready to grant that the present system was indefensible, that would be "an admitted issue." Then it might oppose the affirmative on each of the other three potential issues. If the negative got four men to believe that the proposed lake water was not good enough, but failed to convince them on the other two issues, and then got four others to agree that the lake water would be too expensive to use, and four others that there would not be enough of it, it would win its case by a vote of 12 to 8. If it had limited its efforts to two issues it would have lost by a vote of 12 to 8, and if it had limited its argument to any one issue it would have lost by a vote of 16 to 4. A competent negative opposes the affirmative on every issue on which it sees a good chance to get votes in court, legislature, or on the public platform.

2. **Issues and counter-proposition.** Sometimes the negative sets up a substitute or counter-plan or proposition. When this is the case the negative of course has a burden of proof *on its plan*. The issues of the case are not changed by this plan of defense. If the substitute does not offer an obstacle to the establishing of the affirmative side of the issues, it is a waste of time to talk about it. If the substitute can be so presented as to block one or more of the *vital* points of the affirmative, the case fails—the negative wins. But the substitute may not have won, as explained below.

Suppose in the burglary case already referred to, instead of confining its case to proving unfounded one or more of the five accusations, the defense simply denies them all and offers evidence that proves conclusively that not A, the accused, but X, committed the crime in question. When it accuses X it necessarily takes the burden of proving that X did these things. But its only purpose is to show thereby that A is innocent. And note that X is not declared guilty as the result of this trial. The proposition is that A is guilty. The affirmative has failed to establish its case either by having been blocked on one or more of the issues, or by the negative's offering a substitute. But the substitute did not *win*—not in this trial. It is advanced only enough to show that the claims of the affirmative are unfounded. In such a situation the indictment and trial of X might well follow—but that is another story.

3. **The issues and winning or losing.** In what we have just said concerning issues, burden of proof, and *winning* and *losing*, we have had in mind actual cases in real life, not contest or school debates before judges who are to say *who won the debate*. All that has been said about issues, however, applies in these contest debates exactly as it does in a law court or political campaign, except the remarks on winning or losing. In a law court, in a political campaign, in business, in science, it is *the case* that is being passed on. The decision is on the "merits of the question," not on *the way* in which certain advocates handle the case. But in an intercollegiate debate, for instance, the decision should be determined *always* by the skill of the debaters, *never* on the strength of the case (except in so far as this is indicative of the skill of the debaters). The decision to mean anything at all must be based on the ability shown in debating—not on the strength of the evidence or the merits of the case. A debate should, of course, be worked out and presented *as though the decision were to be made by the audience* or jury or judge on the merits of the case. For only in this way can the contestants show their real ability as debaters, but the judges should know enough about *debating* to render a decision on debating alone.

4. **The issues and conviction and persuasion.** The issues are the points that will have to be established by the affirmative in order to *convince* competent judges that their plan should be adopted. The issues have to do primarily with conviction rather than persuasion. They are the basis of the appeal to the intellect. The work

of persuasion may be done in connection with proving the issues. In selecting evidence, illustration, phraseology, the emotional side of each audience (sentiments, taste, prejudices) should always be kept in mind as one of the guides in all that we do. But in discovering the issues in any case, we must consider only the intellectual side of our case—the facts and the justifiable inferences from the facts. The analysis of the proposition to find the issues should be impersonal—not done with particular audiences or judges in mind. After the impersonal case is discovered then the adjusting of it to any particular tribunal should be carefully undertaken. This, of course, means paying a good deal of attention to persuasion.

H. Number and form of issues. *The number of issues* varies necessarily in different propositions. There are not usually more than three or four, unless in some technical or legal proposition in which there may be a large number. In a great many propositions there is but one issue. The issues are to be discovered. Careful analysis will reveal them. We cannot decide in advance to "pick out" three or four issues. We may find three or four and we may find but one. When we have found the number of points that may be issues from the nature of the case, our next step is to find out if any of them are admitted. If so we place them in the introduction as admitted matter. The others are our actual issues for this controversy.

When found, the issues should be expressed in such *question form* that the affirmative will answer "Yes," and the negative, "No." They should be always so stated in a brief, and usually so stated in a speech or written argument. Do not say, "The issue is, that this plan will be financially advantageous." Do not say, "The issue is, 'What will be the financial effect?'" The proper form is: "The issue is, 'Will this plan be financially advantageous?'" This represents the clean-cut question that must be answered—the exact point which the affirmative affirms and the negative denies.

I. Issues and partition. The partition consists of a statement of the main points to be taken up in the discussion. It is an enumeration of the steps to be taken in presenting the case. It is a plan of campaign determined (and usually announced) in advance. *The parti-*

tion must not be confused with the issues. The points in partition may, it is true, be substantially identical with the issues, but
they may differ widely. There may be one issue and four points
in partition—or three points which cover the three issues. The
issues must all be *vital* points. The points in partition must all be
important but not necessarily vital. If a single issue is lost the case
fails. One or more points in partition may be lost without losing
the case.

Suppose a table is hanging suspended from the ceiling by a
chain of three links. If one link is destroyed the table falls. The
table represents "the case," the contention of the affirmative; the
links of chain represent the issues. Suppose the table is standing
on five legs. One, two, or three legs *may* be removed and still the
table be left standing. It might be that four legs could be removed,
and if the fifth were big enough, and placed directly in the center
of the table, it might hold up the table, especially if the attack on
it were very weak. Here the table again represents "the case," and
the legs represent the points in partition. Or suppose two armies
are contending for the possession of a given territory, the control
of which both understand must depend upon the occupation of two
particular points (the issues), a pass and a certain height of
ground. Now there are various positions which the two opposing
forces may seize and hold, and various lines of attack which they
may adopt, depending upon the peculiar habits and methods of the
respective generals; but these positions and this strategy (the
partition) are valuable only as they serve to give the command
of these two critical points. A partition, then, is a statement of the
points the arguer intends to prove; the issues are the points the
affirmative *must prove* in order to prove its case. If the points of the
partition are well chosen, they will frequently correspond closely
to the issues; but they may be entirely different, and they are
not in any case necessarily identical.

II. FINDING THE ISSUES

The problem of finding the issue or the issues may be simple
or complex. While we usually refer to the issues rather than to the
issue, it must be remembered that often we have but *one issue*. In

many propositions the issues are obvious. All we need to know to discover them is the nature of issues. They are there in sight; we have only to recognize them. In other propositions the problem of analysis is a long and difficult one. For such cases it is well to have in mind specific methods or plans of action. But it must be admitted, and always remembered, that *there is no one method that should necessarily always be applied in all its details* to any case that is to be analyzed. The steps suggested in the following pages should be taken in any case *as far as is necessary* to discover the issues. Tentative issues that we have discovered, or points claimed by our opponents as issues, may be tested by the process here set forth. If one has to analyze a question about which he knows practically nothing, following all these steps in the order presented will discover the issues. But such cases occur rarely. The right thing is to understand the whole system and use whatever part of it seems useful in any particular case.

A. Think. The first thing to do in any case is to *think*. This must always be done. Careful thinking will disclose the issues in many cases. Think the proposition over from all angles. Ask yourself all sorts of questions about it. Who wants this? Why? Whose business is it? Who will pay for it? Who will suffer by it? Who will profit by it? What kind of question is it? What interests are at stake? Economic? Moral? Aesthetic? Social? Political? Commercial? Industrial? Spiritual? Educational? Religious? Literary? Artistic? Which one of these terms, some of which are overlapping or practically synonymous, best characterizes this question? What standards within this field must we be guided by? *What do the terms used mean?* (If you do not know, find out.) How many interpretations could possibly be put on this proposition? Which one best fits the particular circumstances?

B. Study.

1. History. The next step, and one that your thinking will naturally lead you to, is *study*. If we do not already know, we must study the meanings that may be attributed to the terms and to the proposition as a whole. As issues may differ from different propositions, in order to find our particular issues we must learn what interpretation to make and what its vital points are by study-

ing (1) the history of the question with special attention to (a) its origin and (b) the occasion for the present discussion. The nature of any controversy must depend largely upon the circumstances of its origin or the causes of its present importance.

2. All phases. But a study of the origin and history of the question may not reveal the issues. In many propositions dealing with complicated problems we must go further and study (2) all phases of the present situation. Very often issues cannot be found without a complete understanding of the proposition in all its phases. The phase that is, on hasty judgment, passed over as seemingly insignificant often develops with careful scrutiny into some new line of thought and discloses a new and vital issue. We must not consider the economic phase of the question to the exclusion of the ethical or aesthetic phases. If a question has a moral phase and physical phase, an educational phase and a political phase, we must study them all. Nothing that is relevant can safely be ignored, however much it may seem a matter of detail. The question must be thoroughly understood in all its phases before we attempt to make a definitive statement of the issues.

3. Both sides. Akin to this study of all the phases and points of view is the necessity of studying (3) both sides of the question. With a knowledge of only his own side, an advocate may invent or select some points that he decides he will prove; but he cannot know the real issues. While not all points of conflict are issues, the issues if competently found will always be points on which there is a conflict of opinion. To determine where this conflict is, he must obviously know what his opponents maintain, what they are willing to admit, and what they deny. Consequently it will often be helpful in revealing the critical points in any discussion to compare the arguments advanced by the conflicting sides.

C. Exclude. When we have gained the proper knowledge of all the facts, the process is then a process of exclusion and selection. The next step to take is to exclude (1) *admitted matter.* Clearly, if both sides admit the truth of a certain statement, that statement cannot be a critical point. By excluding such facts as these, we can narrow the material down to the significant facts, which alone are valuable.

This is a method often used by great lawyers and deliberative orators. Mr. William Wirt, in the case of Gibbons *vs.* Ogden, finds the issues of the case by first excluding the matters that may be admitted by either side. The legislature of New York had granted to Robert Fulton and others certain exclusive rights of navigation on the waters of the State. Mr. Wirt, in his speech, was endeavoring to prove the grant to be unconstitutional. He began:—

In discussing this question, the general principles assumed as postulates on the other side may be, for the most part, admitted. Thus it may be admitted, that by force of the Declaration of Independence each State became sovereign; that they were, then, independent of each other; that by virtue of their separate sovereignty they had each full power to levy war, to make peace, to establish and regulate commerce, to encourage the arts, and generally to perform all other acts of sovereignty. I shall also concede that the government of the United States is one of delegated powers, and that it is one of enumerated powers, as contended for by the counsel for the correspondent. . . .

The peculiar rule of construction demanded for those powers may also be conceded. But the express powers are to be strictly construed; the implied powers are to be construed liberally. By this it is understood to be meant, that Congress can do no more than they are expressly authorized to do; though the means of doing it are left to their discretion, under no other limit than that they shall be necessary and proper to the end.

It is often a help when we cannot know the minds of our opponents to ask this very question: Can the other side afford to admit this fact? It was in this way that Webster, in the famous White murder trial, established one of his issues in the face of the contradictions of the opposing counsel.

The counsel say that they might safely admit that Richard Crowninshield, Jr., was the perpetrator of this murder. But how could they safely admit that? If that were admitted, everything else would follow. For why should Richard Crowninshield, Jr., kill Mr. White? He was not his heir, nor his devisee; nor was he his enemy. What could be his motive? If Richard Crowninshield, Jr., killed Mr. White, he did it at some one's procurement who himself had a motive. And who, having a motive, is shown to have had any intercourse with Richard Crowninshield, Jr., but Joseph Knapp, and this principally through the agency of the prisoner at the bar? . . . He who believes, on this evidence, that Richard Crowninshield, Jr., was the immediate murderer cannot doubt that both the Knapps were conspirators in that murder. . . . The admission of so important and so connected a fact would render it impossible to contend further against the proof of the entire conspiracy as we state it.

(2) *Irrelevant and* (3) *unimportant matter* must be excluded from the material in which we will find the issues (though not necessarily from any use). There are many ideas and facts that are commonly associated with the proposition which do not really have any logical bearing on it. These should be carefully put aside at the outset. Then, again, there are many other facts properly embraced within the scope of the question which may be very valuable as evidence to prove other facts, but which manifestly are not important in themselves. For instance, in a civil suit for damages in a court of law the honesty or the intelligence of a witness might, under some circumstances, become very significant, the establishment of some vital point depending upon his reliability. Yet the character of this witness would not be mentioned in the pleadings as one of the issues, for his credibility is not important in itself, but only because of its effect upon some other and vital point in the case. In seeking the issues, the first step should be to exclude such facts as these, which are manifestly of only secondary importance.

The following, taken from Mr. Jeremiah S. Black's speech, "In Defence of the Right of Trial by Jury," illustrates the effective use of this method. Here the speaker found his issues by the exclusion of irrelevant matter.

The case before you presents but a single point and that an exceedingly plain one. It is not encumbered with any of those vexed questions that might be expected to arise out of a great war. You are not called upon to decide what kind of a rule a military commander may impose upon the inhabitants of a hostile country which he occupies as a conqueror, or what punishment he may inflict upon the soldiers of his own army or the followers of his camp; or yet how he may deal with civilians in a beleaguered city or other place in a state of actual siege which he is required to defend against a public enemy. The contest covers no such ground as that. The men whose acts we complain of erected themselves into a tribunal for the trial and punishment of citizens who were connected in no way whatever with the army or navy. And this they did in the midst of a community whose social and legal organization had never been disturbed by any war or insurrection, where the courts were wide open, where judicial process was executed every day without interruption, and where all the civil authorities, both State and National, were in the full exercise of their functions. . . .

Keeping the character of the charges in mind, let us come at once to the simple question upon which the court below divided in opinion: Had the commissioners jurisdiction, were they invested with legal authority to try the relators and put them to death for the offense of which they were accused?

(4) *Indirect matter,* furthermore, must be excluded from our issue material, regardless of its general relevancy or great importance. Every important and relevant fact that is denied or that cannot safely be admitted is not necessarily one of the issues. It may be a subordinate point, important only indirectly because the proof of it establishes or helps to establish some larger contention. In that case the larger matter, which the subordinate fact serves to prove, is one of the issues. Usually this discrimination between the issues and the subordinate points is not difficult. The issues are the points the proving of which directly proves the proposition itself; the proving of the subordinate points, on the other hand, helps to prove some larger point, which larger point in turn serves to prove the proposition. The issues are related directly to the proposition; the "subordinate issues," indirectly. For an example, take the question: *Resolved, That labor unions should be compelled to incorporate.* In the consideration of this question the argument might be made that labor unions had very rarely broken their contracts with their employers in the past. This would clearly be only a subordinate point. It would not serve to establish the proposition directly; it would be significant only because it would help to establish the more important contention, that there was no occasion (no cause for action) for compelling the unions to incorporate. This last-mentioned point, on the other hand, would be one of the issues; it would be a vital fact not admitted by the opposing side, on which there was a clash of opinion, and it would stand in direct and immediate relation to the proposition.

D. Select. While this exclusion has been going on we have probably been selecting at the same time, retaining the opposites of the classes of points we have excluded. Our work, then, summed up positively, has been to select (1) points which meet the test of C:

(a) points on which there is a direct clash of opinion (points that are not admitted—that our opponents probably will not admit), (b) relevant points, (c) important points, (d) direct (not indirect or subordinate) points. Our work is about done. These points are necessarily few and may constitute the issues just as they stand. There is one test which will determine this. Our work has been to select (2) points which are *vital* to the establishment of the affirmative side of the proposition. We must select only *vital* points from this small group. Can the affirmative side be established without establishing all these points? If so, they are not all issues. If the affirmative can lose a point and still prove its case, that point is not an issue. When we reach this step in our analysis and find that the points we have selected will not pass this final test, the difficulty is usually that the test for subordinate points and indirectness has not been strictly applied, and that we have three or four points under a proposition in which there are only one or two issues. What we need is a point or two that will group these three or four and connect them to the proposition in a vital way.

Suppose the resolution proposes a new method or process in manufacture, in which there is no question of ethics, or social justice or any such phase to complicate the issues, and suppose you have narrowed the points down to three—the new process will lessen the cost of raw material, will make unnecessary the paying of certain royalties now being paid, and will produce a valuable by-product. These points have passed your tests of importance, relevance, etc., and are all emphatically denied by your opponents. Are they issues? No; they are points in partition. There is not an issue among them, because no one of them is really vital. Suppose the negative shows that you will not lessen the cost of raw material —that this will remain unchanged. But you succeed in proving the saving on royalties and the gaining of a new by-product. Of course you have established your case—that the process should be adopted. Or suppose the negative wins on two of them and shows no change in regard to them, while you show a gain on one. Your case is established. These cannot then be issues. Each issue is so vital that if the affirmative fails to establish one of them the case fails. The difficulty here is that you are trying to get three issues where there is only one, *viz.*, the question, Would this process bring a financial advantage? This is the issue. To establish the fact that this process should be adopted the affirmative must show financial advantage, and this may be shown in any possible way. There is only one issue. The difficulty arose from not applying the test for directness strictly enough.

Summary of method of finding the issues:

A. Think: On the proposition, its possible meaning, all its elements, and aspects, to the limits of your present knowledge.
B. Study:
1. History of question, with especial attention to
   a. Its origin.
   b. Present occasion for discussion.
2. All phases of question.
3. Both sides.
C. Exclude:
1. Mutually admitted matter.
2. Irrelevant matter.
3. Unimportant matter.
4. Indirect matter.
D. Select:
1. Points which meet the test of C.
2. Vital points.

Exercises

1. Phrase a proposition of fact, a proposition of value, and a proposition of policy. Refer to Chapter III. List the potential issues for each proposition.
2. Examine one of the printed debates in the appendixes. State what you believe to be the potential issues, the admitted issues (if any), and the actual issue or issues.
3. Write an expository essay in which you explain how, in terms of section II, "Finding the Issues," you found the issues in an assigned proposition or a proposition of your own choice.
4. State the issues in one proposition of fact, one of value, and one of policy. Indicate the circumstances in which one or more issues might be admitted.
5. Plan an affirmative argumentative speech on a proposition of policy. Present a four-minute introduction which would be appropriate for

this speech. State the proposition, define terms, give background of proposition, exclude irrelevant matter, state the issues, and partition your case. Criticize these introductions from the standpoint of adequacy of analysis.

6. Select a proposition for class analysis. Prepare individual analyses before class and come prepared to participate in class discussion for the purpose of working out an analysis acceptable to the group.

Chapter V · READING AS PREPARATION
FOR DEBATE

I. PRELIMINARY CONSIDERATIONS

A. The purpose of investigation. Investigation is the process of acquiring information about the proposition. This is done principally by reading and discussion, although surveying one's own ideas and listening to subject-matter experts are also helpful procedures. When investigation is thorough, the likelihood of superficiality and mere talk is greatly reduced. To put the idea positively, thorough investigation is undertaken for the purpose of accumulating a general background of information, finding the available evidence, and discovering the specific lines of argument to support an answer to the issues which analysis has revealed.

This general purpose may be served by direct and indirect preparation. Direct preparation is the study and thought which are undertaken in terms of a specific problem for a specific occasion. The work which an advocate does on a proposition after it has been stated is direct preparation. Indirect preparation is that which takes place over a period of time and without reference to a particular occasion. It involves general knowledge and experience. An advocate who is well read and otherwise informed on public questions has an advantage over one who "starts from scratch" with direct preparation. Obviously, both kinds of preparation are useful in that they complement each other.

B. When to read. In case the advocate has an opportunity to phrase his own proposition, part of the reading should precede the act of phrasing. An informed person is better qualified to state accurately a proposition which will express the essence of the controversy.

Similarly, if worthwhile discussion is to precede the wording of a proposition and the subsequent debate upon it, systematic reading is usually indispensable. If five uninformed persons pool their ignorance in a discussion, we may say that five times zero is still zero.

In the instances of school debaters and professional advocates whose propositions are imposed by circumstances, the reading which is direct preparation necessarily occurs after the proposition has been worded. In case the proposition can be altered, it may be that the results of his reading will lead the advocate to revise the original wording. Thus there is something to be said for beginning one's study with a tentative statement and then revising the proposition as the study progresses. In actual practice, however, the advocate whose proposition is given to him is not at liberty to alter the wording of it. His reading is simply a matter of discovering the materials *pro* and *con* on the proposition as phrased.

Whether the reading takes place before or after the proposition is phrased, it may profitably alternate with analysis. In other words, the first step of direct preparation should be a preliminary discovery of issues, the second step should be the reading as directed by these tentative issues, the third step should be a refinement of the issues, and the fourth step should be further reading in terms of the specific issues.

C. Deciding what to read. There is a scarcity of printed material on some debatable propositions, but on most controversial matters there is so much material that wise selection is the chief problem. Two familiar signs of this problem are unevenness in learning and the lack of a comprehensive grasp of the proposition. The proposed remedies have usually included these items of advice: (1) begin with a few required books, (2) begin with a few basic books which are recommended, (3) adopt a reading requirement as in college courses, (4) require debaters to pass a subject-matter test on the proposition, (5) require mastery of one or two comprehensive books. Subject-matter experts can profitably be asked for advice on what to read. Regardless of the method used, the fact is that most debaters need guidance in deciding what to read first. Although school debaters comprise only a small portion of the advocates in our society, their problems with respect to reading may be considered typical.

In connection with this recommended guidance of student debaters in the matter of reading, it is pertinent to suggest a division of labor among the squad members. If the reading list is extensive, it is better at first to divide it and assign specific publications or topics to individuals. Each one will then report to the group or make his reference file available to the others. The following preliminary outline and study outline are readily divisible for this purpose. Advocates who are not school debaters should also find these outlines helpful.

D. The use of original investigation. By original investigation we mean first-hand inquiry as opposed to the reading of the reports of other investigators. It may involve questionnaires, letters, personal observations, interviews, or experiments which are conceived, planned, and conducted by the advocate himself. To supplement their reading on the chain-store proposition, some debaters took shopping trips to independent and chain stores and offered as evidence the prices paid for identical items. In order to obtain evidence on the civic competence of persons between the ages of eighteen and twenty-one, some debaters who advocated lowering the voting age to eighteen years administered current-affairs tests to young persons in that age group.

Wherever conditions are such that it is impossible for the advocate to conduct an investigation as well as it has been done and reported by others, he should rely on reading as the form of investigation. Original investigation requires much time if well done. Therefore, it should be attempted only if the desired data are not available in print.

II. A PLAN TO DIRECT THE READING

A. The preliminary outline. It is helpful to have a plan to guide the reading. For example, in a proposition of policy, one might use an outline such as the one suggested here:

1. What does the question or the proposition mean?
   a) Define the terms.
   b) Identify the class in which the problem belongs; *i.e.,* social

security, international politics, medical economics, labor economics, etc.

c) Isolate the assumptions involved; *i.e.*, the relationship between national sovereignty and world peace in a debate on world organization.

2. How has the problem developed?
   a) Explore briefly its origin and history.
   b) Appraise its present timeliness.
   c) Discover evidence of the existence and the extent of the problem.
3. By what criteria should any solution be evaluated?
4. How does the *status quo* measure up to these criteria?
5. What are the possible solutions?
6. How does each proposal measure up to the criteria?

B. The detailed study outline. The preceding outline can be expanded considerably, if more detail is desired, as in the following sample study outline on National Medical Care:[1]

A. Definitions
   1. What is "complete medical care"?
   2. What does "available to all citizens" mean?
   3. What is "at public expense"?
   4. What is socialized medicine?
   5. What is preventive medicine?
   6. What is curative medicine?
   7. What is health insurance?
B. Analysis of the problem
   8. Are medical costs too high?
   9. Are medical facilities inadequate in quality?
   10. Are medical facilities inadequate in availability?
   11. Do some persons fail to utilize existing facilities for reasons other than cost or availability?
   12. What about the economic needs of doctors, nurses, hospitals, etc.?
   13. To what extent are these conditions inherent in "private medicine"?
C. Goals or criteria
   14. Do we want to reduce the costs of medical care?
   15. Do we want to increase the amount of medical care available?

---

[1] *Resolved, That the Federal Government should provide a system of complete medical care available to all citizens at public expense.*

16. Do we want to improve the distribution of medical facilities?

17. Do we want to preserve the patient-doctor relationship of "private medicine"?

18. Do we want the highest possible level of medical science and technology?

19. De we want the general public to share the costs of medical care?

20. Do we want to encourage fuller use of medical facilities?

21. Do we want to develop preventive medicine?

22. Do we want to maintain the present degree of separation of government and medical practice?

23. Do we want to develop a program that has the support of most of the medical profession?

D. Nature of the proposal

24. What form does this plan of medical care take?

25. How is it to be financed?

26. How is it to be administered?

27. What is to be a doctor's relationship to the plan?

28. What is to be a patient's relationship to it?

29. Will there be minimum or maximum limits on services available to a patient?

30. Will specialized services be available?

31. May doctors and patients disregard the plan except as they may pay taxes to support it?

32. May a doctor practicipate in the plan and have a private practice in addition?

33. What provisions for public health services, hospitals, research, etc., would be made?

34. What medical standards are envisioned, and who would determine them and enforce them?

35. Would medical schools and students be subsidized and controlled by the Federal Government?

36. How would fuller use of medical facilities be encouraged?

E. Relative merits of the proposal

37. Would the plan meet the needs in items 8–13?

38. Would the plan meet the criteria in items 14–23?

39. Would an extension of the clinic plan be better?

40. Would an extension of voluntary plans be better?

41. Would something like the Wagner-Murray-Dingell plan be better?

42. Would a state-administered plan be better?

III. SOURCES OF INFORMATION

A. Reference books and bibliographies. General reference works are useful for background information, specific ideas or facts, cross references, bibliographical items, and similar materials as indicated below. One's choice among the general references must, of course, be governed by the category of the subject under investigation. For background material, consult the *Encyclopedia Britannica,* the *New International Encyclopedia,* the *Encyclopedia of the Social Sciences,* the *Cyclopedia of Education,* the *Cyclopedia of American Government,* and the *New Encyclopedia of Social Reform.* More recent materials are available in the *New International Yearbook,* the *American Yearbook,* the *World Almanac,* the *Statesman's Yearbook,* the *Statistical Abstract of the United States,* and the *Commerce Yearbook.* Personal data concerning the qualifications of authorities are published in *Who's Who in America, Dictionary of American Biography, Dictionary of National Biography* (British Empire), and *Who Knows—And What.*

Special reference works for debaters and others interested in particular propositions include the *Reference Shelf Series,* the *Handbook Series,* and the *University Debaters' Annual,* all published by H. W. Wilson Co., 950–972 University Avenue, New York; the *Debaters' Help Book Series* and *Intercollegiate Debates,* both published by Noble and Noble, 67 Irving Place, New York; and the *Handbook* of the National University Extension Association. We do not recommend the purchase of prepared speeches, rebuttals, evidence files, and case outlines for school debates. The preparation of such materials is properly the function of students under competent faculty guidance.

Ready-made bibliographies on many propositions and questions are available. Among the most familiar sources are the Bibliographical Division of the Library of Congress, the larger city libraries, some state university library extension services, the special reference works listed in the preceding paragraph, and the Public Affairs Information Service, 11 West Fortieth Street, New York. Reference librarians in colleges are usually willing to assist in the preparation of bibliographies if they are given ample notice. However, college students ought not to expect others to do all this work for them.

B. Books. Persons who investigate public questions find helpful information in specialized books in such fields as economics, political science, history, sociology, business, and international relations. These can be traced through the card catalogue under the headings of title, author, and subject. The potential usefulness of a particular book can be estimated tentatively by referring to its table of contents and index.

There are many published book lists, digests, and reviews which provide helpful leads. Some of these are the *Book Review Digest,* the *United States Catalogue* and supplements, the *Cumulative Book Index,* and the *Booklist* of the American Library Association.

C. Periodicals. In this classification are journals of opinion, news magazines, and other regular publications. Students of public questions are familiar with the *American Economic Review, Time, Newsweek,* the *United States News, Harper's, Atlantic, Vital Speeches,* the *Nation,* the *New Republic, Survey, Foreign Affairs, Annals of the American Academy of Political and Social Sciences,* the *Congressional Digest, Speech Activities,* and *Scholastic.*

D. Newspapers. The metropolitan dailies offer reports of current events, texts of speeches, and columns of opinion which are pertinent to current problems. The *New York Times Index* may be used to find the desired items in that paper, and by getting the dates of stories from this source, it is easier to locate similar material in the files of other papers. As we say again in discussing evidence and refutation, it is important to note the editorial policy of the source and make proper allowance for bias or "slant." This advice is not solely applicable to the use of newspapers.

E. Pamphlets on public affairs. *Public Affairs Pamphlets,* a bulletin of the United States Office of Education, provides an index to many inexpensive pamphlets on social, economic, and political problems, and international affairs. These publications of some eighty organizations are listed to meet the needs of public forums. The *Public Affairs Information Service,* published by the H. W. Wilson Company of New York, is a comparable index. The *World Almanac* and other sources list approximately 25,000 organizations, most of which publish pamphlets, and they cover the range of subjects which one is likely to investigate. The Public Affairs Committee, Inc., 22 East 38th Street, New York, issues more than 100 pamphlets at twenty cents each.

There are several discussion and debate programs on the radio networks and many more on local stations. The network programs include the *Northwestern University Reviewing Stand,* the *Town Meeting of the Air,* the *University of Chicago Round Table,* the *People's Platform,* the *American Forum of the Air,* and *Opinion Please.* Printed transcripts of some of these programs are available in inexpensive pamphlet form.

F. Government documents. These documents are so numerous that a large room containing tiers of stacks is required to house the holdings of almost any large university. Obviously, we can refer investigators only to listings of such publications. The single exception is the *Congressional Record,* which reports the day-by-day proceedings of Congress. The document lists are the *Document Catalogue,* the *Monthly Catalogue of United States Public Documents,* the *Price Lists of Government Documents,* and the *Monthly Check List of State Publications.*

G. Interviews and correspondence. In the early stages of investigation it is helpful to have the guidance of a subject-matter expert. Some college debate squads meet with professors of history, of political science, of economics, or of some other pertinent field to receive hints concerning the proper lines of inquiry and the basic types of reading. Later in the process of investigation the needed facts or testimony may not be available in print. Under such circumstances personal letters of inquiry or interviews with source persons may elicit the desired information. Students who are investigating subjects for discussion or argument should not bother busy people needlessly; they ought to exhaust the printed sources first. Those who must write for information should observe the rules of polite correspondence: (1) Use the correct name, title, and address; never write to "Chairman, Department of Economics, Harvard University"; (2) write a brief, neat, literate, typewritten letter; (3) if possible enclose a brief, carefully phrased questionnaire which can be checked in a minimum of time. An inquirer should know that evidence obtained in letters and interviews is not always admissible, according to the rules of some school debating leagues.

IV. HOW TO READ

A. Seek primary sources. Whenever possible, go to primary sources for important facts or statements of expert opinion. It is better to quote from the original document, such as a report of the Committee on the Costs of Medical Care, than to cite a *Reader's Digest* article about it. A secondary source may misrepresent the original. For instance, the headline of a book-review column in a newspaper stated, "How the People Get Pushed Around by War Propaganda," but the book being reviewed dealt with economic, not psychological, warfare. The sense of the original version may be altered unintentionally in the process of condensation.

B. Follow a plan. No single plan is likely to be best for all persons, but some plan is a practical necessity. Unsystematic reading is inefficient if time and energy are valued. Many persons get their best results by reading according to organized topics as in the preceding study outline.

C. Read fast but discriminately. Material that is not relevant to the questions in the study outline can be skimmed, while sentences, pages, or chapters that bear upon the essential points may properly be read thoroughly with the view to taking notes. In general, read rapidly, but not at the expense of comprehension. Avoid the tendency to dismiss lightly the ideas or sources that disagree with your preconceived notions. Apply the tests of evidence as objectively as possible.

D. Read from general to specific. It is obviously better to read general background articles before going to sources that present specific details. This order of reading will reduce the amount of useless note-taking in the early stages of the investigation. General reference works, histories, or other textbooks should take chronological precedence over periodicals and newspapers of recent dates. One who is preparing to discuss or debate some current scheme of world organization may need, first of all, a background knowledge of mankind's attempts in that direction in the past.

E. Assimilate the raw materials. The mere accumulation of quotations and facts is not the real purpose of reading. These items are the raw materials of proof. They should be weighed and related to other similar materials and to the reader's attitudes. Think while you read. Understand not only what was said, but also why it was said. Unassimilated reading notes mean little to the speaker or his audience. The best results are obtained when the product of one's reading is an indivisible composite of the writers' ideas and the reader's reactions.

V. RECORDING MATERIAL

A. Why it is necessary. Even though it is easier at the moment to avoid this bane of preparation by relying on makeshift notes, the advantage is short-lived. The positive advantages of systematic recording make the practice worth-while: it assembles in an orderly fashion the materials for discussion outlines, case outlines, and rebuttals; it prevents the forgetting of ideas and sources; it permits the exchange of notes among persons.

B. What to record. How much should be recorded? The nature of the subject, the investigator's prior knowledge of it, the time involved, and the number, length, and importance of the papers or speeches in which the material is to be used are determining factors. The general tendency is to record too little. Thus it is wise to record, briefly at least, all the apparently significant evidence and argument which the study uncovers.

Enough should be written about each item so that it will be meaningful to the investigator or his colleagues at the moment or even months later. The topic involved, the authority and his qualifications (if opinion evidence), and documentation are minimum essentials. Each note or card should have on it the materials necessary for its defense against the charge that it fails to meet some test of evidence.

C. Methods of recording. One should distinguish between the recording of bibliography and that of evidence and argument. If the bibliography is to be listed on sheets of paper, it should bear a title and be divided into sections on the basis of different types of publications such as books, periodicals, government documents, etc. For details of form, see one of several recently published writer's guides and manuals of style. Usage in the matter of punctuation and the placing of authors' initials and given names varies among editors.

Student debaters are more likely to prepare annotated bibliographies with one item on each card. When debate squad members practice the division of labor which we mentioned earlier in this chapter, they divide the bibliography, make these cards, and exchange them or keep them in a common file. Bibliography cards are 3 x 5 or 4 x 6 inches, but they must be uniform in size and arrangement of data. The following information should be on each card: identification of reference, including person's name, title of article and magazine or book, date of publication, and pagination; where the publication is kept, such as closed reserve, open reserve, stacks, general library, law library, etc.; summary of contents and notation of special-interest items; appraisal of its usefulness to one or both sides. The identification of the reference should be placed at the top of the card.

Students of debate use several methods of recording evidence and rebuttal ideas. Some use loose-leaf notebooks, but that method is cumbersome even if only one item is put on a page. The preferred method is the use of a file box containing 3 x 5 or 4 x 6 cards, alphabetized dividers, and a table of contents in the lid. If cards on one topic are grouped in a section, and if key words and documentation appear at the top of each card, a specific reference can be found quickly. The topics in the detailed study outline or some variation of them may be used as a basis for grouping the cards, placing the dividers, and itemizing the table of contents. The following samples indicate the most common practices.

Suggested Solutions: Inflation or Deflation

John T. Flynn, economist and journalist

"This Setback in Business," *Harper's Magazine,* No. 1052, January, 1938, p. 204.

"The choice is a simple one, even though it be an appalling one for a political government to make. We must make up our minds either to inflate or deflate. If we decide that we want to hold up prices we must decide to inflate. The government must make an end of talk about balancing the budget. . . . If we decide that inflation by government credit is too dangerous—which is the fact— then we must decide to move down to a lower price level."

Low income and high mortality	Selwyn D. Collins (add qualifications in case of opinion evidence)	*Economic Status and Health,* U.S. Public Health Bulletin, No. 165, 1927, p. 49

Various studies of infant mortality by the U.S. Children's Bureau have shown marked correlation between low incomes and high infant mortality rates . . . A 5-city survey in 1912–1914 showed a death rate of 49.2 per 1000 live births in laborers' families with incomes $1,250 and over. In groups under $450 annual wage the rate was 179.3, or almost four times as great.

Exercises

1. Investigate a chosen or assigned proposition which may be used for this and subsequent exercises.
   a. Record the material on cards as shown in this chapter.
   b. The assigned number of cards may be divided among a stated number of points in the detailed study outline.

   c. Prepare a classified bibliography or a set of annotated bibliography cards.

2. Class committees may be assigned to prepare sections of a detailed study outline on a proposition.

3. If a division of labor, as suggested in this chapter, has been practiced, the teacher might designate a period in which questions from the detailed study outline will be asked, and students will be called upon to read cards of material which provide answers.

4. Comment on this advertisement which was sent to debate directors: "Why spend your valuable time looking for debate materials when you can get a complete service at a very low cost?"

Chapter **VI** · DISCUSSION AS PREPARATION FOR DEBATE

Inquiry of one kind or another normally precedes advocacy. It may take the form of private reflection, reading, experimentation, or discussion—one or more of these or other methods of exploration and investigation. Such inquiry may be a precursor *of* debate or a preparation *for* debate. In other words, the propositions which people choose to defend as advocates and debaters are typically the *outcomes* of inquiry; and secondly, the planning of the debater's case, *after the proposition has been formulated,* can usually benefit by one or more of these investigative techniques. In this chapter we are primarily interested in *discussion* as a means of preparing for debate—helping to explore, assess, and assemble the evidence and argument best adapted to support a proposition to which the advocate is already committed.

I. THE NATURE AND PURPOSE OF DISCUSSION

Discussion may be defined as *"the cooperative deliberation of problems by persons thinking and conversing together in face-to-face or coacting groups under the direction of a leader for purposes of understanding and action."*[1] A brief analysis of this definition will provide an adequate understanding of discussion for our purposes here.

Discussion begins with a problem (rather than a proposition) and seeks a solution to this problem (which can be phrased as a proposition) through cooperative (rather than competitive) thinking; this thinking is reflective (rather than intentional) in character and proceeds through the usual steps in such thinking —problem, analysis, suggested solutions or hypotheses, reasoned

---

[1] James H. McBurney and Kenneth G. Hance, *Discussion in Human Affairs,* New York, Harper and Brothers, 1950, p. 10.

development of these hypotheses, and acceptance or rejection of the hypotheses (rather than an organized structure of evidence and argument offered as proof). As a group undertaking, discussion is normally under the direction of a leader who seeks to provide guidance and direction. The purposes may be a better understanding of the problem under consideration, or the determination of policy as a basis for action, or both. The typical situation for discussion is the small face-to-face group so arranged that everyone can be seen and heard in normal conversation. With some adaptations, discussion can also be conducted in coacting groups where a speaker-audience situation obtains, *viz.* the panel discussion or symposium.

Discussion is pre-eminently a problem-solving method which attempts to bring the best reflective effort of groups to bear on personal and social problems. As such, it has wide scope and usefulness in a democratic society. In spirit and method, it is a close neighbor to scientific method.

II. DISCUSSION AS A PRECURSOR OF DEBATE

Discussion makes its greatest contribution in groups whose purpose is better understanding of a problem or of the attitudes of the people associated with the problem. In this kind of situation, people do not have to be brought to agreement or consensus. Better understanding has high personal and social values even though differences persist. There are countless practical situations confronting groups of all kinds, however, in which decisions must be reached, where understanding is not enough. If differences cannot be resolved by discussion, and policy must be determined and action taken, debate is the logical recourse. Under such circumstances, dicussion gives way to debate, and motions are made, debated, and voted. Such debate is usually conducted under the rules of parliamentary procedure (Chapter xviii). Such legislative debate is one of the most frequent and most important kinds of debate.

Even if discussion yields a working consensus in a committee or other small group without recourse to debate, however, this decision will very often have to be "sold" to parent legislative bodies or to the public at large by means of argumentation and debate.

These are the usual contexts in which discussion is a forerunner of debate. Properly understood, discussion and debate play complementary roles. Discussion is not antagonistic to debate nor is debate hostile to discussion. Both merit serious attention and study. Every student of argumentation should understand these relationships between discussion and debate.

III. DISCUSSION AS A PREPARATION FOR DEBATE

In this book we make no attempt to deal with discussion except as means of preparing the debate *after the proposition has been formulated*. While this is a secondary and ancillary function of discussion, it can be of real assistance to the advocate. Many professional advocates such as lawyers, public relations counselors, and salesmen are "handed" their propositions by clients or employers. For that matter, all persons find themselves in countless situations where the proposition is dictated by the exigencies of the moment, by circumstances to which previous actions have committed them, or by the conduct of others in whom they are interested. Not all propositions, by any means, are calmly and reflectively arrived at by discussion, or by any other careful, deliberative procedure; nor does this fact necessarily cast any aspersion on men who defend these propositions.

Given a proposition, by whatever means, both personal and social interest will dictate as much preparation for its defense as circumstances require and permit. In Chapter v we considered *reading* as a method of preparation. Discussion can be a valuable supplement to such reading in many cases.

IV. USES OF DISCUSSION

Advocacy is often a joint enterprise. In a large-scale campaign many people are interested and many people participate in the formulation of the case or the platform. In many debates (school or other contest debates, for example) the affirmative and the negative will be represented by teams. Wherever such a joint enterprise is involved, there must be close coordination of effort and cooperative planning by the affirmative, on the one hand, and the negative, on the other. Without it, even the closest partners in a cause may find themselves at cross purposes and needlessly divisive and ineffectual in their efforts. Discussion is the best means of getting together. Ordinarily many conferences, "debate meetings," or planning sessions will be useful.

No matter what the source of the proposition, it is presumably an answer to some kind of problem. Propositions of fact are answers (or alleged answers) to questions of fact; propositions of value are appraisals growing out of questions of value; and propositions of policy are proposed courses of action designed to meet problems which appear to require action. No preparation for the defense or attack of a given proposition can be more searching than one which defines the problem that the proposition is designed to answer, analyzes this problem carefully, compares the proposed answer critically with other possible answers to the same problem, and considers the available means of confirming or implementing the proposition. Since these are the logical steps in solving a problem or arriving at a proposition, they quite obviously recommend themselves to anyone who wishes to prepare himself to defend a proposition. This kind of preparation will give debaters a broad understanding of the problem area and provide the basis for a much more mature defense than would otherwise be possible. Actually, such an investigation is the basic means of determining whether one wishes to defend or oppose a proposition. If he has this choice, he is prepared to defend his convictions with maximum insight. If he is committed to the affirmative or the negative of a specific proposition, he is in a position to present *the best possible case for the proposition*. No advocate can do more, nor should be expected to do more.

Discussion is uniquely helpful to the advocate in making this kind of preparation because properly conducted discussion is concerned with precisely these steps in reflective thinking, and because it presents an opportunity to share the ideas and attitudes of others. Any advocate who prepares in solitude is likely to have a rude awakening when he faces an audience or an opponent. In many cases the ideas, attitudes, emotions, and prejudices of those who are affected by the proposition, or those who are expected to accept it, are of enormous importance in preparing defense and attack. Discussion provides the best kind of opportunity for realistic insight into these personal factors.

The experience of participating in discussion is also of value to debaters as speakers. The quick give-and-take of discussion is good experience for any advocate. He learns to meet objections immediately in a situation where those who disagree can ask questions which cannot easily be parried or ignored. The spirit and temper of a properly conducted discussion develop emotional control and vigorous forthrightness in those who participate. Speakers with considerable experience of this kind behind them are less likely to become intemperate, injudicious, or otherwise obnoxious. They are less likely to resort to petty sophistries, dodges, and tricks which frequently tempt the advocate.[2]

V. SUGGESTIONS FOR CONDUCTING DISCUSSION

If discussion is to have maximum value for the advocate, quite obviously it should bring together the best informed people available. Little or nothing is gained by pooling ignorance. If a team effort is involved, it is often wise to include experts who are not directly concerned with the debate in preparation. It is often wise, too, for affirmative and negative groups to meet together, at least in the preliminary stages of preparation.

It is of great importance that these preparatory discussions be conducted on a completely frank and fair basis. Even though the debater is thoroughly and completely committed to a given proposition, the preparatory discussion should be conducted in an exploratory rather than an argumentative mood. This is the time, if ever, to face all of the available facts and opinions and to assess them as fairly as possible. Nothing is gained by glossing over or covering up. On the contrary, much can be lost by failing to deal with the problem as objectively as possible. The purpose of the discussion is to discover strengths and weaknesses; it is much better to encounter them and get their full measure in preparatory discussion than it is to meet them for the first time in the hands of an opponent or in the minds of a hostile audience.

The objectives of the discussion, as we have said, are: (1) to define and delimit the problem which the proposition under con-

[2] William M. Sattler, "Some Values of Discussion in the Investigation and Analysis Phases of Debate," *The Gavel*, March–May, 1943, Vol. 25, Numbers 3 and 4, pp. 54–55.

sideration is designed to answer, or appears best to answer; (2) to analyze this problem in terms of the factors which constitute the problem and what is causing them (including personal factors and human values); (3) to discover and define all solutions to this problem (including the proposition at hand) which have any reasonable claim to credence; (4) to compare the relative advantages and disadvantages, merits, and demerits of these hypotheses; and (5) to select the one which appears best to meet the problem for further study and implementation. The fifth step may require a little "soul-searching," if the answer to the problem which "your" proposition is best designed to meet turns out to be some other proposition. As we have said before, under these circumstances, if you have no irrevocable commitment, you will be negative on the proposition which instigated the investigation. If you are committed, you will at least know what you are up against.

The five steps in reflective thinking outlined above constitute the best organization for most discussions. In most cases, it is wise to appoint (or accept) a leader who will guide the discussion in terms of these five steps. The goal of *all* participants should be to contribute *all* the ideas and attitudes which have any significant bearing on the problem. Moreover, these should be contributed in the spirit and manner which will best help the members of the group to think their way through the problem. The best approach is one of explaining *how* you feel or think and *why* you think and feel as you do. This should be presented as an "invitation" to others to criticize your position and the reasons for it. Remember that you are using this discussion as a *preparation* for debate—you are trying to learn, to understand, to profit by criticism. There will be time enough to organize your resources for defense and attack *after* you know the "lay of the land."

Exercises

1. Define discussion and distinguish between discussion and debate. In what ways is discussion a precursor of debate? A preparation for debate?
2. Select a problem for class discussion. Phrase the subject for discussion as a question. Appoint a leader and conduct a discussion organized in terms of these steps in reflective thinking:

    a. Definition and delimitation of the problem
    b. Analysis of the problem
    c. Possible solutions to the problem
    d. Comparison of advantages and disadvantages of solutions
    e. Selection of best solution and consideration of ways and means of putting it into operation.

3. Phrase the solutions in Step C above as propositions for debate.
4. Divide the class into affirmatives and negatives on a proposition of policy. Convene the affirmatives and the negatives as separate discussion groups for the purpose of planning affirmative and negative cases.

Chapter **VII** · EVIDENCE

I. THE NATURE OF EVIDENCE

A. Evidence and proof. Evidence consists of facts, opinions, or material things that are used in generating proof. It is the raw material from which the finished product, proof, is manufactured by the process of reasoning. Proof is the effect, the result aimed at, the objective of the arguer.

B. Argument. In its restricted meaning, this is the name used to designate the process by which, from knowing the existence of one fact, or a certain number of facts, we infer the existence of other facts. This meaning of the word "argument" must not be confused with other meanings. The word may be used to refer to a finished discourse as a whole; it may refer to an entire debate or discussion; or, as here, it may mean simply a single process of reasoning. There is, perhaps, no better definition of an argument, in this sense, than Cardinal Newman's definition of reason as "any process or act of the mind by which, from knowing one thing, it advances on to know another."

C. Persuasion and conviction in evidence. In choosing from whatever materials we have been able to gather—those facts, arguments, or appeals that will best serve our purpose in a particular case— we must remember the dual nature of all argumentation: our materials must be judged and chosen in accordance with the standards of both conviction and of persuasion. *Persuasion* requires that we consider the character, intelligence, and personal interests of our audience or readers, and the circumstances in which we are arguing, so that we may make use of the ideas and methods that will strike most directly and forcibly upon the imagination and emotions of those we address. While evidence must be chosen primarily on the basis of its logical sufficiency, it is well to consider also its persuasive possibilities. When a choice is possible between

73

evidential facts, witnesses, or methods of proof, that which will have the more persuasive effect should be chosen. But persuasion is a secondary consideration here. Nothing can be good *evidence* that does not qualify as a sound basis for conviction. *Conviction* requires that we understand the inherent strength of the various kinds of evidence, so that we may employ only the best evidence to accomplish our purpose.

D. Evidence in law. Before discussing the classification and tests of evidence in general argumentation, we should have clearly in mind what legal evidence means as distinct from evidence used in ordinary discussion outside of court trials. We should know the fundamental precepts and purposes of the law of evidence in order to understand, and to be able properly to apply, whatever borrowings we may make from this division of legal practice. A clear understanding of the law of evidence will show us why evidence in argumentation outside of law courts should not be rigidly subjected to the *legal* tests.

The law of evidence concerns itself with furnishing to courts the kinds of evidence suited to their function of arriving at *judicial* decisions in regard to questions before them. In discharging their proper functions the courts of law are not engaged in academic discussions nor in the work of discovering and enforcing abstract truth or abstract justice. Their purpose is to settle disputes and award justice as fairly and accurately as may be under the limits imposed upon them, such as time, expense, etc., and by the use of such instrumentalities as are available for their employment. The law of evidence has developed to meet the requirements of this practical situation, and is not a set of rules to be followed outside of the courtroom by those working upon questions which are not to be decided in courts of law.

The relevancy of a piece of evidence cannot be settled by law. Matters are relevant or not according to the tests of logic and general experience. The law of evidence simply says that under certain circumstances certain *relevant evidence shall not be admitted.* It consists of a set of excluding rules which exclude certain classes of relevant evidence, and consists further of certain exceptions to these rules, which admit subdivisions of classes of evidence excluded by the general rules. Legal tests of evidence are not, therefore, tests of logical relevancy, but tests of legal admissibility. The grounds upon which legal admissibility has been denied to certain classes of evidence are various. Some kinds of evidence are thought to be of too little importance, in some the connection is too far-fetched. Some kinds of evidence are excluded because it is feared their effects upon the juries would not be salutary; others are excluded on grounds of general public policy, etc. It is well for the student of general argumentation to be as familiar as possible with the law of evidence in order to understand what use may properly be made outside of the courtrooms of suggestions to be drawn from rules which are rigidly enforced in the courts themselves.

E. Evidence in general argumentation. In brief, then, in general argumentation we may have good evidence that would not be admitted in law courts. Relevancy, logical sufficiency, is what we demand of evidence outside of courts. But in law, evidence must meet this test and then also meet the requirements of the law of evidence. There is no "law of evidence" as such outside of the

TEST FORM FOR EVIDENCE

1. Point, Contention, Argument	2. Evidence	3. Personal Source-Witness	4. Documentary Source-Where Found
Proposed plan would fail to produce the needed revenue.	It has failed in six similar American cities. Toledo, O. Buffalo, N.Y. Hartford, Conn. Denver, Col. Spokane, Wash. Rochester, N.Y.	Dr. X.Y.Z., Professor of Municipal Administration, Yale University.	*Relief Financing and Administration.* New York, Prentice-Hall. 1949, pp. 61–83.

courts. So the oft-heard statement that such and such evidence "would not be admitted in any court in the country" has really very little force if the discussion is being carried on outside of a court. It is usually sufficiently answered by reminding its user that we are not in court. However, it is probably well to scrutinize very carefully in general argumentation evidence that courts have thought it best to exclude entirely from the consideration of juries. In order to be able to do this, on the one hand, and to be ready, on the other, to thwart whoever (either in ignorance or cunning) tries improperly to apply in general discussion the excluding rules of the law courts, it is well to be familiar with some of the basic legal tests of evidence which follow in Part II.

Any advocate preparing to debate a case in court, legislature, or public forum should always have ready full and accurate information of the sort called for in columns 2, 3, and 4 of the above form. Such information may be used in constructive main speeches or in rebuttal, or at any time when a challenge or other circumstance makes its use advisable. The well-prepared debater will always have it available. Many poor debaters never get out of column 1 or at best stop at 2. The good debater always has *accurate and complete data for columns 3 and 4 for all important evidence.*

F. The sources of evidence. Evidence which seems on its face to be credible, consistent, and convincing may be rendered of no account by an exposure of weakness in the source from whence it comes. The sources of evidence are three—*persons, documents, and things.* Persons are of course the most important source. The testimony of persons may be written as well as spoken. Not all written evidence is documentary. Books, magazine articles, etc., used in general argumentation should be used as the personal testimony of their authors. When a writer states in a book that a certain thing is true, this is personal testimony that the thing is true and documentary evidence that he stated that it is true. The person behind all personal testimony should be tested alike in written and oral evidence. As the term is used in this book "witness" covers both "speaker" and "writer." It may be said, however, that written testimony is less likely to contain such errors as are due to simple thoughtlessness. But in all cases the sources of evidence should be carefully examined. If it can be shown that the statements, however plausible, are mere careless assertions of unreliable persons, or that the testimony was given with some dishonest motive, its value is gone. So it is always necessary in selecting one's own proof or in attacking the proof of an opponent to know what kinds of witnesses give good evidence, and what kinds bad evidence.

G. Prejudiced witnesses. Before passing on to a consideration of the kinds of evidence and the tests of evidence, it may be well to state what the function of the witness is, to analyze his operations, and to give a warning concerning a big question that is important in connection with the testimony of all kinds of witnesses. A witness has to *gather* impressions, facts, information, and then *present* these to others. He must learn the truth and tell it. *A good witness must be capable and desirous of finding out or receiving the truth, and capable and desirous of reporting the truth.* The big question that we must ask in regard to each witness is "with what prejudice, if any, does he look upon the matter concerning which he is testifying?"

Prejudice, bias, self-interest, personal liking for one thing and dislike for another, affect the *truth-finding* as well as the *truth-telling* of many men who are *desirous* of finding and telling nothing but the truth. It is to a great extent true that men (all men—and women—not simply the less intellectual) believe what they want to believe. They are *not capable* of finding the truth in regard to some things because they look at these things through the colored glasses of extreme bias. What many honest men see, hear, and even taste and smell, depends to a certain extent upon their prejudices. The solution of the difficulty thus presented is not to resolve not to use prejudiced witnesses, but to use the least prejudiced witnesses possible. To decline to receive or accept the testimony of prejudiced witnesses is to decline all testimony on most of the important questions of the day. Of course there are many mere questions of fact in which prejudices are of no account. But in general argumentation, in politics, economics, sociology, religion, literature, education, etc., most men who are discussing questions and writing articles and books, have definite opinions, beliefs, interests, and prejudices. This does not mean that we must disregard what they testify to, but that we must weigh their testimony with reference to their preconceived notions. We must be sure that they *accurately report* what they found by *competent investigation* or learning, and we must *always listen to the testimony on both sides*. Read what both the advocates and opponents of a certain measure find in the facts of a given event, and then draw your own conclusions as to the truth. Do not try to get the truth concerning something from those who are naturally prejudiced against it, and do not accept, without comparison with the statements of opponents, the testimony concerning anything of those who are naturally prejudiced in its favor, or against it.

II. THE KINDS OF EVIDENCE

Evidence is usually classified in a series of pairs of labels. We give seven such pairs. It is substantially accurate to say that every item of evidence will bear *one* label from each *pair*. That is, all evidence is either direct or circumstantial, either real or personal, either original or hearsay, etc. Some of the divisions made are more or less arbitrary and there is slight disagreement among authorities, especially as to nomenclature. It is well worth-while, however, to examine the commoner classifications and definitions, at least to the extent of learning what is meant by the terms used.

A. Direct or circumstantial. The most common classification of evidence is into (1) direct and (2) indirect or circumstantial.

Direct evidence is evidence which, if accepted and believed, establishes *immediately* the truth of the contention at issue. If the question is, *Did A shoot B?* the testimony of eye witnesses that they saw A shoot B is direct evidence. Circumstantial evidence is evidence from which an *inference* may be drawn as to the truth of the contention at issue. It establishes the main contention only *mediately*. It is a circumstance from which one might infer the truth of the proposition. In the question suggested above, if the witnesses testify that they saw A running away from the place where they found B just after he had been shot, that is circumstantial evidence.

In law the term "direct evidence" is usually applied to the testimony of persons who declare the existence of the fact in issue, speaking from their own personal knowledge. The important factor is that these persons testify directly as to the existence of the fact in issue. The testimony is required to be based on their own personal knowledge by the hearsay rule. The evidence would still be *direct* as distinct from *circumstantial* if the information were second-hand or "hearsay," but since as such it would normally be inadmissible in a law court, direct evidence in law is defined in terms which cover direct *original* evidence. If the witness testified that C told him that he (C) saw A kill B, the evidence would still be direct (*i.e.*, not circumstantial) but it would be inadmissible as *hearsay* in law. Outside of law courts, however, we act on this kind of direct evidence every day. It is obviously impossible to classify evidence as direct or circumstantial until we know the "fact in issue" to determine which this evidence is advanced. The words "direct" and "circumstantial" are only labels of the *relation of the evidence to the issue*. If it immediately affirms or denies some fact *from which an inference* is made to the "fact in issue," it is circumstantial. If it immediately affirms the "fact in issue" itself without the use of any inference, it is direct.

The most effective proof is gained by the use of these two kinds of evidence *in combination*. Direct evidence may be untrustworthy because of mistakes in the observation of the witness, inaccuracy in reporting, or because of prejudice. Circumstantial evidence may be inconclusive because of a possible ambiguity in the inferences to be drawn from it. But when the two kinds are used together, each confirming the other, the evidence becomes of the highest possible efficacy.

B. Written or unwritten. With respect to its form, we may classify evidence as: (1) written and (2) unwritten. In courts of law a considerable part of the evidence is unwritten. It consists of the spoken testimony of witnesses present before the judge or jury. In formal debate elsewhere, however, the evidence is largely written. It is often akin in its nature to the spoken testimony of the courts, in that it expresses the beliefs of different persons as to the existence of certain facts. But the persons themselves are rarely present to express their beliefs orally. Their opinions and the facts they report are gathered from books, magazines, newspapers, and documents.

C. Real or personal. Evidence is either (1) real or (2) personal. Real evidence is evidence of which any object is the source—persons may be included—in regard to qualities which belong to persons as well as to things. Real evidence is obtained when weapons or wounds are exhibited to the jury, or fences or railroad crossings are examined by them, or a person whose age or parentage is in issue appears before the jury to be *seen* by them. Real evidence, of course, cannot be hearsay. It is evidence presented directly to the senses of those who are to judge, without any interpretation by a person. The evidence speaks for itself. There is no "thought communication." It may of course be presented to any of the senses—sight, hearing, taste, smell, etc.

Personal evidence is that which is afforded by a human agent, either in the way of discourse, or by voluntary signs (made for the purpose of communicating thoughts). Evidence gained by observation (of the person of the witness) or that afforded by *involuntary* changes of countenance and deportment comes under the head of real evidence. Whenever a witness communicates thought to a judge or jury either by spoken language or by signs, he is giving personal evidence; while if he *shows* the jury a wound, or that he can raise his arm by raising it for them to see, he is giving real evidence. Problem: If a man on the witness stand is asked if he has a stiff neck and by way of answer he moves his head from side to side, is he giving real or personal evidence?

D. Original and unoriginal. A division of evidence that is important because under it we get one of the terms ("hearsay") that we note frequently in discussions of evidence, is the division into (1) original and (2) unoriginal evidence. Original evidence is that which is reported to those who are to judge by the person who originally obtained the evidence—who by the use of his senses saw, heard, felt, smelled, tasted the evidence at its source. Unoriginal, or hearsay, evidence is that which is reported to those who are to judge by someone other than the person who originally obtained the evidence. When A testifies that he saw B at a ball game on June 1, that is original evidence. If C testifies that A told him that A saw B at the ball game, that is hearsay evidence that B was at the ball game. For us it is substantially correct to say that unoriginal evidence means *hearsay* evidence.

What the courts exclude, argumentation elsewhere should treat with suspicion, but should not necessarily rule out. Courts must have rules that will apply to all alike. But we are not so bound in general argumentation. Of course, the hearsay evidence of the ignorant, the careless, the vicious, is worthless. But hearsay evidence coming through accurate, trained minds may be of such a character that it would be absurd to question it on the ground that it is hearsay. Second-hand evidence, however, is usually less convincing than original evidence. The testimony may be too many stages removed from the fact itself. An audience will often suspect that the arguer cannot or dare not produce the original authority. Again, it is too easily overthrown. If a reliable witness who has a first-hand knowledge can be brought to testify to any fact of a contradictory nature, the hearsay evidence is immediately brought to the ground.

Care must be taken not to confuse direct and original evidence. If A testifies that B said that he saw X kill Y, this is direct but hearsay. If A testifies that he saw X running away from the scene of the murder of Y at about the time Y must have been killed, this is original but circumstantial evidence that X murdered Y.

E. Preappointed or casual. Evidence may be divided into (1) preappointed evidence and (2) casual evidence. Wherever "the creation or preservation of an article of evidence has been, either to public or private minds, an object of solicitude, . . . (*viz.* in the view of its serving to give effect to a right, or enforce an obligation, on some future contingent occasion), the evidence so created and preserved comes under the notion of preappointed evidence." Deeds, notes, written contracts, etc., are forms of written preappointed evidence. When a man arranges to have certain persons witness his words or actions in order that they may testify to what he said or did, we have unwritten preappointed evidence. Any evidence not coming under the head of preappointed evidence is casual or undesigned evidence. It is evidence that has been neither created nor preserved for the purpose of using it as evidence of the fact now being substantiated by it. This kind of evidence consists of testimony given by persons who, when they obtained it, had no thought that it would ever be used as evidence in the case in question. Speaking for another purpose a person often lets fall a statement that is merely incidental. The value of such evidence lies in its freedom from the suspicion of any hidden motive. It is ingenuous and presumably honest. But it has very serious weakness. The testimony may well have been careless. The witness, thinking the assertion of slight importance, may have been indifferent as to its accuracy.

Mr. Daniel Webster, in the following selection from his famous argument in the White murder trial, enforced the value of some of his evidence by showing that it was casual.

Mr. Southwick swears all that a man can swear. He has the best means of judging that could be had at the time. He tells you that he left his father's house at half-past ten o'clock, and as he passed to his own house in Brown Street, he saw a man sitting on the steps of the rope-walk; that he passed him three times, and each time he held down his head, so that he did not see his face. That the man had on a cloak, which was not wrapped around him, and a glazed cap. That he took the man to be Frank Knapp at the time; that, when he went into his house, he told his wife that he thought it was Frank Knapp; that he knew him well, having known him from a boy. And his wife swears that he did so tell her when he came home. What could mislead this witness at the time? He was not then suspecting Frank Knapp of anything. He could not then be influenced by any prejudices. If you believe that the witness saw Frank Knapp in this position at this time, it proves the case.

F. Positive or negative. This classification is important because of the peculiar nature and significance of what has long been called (especially by rhetoricians) "negative evidence." The term (1) "positive evidence" is rarely used. It is needed simply to balance the negative. Positive evidence is all actual evidence. (2) "Negative evidence" is the term applied to a *significant absence of evidence:* as, for instance, the absence of signs of campfires as *evidence* that campers have not preceded you along a certain trail; or the failure of a member of a dinner party to mention, while discussing the dinner later, that one of the guests died at the table of heart failure, as *evidence* that this did not happen.

Such negative testimony, or the testimony of silence—the failure of a witness to mention something so striking that he must have noticed it if it had occurred—has often been mentioned by writers on argumentation as evidence of special value.

For instance, the absence of a man's name from the list of students published in a college catalogue is negative evidence that this man is not a student at this college. The failure of the newspapers of a certain city for the month of May, 1888, to mention a sensational murder trial alleged to have been held in that city during that month is negative evidence that no such trial took place. If we fail to find in the standard biographies of a man any reference to his having been elected to an important public office, it is safe to conclude that he never was so elected. The strength of this evidence is similar to that of casual evidence. It lies in the difficulty of "manufacturing" or manipulating it. The absence of evidence to support a claim where we have a right to expect it to be found if the claim is true, is in many cases more convincing than positive assertions. The common expression, "If that were true, we would have heard about it," expresses the universal faith in negative evidence.

G. Ordinary or expert. Looked at from the point of view of the sources from whence the evidence is derived, there are two kinds of evidence: (1) ordinary evidence, and (2) expert evidence. There are certain tests that may be applied to all witnesses; these are the tests of the sources of ordinary evidence. Then the examination of the class of witnesses known as "experts" demands the application of certain additional tests.

Most evidence is *ordinary*. This term covers all that is not *expert*. Expert testimony, strictly speaking, is called in law "opinion evidence" and in general argumentation, "argument from authority." These two terms cover practically parallel things, and we will gain considerably in general argumentation if we understand the legal doctrine of "opinion evidence" and follow it in dealing with "argument from authority." In law the testimony of an "ordinary" witness is not always limited strictly to matters of fact. There are at times circumstances under which an ordinary witness is allowed to testify in regard to matters of opinion, such for instance as his opinion regarding the "character" or the "sanity" of some other person. Also, there arise at times in law trials circumstances under which an "expert" witness testifies to matters of fact rather than to matters of opinion. For instance, an expert chemist might very well testify as to matters of fact in the realm of chemistry, under which circumstances he could not be called strictly an "opinion" witness. However, the expert is usually asked to interpret facts which he or other witnesses establish, and this interpretation, which is the expert's principal function, usually is, of course, opinion evidence in law, or argument from authority in general argumentation.

The ordinary witness testifies that a certain alleged fact is true because he actually observed it to be so; the expert testifies that the same alleged fact is true because certain other facts exist, and his peculiar and exceptional knowledge justifies him in inferring the existence of the fact in question. The ordinary witness in a law court is usually not allowed to express an *opinion* or even to use a word which shows his opinion. He must state what he saw, heard, etc., without characterizing it in any way. Under certain circumstances "experts" are called who are allowed to express opinions—or give opinion evidence.

To take a simple illustration, the question is whether a certain man who was shot and killed wore a certain coat on the day of the murder. The ordinary witness may testify that he saw the deceased near the place of the murder a short time before the deed, and that he was wearing the coat in question. The expert finds certain stains on the coat and with the aid of his exceptional knowledge of chemistry, he infers that the stains are blood stains and freshly made. This is his opinion. He is allowed to give this opinion to the jury. An ordinary witness may tell the jury that he saw A strike B in a certain manner. The expert can tell the jury whether such a blow would be fatal to a man in B's condition. Clearly in these cases the value of the testimony of the expert depends upon his special technical skill. This is always the primary test of expert evidence: Is the witness possessed of such knowledge that he will draw the correct conclusions from the facts presented to him? Such evidence is usually used only when the expert is dealing with aspects of the question on which the layman cannot be expected to draw valid conclusions. Then the expert is allowed to give opinion evidence. Until this point is reached he is only an ordinary witness, regardless of his position or reputation.

1. **Argument from authority.** In general argumentation opinion evidence is frequently called the "argument from authority." This

is an inaccurate label for it is not properly an argument—*i.e.*, a process of reasoning—but evidence. It consists in establishing a fact by quoting the opinion of some person whose knowledge is such as to justify the acceptance of his inferences as truthful. The legal procedure in this matter should be followed closely in all argumentation. This will, among other things, do away with one of the most stupid and harmful of the bad practices in contest debating— that of quoting alleged "authorities" on all sorts of questions. The people quoted are (1) usually not authorities—not experts—not people specially qualified to express opinions on the questions discusssed, and (2) the questions on which the authorities are cited are not questions which call for expert testimony. Very often they are plain, ordinary, everyday propositions on which all citizens are supposed to be qualified to pass judgment. Moreover, authorities are rushed in (3) without being so produced as to be accepted by anyone as authorities whose opinions might be helpful.

It must be remembered that a distinguished man is not necessarily an authority on any question on which he has expressed an opinion. The fact that a man is a distinguished scientist gives him no standing as a critic of literature. Success in politics does not make a man an authority in education. Dramatists are not *per se* entitled to the privileges of opinion witnesses on questions of sociology, and the opinions of famous clergymen in the field of economics should usually be accorded the same good-humored disregard that ought to greet the pronouncements of learned scientists on questions of religion and theology. We are not saying that a man should have no opinions except in his special field of work— but simply that the fact that a man is an authority in one field does not make him *an authority in other fields.*

2. **Documentation of sources.** This is neither evidence nor argument from authority. Care should be taken to avoid the common error of treating all documentation of sources and identification of witnesses as arguments from authority. When a great jurist is quoted as saying that a certain law was passed in a certain state on a given date, he is an ordinary witness to be tested precisely as the farmer who testifies in regard to an accident on the highway. When the judge is quoted, and the place where his statement was found is given, the witness is identified, and the source of information

documented, as should usually be done; but there is no expert testimony offered, no opinion evidence given, no comment from authority used. We have the latter situation when we quote the judge as saying that such and such a law would be unconstitutional.

III. THE TESTS OF EVIDENCE

Very important for our purposes are the tests to be applied to determine the value of evidence. To know whether a piece of evidence is strong or weak is essential to the intelligent conduct of a case. We can frequently use only a limited amount of all that is available. We must have the power to discriminate. Then, too, we must know what is strong enough to be put in the forefront of the proof, and what is so weak as to be valuable only for the purpose of "filling in" and reinforcing the more important parts. For these purposes we have two vital tests of evidence: (A), the test of the *quality* of the evidence itself, and (B), the test of the *sources* from whence it comes. For convenience in our discussion, the sources of evidence will be referred to as "witnesses."

A. Tests of the quality of the evidence itself.

1. Is the evidence consistent with human nature and human experience? Any man properly hesitates to accept as a fact anything that runs contrary to his own past experience or the experience of his fellow-men. To make him believe in any evidence that contradicts the beliefs of his life and his habits of thinking requires explanation, enforcement, and substantiation that soon become an argument in themselves, and even then the unqualified acceptance of the proof may be a matter of doubt. If the evidence is in this way contrary to ordinary human experience, one must never neglect to maintain its truthfulness by explaining just why it is credible and valuable. Campbell, in his *Philosophy of Rhetoric*[1] expresses the situation, when he says: "From experience we learn to confine our belief in human testimony within the proper bounds. Hence we are taught to consider many attendant circumstances which serve . . . to corroborate . . . its evidence. The reputation of the attester,

[1] P. 77.

his manner of address, the nature of the fact attested, the occasion of giving the testimony, the possible or probable design in giving it and several other circumstances have considerable influence in fixing the degree of credibility." Evidence, then, should as far as possible be consistent with ordinary human experience and the natural course of affairs. If it is of any extraordinary nature, its credibility must be shown before it will be of value or effect.

The weakness of evidence that is of an extraordinary nature and contrary to common experience, is exposed in the following selection from the speech by John Henry North in the case of Rex *vs.* Forbes and others. Mr. North's client was charged with committing criminal assault upon the Lord-Lieutenant of Ireland. Testimony was given by a certain Dr. M'Namara, who said that he actually saw the defendant hurl a bottle at the Lord-Lieutenant in a public theatre. Mr. North attacks testimony as follows:—

The Doctor in the middle gallery sees Handwich in the third row of the upper one, though between them there were two benches covered with people, and the boarded parapet in front of the upper gallery besides! Through all these obstacles he sees him in that dark corner of the gallery where he represents him to be placed; sees him fling the bottle, and is now able, at this distance of time, to identify his person. The bottle itself he saw in what he learnedly calls its transit. A word or two on that same transit. I hold it physically impossible that a bottle could have taken the course described by Farrell and M'Namara, from the upper gallery to the stage, without being observed by four or five hundred spectators. Just think what the theatre is: a wide, illuminated area, whose bounding surfaces are studded with eyes as numerous as those of Argus. Not a square inch in that field of view which was not painted on the retina of some one eye or other in that vast assembly. Consider, too, the time—the interval between the play and farce—when the attention of the audience was not fixed upon the stage, when people were all looking about them, recognizing and greeting their friends and acquaintances. Was there no one to mark this bottle but Farrell, M'Namara, and the young medical student? What, not one giggling girl in the boxes, glancing round for admiration! not an opera-glass pointed! no fortunate observer of the transit but the astronomer from Ballinakill! Is all this credible? But this is not all—voonders upon voonders, as the Dutchman said when he got to London—the greatest miracle is to come. Down comes the bottle, thundering from the upper gallery to the stage, and falls unbroken!

2. Is the evidence consistent with known facts? The necessity is apparent of avoiding contradiction between evidence presented and other well-known facts. Its discovery by an opponent or by the audience will ruin all confidence in the offending person. The mistake of adducing evidence that is contradicted by the commonly known or easily proved facts of the question is illustrated by the following examples.

A few years ago in a trial of a civil suit the defendant, on the witness stand, was seeking to establish an alibi. In the course of his testimony he was asked to tell of all his movements and doings on a particular day. He told of several purchases he had made in the stores of the city, of his visit to a barber's shop, and of various other incidents. When this testimony was finished, the examining lawyer stated the simple fact that the day in question had been the day of the observance of President William McKinley's burial. Every shop and store had been closed. The testimony was not to be reconciled with the facts well known to the judge and the jury, and was discredited.

Webster used this test effectively in the White murder trial to overthrow the testimony of one of the witnesses of the defence:

Balch says that on the evening, whenever it was, he saw the prisoner, the prisoner told him he was going out of town on horseback, for a distance of about twenty minutes' drive, and that he was going to get a horse at Osborn's. This was about seven o'clock. At about nine, Balch says he saw the prisoner again, and was then told by him that he had had his ride, and had returned. Now it appears by Osborn's books that the prisoner had a saddlehorse from his stable, not on Tuesday evening, the night of the murder, but on the Saturday evening previous. This fixes the time about which these young men testify, and is a complete answer and refutation of the attempted alibi on Tuesday evening.

3. Is the evidence consistent with itself? Evidence that contradicts itself is of course the worst possible kind. Some answer may be made, some explanation given, to save the situation when one's evidence is shown to be inconsistent with human experience or known facts. Is human experience correct and complete in regard to the matter in question? Men are continually accepting beliefs that are inconsistent with the experiences of their fathers. Are the *known* facts really known or only *supposed?* Has there been a mistake? Must we abandon some of the presumably established facts in the light of new evidence? But when our evidence has an inconsistency within itself we cannot escape without suffering some disadvantage. We cannot go outside and show the error is on the other side. There is something wrong with our own evidence, and when this is exposed by our opponent, or detected by readers or hearers, our cause has suffered more than would have been the case had we failed to meet any other test. Inconsistency in the disputant himself is unpardonable. So, when Oppius was charged with defrauding the soldiers of their pensions, Cicero refuted the charge by proving that the *same persons* charged Oppius with a design to corrupt the army with his extravagant gifts and liberality. So a man who, in explaining irregularity in regard to advertising a certain function, based part of his case on the fact that a large crowd was neither expected nor desired because the patronage was a fixed and assured one, and based a second part of his case on the assertion that he had to do what was done in order to catch the public and get as large an attendance as was possible, lost greatly in the minds of the judges when this inconsistency was pointed out.

4. **Can the evidence pass the "hearsay" test?**

a. **In the law courts.** Of course, hearsay evidence is ruled out in the courts unless it comes under one of the recognized exceptions to the hearsay rule. But it is well to note that evidence may be hearsay and therefore inadmissible if offered to prove one thing, and original evidence and admissible if offered to prove another. Evidence is inadmissible as hearsay only when offered as evidence of the thing stated—of the truth of the remark made. For instance, W testifies, "I heard J say to B, 'The horse is sound.'" This is hearsay evidence if offered to prove that the horse was sound. It is original evidence if offered to prove that J warranted the horse.

b. **In general argumentation.** Here, as a matter of fact, hearsay evidence is often good. The question here is (1) whether the evidence itself is of such a nature that it may be safely passed from person to person with substantial accuracy, and (2) whether or not the channel through which the evidence comes is satisfactory. The reasons for excluding hearsay at all are: no chance for cross-examination of witness, witness not under oath, the opportunity of someone in the chain not saying what he meant, or someone not understanding correctly what was said. When by the mental and moral character of the persons forming the channel, and by the definite, clean-cut nature of the evidence itself, these objections are met, the fact that the evidence is hearsay amounts to very little. For instance, we would give little credence to a village story, vague "undocumented" rumor, or neighborhood gossip, in regard to the behavior of newcomers to a neighboring estate—people who would naturally be misunderstood and mistrusted by many of the villagers. But if the dean of X College announced in faculty meeting that the dean of Y College had said that the president of Y had telephoned that the governor had just vetoed a certain bill, the hearsay evidence would be accepted and acted upon without question.

5. **Is the evidence of a kind that is exceptionally valuable?** Under this head it is well to mention four kinds of evidence that have special value. We should keep these in mind when testing evidence —either our own or our opponents'.

a. **Admissions and declarations against interest.** These are the terms given in the courts to the testimony of persons contrary to what their own concern in the cause would suggest. This testimony is regarded in law as of such importance and so free from doubt that second-hand evidence of such statements is made admissible, contrary to the general rule excluding all hearsay evidence. When people make deliberate statements to their own disadvantage the statements are usually true; when people deliberately lie it is usually because they think the lie is to their advantage. Sometimes the admission or declaration is made when the person is aware of its damaging nature; sometimes, when unaware. Such testimony is ordinarily reliable, but there are exceptions. If the statement is made by a person unconscious of its effect on his own interests, we must be sure that it was not made carelessly, or under the influence of an intent to gain some other end. If it is a deliberate admission or confession, there may have been some hope of reward that led the witness to suffer a lesser evil for a greater gain; or the statement may have been given under compulsion. In either case its value is reduced or open to serious question. But the presumption is always in favor of the trustworthiness of this kind of evidence. To take an example: a statement by any "protected" manufacturer that tariff duties were too high—if such a thing were possible—would be a worthy bit of evidence. But if it could be proved that he was about to embark in some new enterprise where the tariff could not help him, that his purpose was the destruction of some greater rival, or that he was in the hire of a political manager, its force would be destroyed.

b. Casual or undesigned evidence. This kind of evidence, whose character has already been discussed, is especially valuable because of its freedom from suspicion.

c. Negative evidence. Negative evidence has also been fully explained. It is a third type that is generally considered especially valuable because it cannot be easily manufactured or "doctored." It is difficult to tamper with an absence of evidence. Though sometimes, of course, the significant absence may be artifically brought about.

d. Real evidence. If the nature of the controversy is such as to permit the use of real evidence, this sort (already discussed) is of course much better than personal evidence to the same effect. When one can exhibit the condition of a wound, the ill fit of a coat, the dangerous condition of a bridge or railroad crossing, such exhibition will be better than oral descriptions of these things.

B. Tests of the sources of evidence.

    1. Tests of ordinary —"fact"—witnesses.

    a. Is the witness physically qualified? Most human knowledge comes through the avenues of the five senses, and it is from the information so received that we get evidence. Clearly, then, the physical powers of a witness may have great influence upon his reliability. If a witness is color-blind, his testimony that green signal lights were displayed at the time and place of a railroad accident must be ignored. However, this test is not very common outside of the courtroom. The writers that furnish the materials of student debate and of ordinary argument everywhere are usually beyond the reach of such examination, and their testimony is not commonly of such a nature that it makes much difference whether they are blind, deaf, or otherwise physically handicapped. But whenever physical weakness may have any important effect on the testimony, the test should be rigorously applied. It is one of the most effective of all possible tests, for such a defect in a witness is conclusive against his testimony.

b. Is the witness mentally qualified? More important for the purposes of general argumentation than the test of physical endowment is the test of mental powers.

(I) *Memory.* The test of the memory of a witness is applicable everywhere. In the courts, it is a part of the "stock in trade" of a cross-examiner. In ordinary argument it is less significant. A defective memory is damaging, because it raises a strong presumption of error in the statement of testimony. If the witness cannot remember things in general, it is probable that he cannot clearly remember about the particular fact in question. His impressions will probably be vague and indistinct, and so his statements will be unreliable.

In the White murder trial, Webster used this test in attacking a witness of the defense:—

Mr. Burchmore says, to the best of his belief, it was the evening of the murder. Afterwards he attempts to speak positively, from recollecting that he mentioned the circumstance to William Peirce as he went to Mineral Spring on Fast-day. Last Monday morning he told Colonel Putnam he could not fix the time. This witness stands in a much worse plight than either of the others. It is difficult to reconcile all he has said with any belief in the accuracy of his recollections.

(II) *Accuracy of statement.* The accurate use of words and phrases is not by any means universal. We shall treat later of the different kinds of "liars"; but many mistakes of verbal expression are wholly undesigned. Provincial phrases, personal peculiarities in speech, a tendency toward exaggeration, may often lead a witness to say what he does not really mean. In getting written evidence, to avoid the mistake of misunderstanding the witness, the real import of the testimony should be gathered from the evidence as a whole rather than from the exact words of any particular sentences. Witnesses who are habitually inaccurate must, of course, be treated with suspicion. There are many writers whose practice it is to deal in generalities and bold overstatements. If a man has a reputation for that style of writing, his testimony should be discounted in proportion to the relevancy of his style to the type of evidence he is giving.

(A) *Thoughtless exaggeration.* Accidental or thoughtless exaggeration is very common in oral testimony, and arises from habits of mind in the witness. Some men have an irresistible impulse to "make things big," like Falstaff, with his "eleven men in buckram." Intentional exaggeration is simply one kind of deliberate lying. A witness who exaggerates can best be exposed by investigating his accuracy in other instances.

c. Is the witness morally qualified? *Deliberate perversion of the truth implies some motive. With an expert* the motive is often that of pride. One expert is opposed to another in some court trial or perhaps on some economic question in general argument. Each feels that his reputation depends on the overthrow of his rival. Consequently, though they may begin with the most honest intentions, they yield to the demands of the occasion, their testimony degenerates into a spirited argument, and exaggeration and misrepresentation are bred. *With an ordinary witness* the motive is likely to be some interest in the question at issue. He may feel some sympathy with the parties most deeply involved in the outcome, or he himself may have some interest in the question at issue.

A witness must be tested with these possible weaknesses in view, in two respects: (1) *Is he unduly interested in the outcome?* and (2) *what is his general moral character?* This second test is significant, because it tells us to what extent the witness would permit unworthy motives to influence his words. A reputation for low moral character in a witness makes his testimony of little or no value.

This test is one of the most common in the courts. Rufus Choate gave a good illustration of its effectiveness in his speech in the Dalton divorce case. While attacking one of the leading witnesses of the plaintiff, he said:—

I begin, therefore, with the foundation witness in this case, John H. Coburn, and I respectfully submit to you, that tried by every test of credibility which the law recognizes, on your oaths you are bound to disbelieve him. It is not that a laugh can be raised against Coburn or his testimony—that is nothing; it is that, according to those tests which are founded on the longest and widest experience the law deems satisfactory to show whether a jury can safely believe or not, he is not to be believed. I submit, then, that John H. Coburn is not an honest man, and is not, therefore, entitled to be heard in so delicate a work as bringing every word my client spoke on that evening to her husband; he is not an honest man, and I put it on your solemn oath to you, that there is not a man on that jury who, on the exhibition of John H. Coburn, would intrust him to carry a bundlle worth five dollars from this court-house to the depot.

d. Did the witness have an opportunity to get the truth? This is an obvious and important test. If the situation or experience of the witness has been such that he has not had a chance to observe the facts to which he testifies, and to observe them closely and care-fully, his statements are clearly untrustworthy. In the courts it is a common method of impeaching testimony to show that a witness was too far from the scene to see clearly, that he did not have time to observe carefully.

This test is of first importance in all kinds of argumentation. Innumerable writers are ready to venture the most positive state-ments on the foundation of a few weeks' investigation, or to make bold assertions of some general truth when they have observed only a few phenomena, and when those they have observed are excep-tional or sporadic in nature. It is not uncommon that a traveler visits a foreign country for a few months or a year, and, on his return, writes articles or a book on the society, political methods, or eco-nomic prospects of the unfamiliar land. Such a man is not to be criticised for writing in the magazines or publishing a book; his narrative may well be interesting. But *as evidence, his statements and prophecies generally amount to little.* The opportunities for observation are insufficient to make good evidence.

2. The tests of the sources of expert evidence. This in general argumentation is testing the authorities in "arguments from author-ity." The "authority" used for the purpose of such argument or such evidence as this must bear three special tests:

a. Is the case such as to make the introduction of opinion evidence —arguments from authority—warrantable? Do not offend your audience by giving the *opinions* of alleged authorities on questions on which the facts are available and understandable to any intelli-gent man. Do not ask A to believe a thing *because* B believes it, when A's opinion is just as good as B's. No authorities, no matter how good, should be used to settle questions where opinion evi-dence is not *needed.*

b. Is the witness possessed of the knowledge and experience neces-

sary to justify his acceptance as an expert in the matter in question?

c. Is his authority recognized by the audience or reader? However great the knowledge or skill of an expert, if his greatness is unknown to the hearer or reader, the effect of quoting him will be of little benefit and may do harm. The audience or reader will see in the pretended "authority" nothing more than a meaningless name, and so may ignore or resent his statement. The advocate must always be sure that the worth of his expert is accepted; and if there be any doubt, his first duty is to establish, for his expert, a satisfactory reputation.

Exercises

1. Prepare and deliver a five-minute argumentative speech in which more than one kind of evidence is used to support the point or points in partition. Quote the evidence from cards like the "Test Form for Evidence" in this chapter.
2. Apply the appropriate tests of evidence to one specimen which you select from a printed debate.
3. Quote an argumentative editorial and analyze it in terms of the kinds and tests of evidence.
4. Perform the operation as in question 3 with an advertisement which contains argumentative copy.
5. Cite examples of items of evidence which may be classified as follows:
   a. Personal, circumstantial, and original
   b. Negative, real, circumstantial, and ordinary
   c. Direct, unwritten, hearsay, personal, and casual
   d. Negative, real, casual, and circumstantial.

Chapter **VIII** · KINDS OF ARGUMENT

The term "argument" has at least two meanings which should be distinguished. When one refers to a debate, or a controversy, or a dispute, as an "argument," he is using the term in its broader sense. In a more limited sense, argument may be defined as *the process of reasoning by which conclusions are inferred from premises*. In this chapter we are using the term in the second, more restricted sense. Thus, an argument is a line of reasoning or an inference from premises, offered to support a conclusion; and the kinds of argument reported here are the several types of reasoning which can be so employed.

Proof is a result of evidence *and* argument; evidence and argument are the two essential elements of proof. In proving a proposition, then, evidence and argument are presented for the purpose of establishing the "truth," justice, or wisdom of this proposition. The sounder the evidence and the more conclusive the argument, the greater is the probability of the conclusion.

I. ARGUMENT FROM SIGN

An argument from sign is one which gives an indication that the proposition *is* true without attempting to explain *why* it is true. It is a *ratio cognoscendi* or reason for acknowledging or recognizing the truth of a proposition as distinguished from a *ratio essendi* or reason why the proposition is true. A few simple examples will explain the nature of signs.

We may offer as signs of the coming of spring such indications as the northern flight of migratory birds, longer days, the breaking up of ice on lakes and streams, the budding of trees, the appearance of farmers in their fields, etc. All these are familiar signs of spring which in no sense explain *why* spring is coming. Similarly, the presence of picket lines might be offered to prove that a plant is on strike; boarded-up windows and an unkempt lawn might be taken as signs that a property is vacant; applause as an indication of approval; or rusty rails as an argument that a railroad track is used infrequently.

All arguments from sign are based on the assumption (stated or implied) that two or more variables are related in such a way that the presence or absence of one may be taken as an indication of the presence or absence of the other. Such relationships are *reciprocal* when either variable may be taken as the sign of the other. Thus, a thermometer showing freezing temperature may be taken as a sign of ice on the pond, and ice on the pond may be taken as a sign that the thermometer will register a freezing temperature. Sign relationships are *nonreciprocal* when one variable serves as a sign of a second, but this second *cannot* be reliably deduced from the first. For example, it might be inferred that a book is good because it bears the Macmillan imprint, but it cannot be concluded with equal force that a good book is a sign of the Macmillan imprint.

These sign relations are sometimes referred to as *substance-attribute* relations. Since every substance (object, thing, person, event, item, etc.) has certain distinguishing attributes or characteristics (size, shape, color, speed, number, etc.), the attributes may be taken as signs of the substance or the substance as a sign of the attributes.

All arguments from sign are based on generalizations either stated or implied. Thus, if it is contended that a certain publisher's imprint raises a presumption in favor of a book which bears this imprint, there is an implied assumption that this publisher usually brings out good books. In the arguments from sign given below, the assumed generalization upon which the argument is based is stated parenthetically.

CONCLUSION— The temperature is below 32 degrees, because

PREMISE— 1. It is snowing.

ASSUMED
GENERALIZATION— (1′. It never snows unless the temperature is below 32 degrees.)

CONCLUSION— This penal institution is failing to rehabilitate criminals, because

PREMISE— 1. Persons released usually return to a life of crime.

ASSUMED
GENERALIZATION— (1′. If released prisoners return to crime, the prison has failed to rehabilitate them.)

The basic test of any argument from sign lies in the reliability of the generalization upon which it is based. How perfectly, or reliably, or surely are the variables correlated? The following questions may be applied as tests in constructing and appraising such arguments.

A. Is the sign relationship accidental or coincidental? Quite obviously an accidental or coincidental association between certain phenomena cannot be regarded as a reliable basis for argument from sign. Many unfair attitudes toward people of different races and creeds are based upon such accidental associations. If a man has been unfortunate enough to meet a few Catholics or a few Methodists or a few Jews with undesirable characteristics, he must be exceedingly careful about imputing these characteristics to others of the same faith.

B. Is the sign relationship reciprocal? As we have already seen, X may be a reliable sign of Y without Y being an equally reliable sign of X. Even though we may be able to argue that pablum is nourishing because baby grows fat on it, we cannot with equal propriety take plumpness in baby as a sign that he eats pablum.

C. Have special factors intervened which alter normal relations? Time and space affect many sign relationships. Things that are related at one time may not be similarly related at a later time, and things which are related in one context may not be related in another. A crowd in Wrigley Field may be taken as a fairly reliable sign that a baseball game is scheduled, *if it is during the baseball season;* later in the year, such a crowd would probably mean a football game. High temperatures in one city are usually a reliable sign of high temperatures in a neighboring city, but if a high mountain range separates the two locations, this may not be the case.

D. Is the sign reliable without the collaboration or concurrence of other signs? The probative force of argument from sign is usually greater as additional signs are presented to support the same conclusion. A quite inconclusive sign may become significant when offered in concert with others. Thus, the presence of a man at the scene of a crime might not establish his guilt, but if it could be shown that he attempted to flee and that he possessed a weapon of the type that was used to commit the crime, the inference would be much more compelling.

II. CAUSAL ARGUMENT

A causal argument is one which serves to *account for* or *explain why* the proposition is true. Such an argument does not attempt to establish the proposition as being true, but, assuming its truth, attempts to show what causes it to be true. Typically, causal arguments follow arguments from sign in a rhetorical demonstration. The speaker first presents signs to show that the proposition *is* true, and then goes on to present arguments which show *why* it is true.

It is often difficult to distinguish between sign and causal arguments because the English connectives commonly used in argumentative discourse are ambiguous with respect to this distinction. Such words as "because," "for," "hence," "therefore" may be used to express either the relation of cause *or* sign between premise and conclusion with equal acceptability. The word "because," for example, does not necessarily imply causation. Whately's advice on the point is helpful:

The only decisive test by which to distinguish the Arguments which belong to the one, and to the other of these classes, is to ask the question, "Supposing the proposition in question to be admitted, would this statement here used as an Argument, serve to *account* for and explain the truth, or not?" It will then be readily referred to the former or to the latter class, according as the answer is in the affirmative or the negative; as *e.g.* if a murder were imputed to anyone on the grounds of his "having a hatred to the deceased, and an interest in his death," the Argument would belong to the former class; because, *supposing* his guilt to be admitted, and an inquiry to be made how he could have committed the murder, the circumstances just mentioned would serve to *account* for it; but not so, with respect to such an Argument as his "having blood on his clothes"; which would therefore be referred to the other class.[1]

Causal arguments are analytical in nature and usually require more insight and discernment than inferences from signs. In other

[1] Richard Whately, *Elements of Rhetoric*, London: John W. Parker, West Strand, 1846, pp. 46–7.

words, it is usually easier to *identify* than it is to *explain*. It might not be difficult to convince a person that the atomic bomb is capable of vast destructive power (Hiroshima and Nagasaki provide ample signs), but it is exceedingly difficult to explain *why* this bomb works as it does. We "know" many things on the basis of *signs* which we do not understand *causally*. I know *what* to expect when I push certain buttons and work certain pedals in my car, but I do not know *why* they operate as they do; a garage mechanic knows more of the explanation than I do; and the automotive engineer can provide a more basic explanation than the mechanic. As this example suggests, even a causal argument may be relatively superficial, or it may be fundamental and basic. The speaker's purpose (to say nothing of his capacities) and the demands of the occasion will usually dictate the extent to which causation should be pursued.

All causal arguments (as is true of signs) are based on generalizations either stated or implied. In the examples cited below, these generalizations are given parenthetically.

CONCLUSION— The temperature is below 32 degrees, because
PREMISE— 1. A cold mass of air is blowing in from the north.
ASSUMED
GENERALIZATION— (1'. North winds often bring in freezing temperatures.)
CONCLUSION— This penal institution is failing to rehabilitate criminals, because
PREMISE— 1. The warden is not a trained criminologist.
ASSUMED
GENERALIZATION— (1'. We can seldom expect competent rehabilitative measures from wardens with little or no training in criminology.)

The basic test of any causal argument lies in the reliability or universality of the generalization upon which it is based. The following questions may be applied as tests in constructing and appraising such arguments.

A. Is the connection between the cause and effect broken or incomplete? In causal argument the cause and effect are often separated by several intermediate steps. In other words, the cause is often *mediate* rather than *immediate*. The pull on the trigger will fire the shot if, and only if, the catch, the spring, the hammer, the cap, and so on, all act in the expected manner. The closer the causal connection, the surer is the argument, and any argument can be destroyed by showing that some of the intermediate links are lacking. It might be proved that A was inspired with a most malevolent hatred of B, that he would welcome any favorable opportunity of attacking him, even that he had actually sought to do him injury; but in order to connect this motive with the murder of B, it must be shown that none of the necessary intermediate steps was lacking. It must be proved that A was present at the time, that he had the necessary weapon, that he was physically strong enough to do the deed. The destruction of one of these links of the chain destroys the argument.

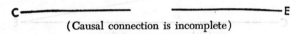

(Causal connection is incomplete)

B. Have other causes operated (or will they operate) to prevent or alter the cause under discussion? The normal progress between the cause and the effect is often stopped or turned from its course by the intervention of some other cause which destroys or turns aside the natural result of the first cause. If a man takes a dose of deadly poison, the chances are that it will cause his death; but it may be shown that this effect will not actually follow in this case, by showing that the man took an antidote. The antidote prevents the occurrence of the natural effect. One may argue that capital punishment will serve as a deterrent to crime because of the severity of the penalty; but this reasoning may be questioned by showing that the very severity of the punishment is such that juries will not convict where the penalty is mandatory and that judges are reluctant to impose it for the same reason.

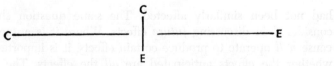

(Other causes may prevent expected effect)

C. To what extent is the effect the result of the cause? In other words, is the cause adequate to produce the effect? One of the most common mistakes in causal argument arises when a speaker offers an explanation which is inadequate, or anticipates results greater than can be reasonably expected. This gives rise to the fallacy of *part cause*. To argue that college athletes are healthier than non-athletes because they participate in sports, neglects the probability that they were selected for athletics because of their superior health; even if it is conceded that athletic participation is a contributing cause, this additional factor must be recognized. Similarly, to contend that a tax will yield certain required revenue without considering the cost of collection, is to suggest an inadequate cause; additional sources will have to be tapped to raise the required amount.

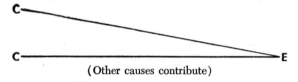

(Other causes contribute)

D. Does the cause produce other effects? If it can be shown that a cause may be expected to produce effects other than those in question, the absence of these side effects will throw doubt on the analysis. Thus, an argument that death was caused by drowning would be seriously questioned if it were shown that the lungs of the victim were not filled with water. Or a contention that a short supply of wheat caused a certain brand of flour to increase in price would be doubtful if it could be shown that other brands of wheat flour

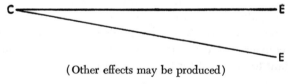

(Other effects may be produced)

had not been similarly affected. The same question should be considered in discussing *future* effects. Where it is argued that a cause *will* operate to produce certain effects, it is important to ask whether the effects anticipated are *all* the effects. The negative argument that the affirmative plan will produce "new and greater evils" is a familiar one in debate.

It is helpful to note that a speaker may consider causation in relation to *past fact, present fact,* or *future fact.* While this has been implied throughout our discussion of causal argument, we make it explicit here. If an event has already occurred, we necessarily discuss its cause in retrospect. If it is occurring now, we examine the cause while it is operating. If the cause has not yet operated, we then anticipate effects on the basis of past experience. The tests of causal reasoning apply in all cases.

III. ARGUMENT BY EXAMPLE

In most argumentative discourse, the speaker begins with his proposition and then presents argument from sign to prove the proposition *is* true, and causal arguments to explain *why* it is true. All of these arguments may have to be supported by examples to make them convincing. An example is a case or instance in point, and argument from example is the process of inference by which a conclusion is drawn from one or more such cases or instances in point. Examples or cases offered in argument constitute evidence. The immediate inference from such evidence is argument from example. As we shall see in the next chapter, the kinds of propositions argued in public debate can rarely be supported *directly* by examples. The arguments from example are ordinarily connected with the speaker's proposition through the mediation of arguments from sign and cause. Thus, the premises of these arguments (sign and cause) become the conclusions of arguments from example in connected discourse.

Argument from example is sometimes called "generalization" or "argument by generalization." These labels are appropriate because such a generalization, a general law or principle, is the object in view in argument from example. This kind of argument involves an examination of the real, phenomenal, existential world for the purpose of making accurate statements about it. As I look out of my study window, it is possible for me to make dozens of generalizations from the "examples" which are spread before me: snow is white; oak trees lose their leaves in the winter; my property is contiguous with the Cook County Forest Preserve on the south; mallard drakes have green heads; wood ducks have brilliant plumage; these ducks usually alert when a car passes on Lake Avenue; the trees bend south against a north wind. Having made these observations, I can pull the drapes, shut off the view, and make a number of inferences *based on* these observations. I hear a car passing on Lake Avenue and infer that the ducks have alerted; I hear the wind and infer that the trees are bending, etc. These inferences may be stated as causal arguments, *viz.*, that the ducks have probably alerted because a car is passing on Lake Avenue. Having observed this phenomenon, I can infer it in a particular case on the basis of these observations. As we have seen, all arguments from cause and sign are premised on generalizations either stated or implied. It is the business of argument from example to supply these generalizations.

The crux of argument from example consists in presenting one or more individual objects or instances, of a certain class, as fair specimens in respect of some point or other, and drawing an inference from them respecting the whole class. The following questions may be applied as tests of such argument.

A. Are the specimens fair in respect to the point in issue? The failure to meet this test is very common in dishonest and partisan controversy. The statement that "100 students were asked if they wanted the _____ system introduced, and only three said 'Yes'" has no valid force whatever if the 100 students were all unfair specimens of the general student body of 5,000 in regard to the particular point in issue. Choosing unfair specimens and making out a plausible, but dishonest and worthless, generalization is a favorite trick of partisan investigators and advocates who have to make out a preconceived case regardless of truth.

B. Has a large enough part of the class been observed to justify an inference regarding the whole class? To apply this test, as in applying the first one, it is necessary to know the exact nature of the question at issue. In questions which concern the working out of natural laws, as in chemistry, physics, biology, etc., a very small number of specimens are needed to determine the rule. If a certain treatment of a dozen rabbits results in each case in the same way, it is reasonably safe to formulate a rule for all the millions of rabbits, or for other animals as well. In chemistry or physics one very carefully performed experiment may well settle some question for all time. A rule can be formulated and followed with confidence in every case. *This is generalization from a single in-*

stance. It is usually allowable when dealing with the working of natural laws on inanimate materials, and sometimes on plants and animals. Of course, many questions, such as questions in chemistry or physics, plants and animals, even human beings, are to be tested in the same manner as inanimate materials. It is as we get further and further from this type of question, and nearer to questions involving personal taste, ability, prejudice, opinion, belief, etc., that we must increasingly enlarge the proportion of observed instances. The greater the possible variations in answer to our question, the wider must be the field of observation, in order to justify a generalization. And, of course, the very nature of many questions precludes the possibility of getting a rule that will work without exceptions. In practically all questions affecting human conduct a high degree of probability is all we can hope to get for any general rule.

There is another circumstance under which generalizations can be drawn from a single example: in those cases in which the example used is demonstrably least favorable to the generalization. Some years ago the colleges debated the proposition that the several states should derive at least 50 per cent of their tax revenue from sources other than tangible property. One affirmative team undertook to show that this tax program would be at its worst in North Dakota because the wealth of this state, more than any other, lay in tangible property. Having established this, they went on to show that the proposed distribution of taxes would be wise even in North Dakota, and concluded that if the program was advisable in the state least favorable to it, then surely it should be adopted in the others.

What is sought, of course, in making a generalization is a fair sample of the phenomena about which a generalization is being made. An ideal sample will represent all the significant variables entering into the generalization, with proper regard to the weight or frequency of each. If the cross section is carefully chosen, a relatively small sample will often permit a sound generalization.

C. Are negative instances accounted for? Whenever a generalization is drawn in which there are negative instances, *i.e.*, cases in which the relationship alleged is not borne out, it is advisable to account for these cases. Failure to do this paves the way for an opponent to produce these cases and thereby throw doubt on the entire matter. In the first place, every generalization should be qualified as accurately as possible in terms of the available data; and in the second place, instances which do not conform to the rule should be shown to be exceptional cases, or cases which are not significant for other reasons.

D. Is the relationship generalized apparent in the examples adduced? Examples are presented to support a generalization. These generalizations assert sign relations (mallard drakes have green heads) or causal relations (loud noises cause ducks to alert). To be effective, such examples should clearly exhibit the relation which is being generalized. Unless this is the case, the examples themselves become subjects for argument. Suppose it is contended that city X should adopt the city manager form of government because it has succeeded in cities A, B, and C. If A, B, and C exhibit this success without further argument, they may be regarded as examples. If not, they must, in this case, be taken as signs, and arguments must be offered to prove the allegation with respect to A, B, and C. These arguments must, in turn, be supported by further arguments. This process is refined until premises are reached which can be supported by examples—examples in which the relationship generalized is apparent. In any chain of argument which begins with the proposition, the arguments from example, if such appear at all, are the last arguments in this chain.

IV. ANALOGY

In argument from analogy, the ground of inference is the resemblance between two individual objects or kinds of objects in a certain number of points, and the inference is that they resemble one another in some other point, known to belong to the one, but not known to belong to the other. Whereas argument from example generalizes from one or more cases, analogy infers a conclusion about one case by comparing it with another. "Two things go together in many cases, therefore in all, including this one," is the argument in extending a generalization; "two things agree in many respects, therefore in this other," is the argument from analogy—"If two cases are alike in all essential respects, they will (in all probability) be alike in the respect under question." The classic example of argument from analogy is that given by Thomas Reid in his *Intellectual Powers:*

We may observe a very great similitude between this earth which we inhabit, and the other planets, Saturn, Jupiter, Mars, Venus, and Mercury. They all revolve around the sun, as the earth does, although at different distances and in different periods. They borrow all their light from the sun, as the earth does. Several of them are known to revolve around their visible axis like the earth, and by that means have like succession of day and night. Some of them have moons, that serve to give them light in the absence of the sun, as our moon does to us. They are all, in their motions, subject to the same law of gravitation as the earth is. From all this similitude it is not unreasonable to think that these planets may, like our earth, be the habitations of various orders of living creatures. There is some probability in this conclusion from analogy.

There are two kinds of analogies: *literal* and *figurative*. The analogy is literal when the cases, objects, or things compared are in the same general class, *viz.*, two dwellings, two farms, two cities, two planets, etc. The analogy is figurative when the cases, objects, or things compared are in different classes, as in the following example: "You should not change horses in the middle of a stream; you should not, therefore, change generals in the middle of a campaign." Figurative analogies are useful for illustrative purposes only and have no probative force. Literal analogies, on the other hand, may be used to prove a point in argument if they are carefully constituted. The questions which follow may be used as tests.

A. Are the compared cases alike in all essential respects? This is the vital test in analogical reasoning. And the important word in this question is "essential." If I reason that a fireplace is adequate in my neighbor's cottage and therefore should be adequate in mine, the fact that my cottage is white and his green is completely immaterial. It is not an essential difference for purposes of this analogy. Essential factors would certainly include the size and construction of the two buildings. In order to give grounds for any analogical argument, it is important not that the resemblances are many, but that they are such as bear directly on the argument. "Caesar had his Brutus, Charles I his Cromwell, and George III may profit by their example." Caesar was unlike Charles I in most of his personal qualities; he ruled a different country, in a different age. George III was the very opposite of the Roman in temper and character; his people, his advisers, his century, were not similar to those of either of the men with whom he was compared. But the three cases were similar in the essential element: Caesar, Charles I, and George III all represented the pressure of tyranny upon a spirited, liberty-loving people. In each case, oppression was the cause of the effect, rebellion; and whatever other differences there were in the circumstances, the *causes* were similar in nature.

B. Are differences in the compared cases accounted for? Any differences which *appear* to be essential should be shown to be non-essential, nonexistent, or disposed of in some other manner.

C. Is the argument from analogy cumulative? Analogical reasoning becomes cumulative when more than one comparison is adduced to support the conclusion. For instance, if we were arguing that a certain project would be successful in Michigan, it might be possible to draw analogies with several other states where this project was in operation. Cumulative analogy is not identical with generalization as it is sometimes claimed, because a particular conclusion regarding some specific case is always drawn in analogical reasoning, while a general conclusion pertaining to all cases is the result of generalization. From a series of analogies showing the success of a certain project, we argue that it will be successful in a particular case. From a series of cases in generalization we conclude that the project will be successful in all cases. Reasoning from analogy becomes increasingly strong as the number of comparisons is increased, or in other words, as the analogies are cumulated.

❋ ❋ ❋

In concluding this chapter, it should be pointed out that argument from sign and causal argument are *deductive* in character as here discussed, and argument from example and analogy are *inductive*. Inductive argument may yield conclusions which become the premises in deductive arguments. Sign relationships and causal relationships enter into all argument. Induction is the process by which these relationships are discovered and generalized. Deduction is the process by which such generalizations are applied to particular cases. In the next chapter we explain how these different kinds of argument are related and expressed in argumentative discourse.

Exercises

1. Bring in five original examples of each of the four kinds of argument discussed in this chapter. Criticize these examples in class. Apply the appropriate tests to them.
2. Present an affirmative or negative argumentative speech which will illustrate the four kinds of argument. Hand in an outline of this speech in which the kinds of argument are identified marginally.
3. Identify and criticize the kinds of argument in an article selected from a contemporary journal of opinion such as *Harper's* or the *New Republic*.
4. Select a proposition of policy for class debate. Divide the class into an affirmative group and a negative group. Alternate affirmative and negative speeches with attention to the kinds of argument used and refutation which points out weakness in argument.
5. Conduct class debates on the following plan: affirmative constructive case, six minutes; negative rejoinder, nine minutes; affirmative rebuttal, three minutes.

Chapter **IX** · THE STRUCTURE
OF ARGUMENT

In Chapter vii we discussed evidence—the kinds of evidence and the tests which can be applied to it. In Chapter viii we explained the four basic kinds of argument—example, analogy, cause, and sign. In this chapter we point out the forms which these proofs take in argumentative discourse and how they are related to the brief or the outline of argumentative discourse. The problem is one of giving the evidence and argument (reasoning) of the speaker a context and structure which will recommend his proposition to the listener; it is a matter of expressing in language the grounds from which another can reason to the conclusion upheld by the advocate.

I. DEDUCTIVE REASONING IN ARGUMENT

In preparing his brief and presenting his case, the advocate usually begins with his proposition. He then sets forth the primary arguments (main points) in support of this proposition. These primary arguments must usually be supported by secondary arguments (subpoints), and the secondary arguments may need to be supported by tertiary arguments, etc. This process of refinement results in chains of argument in which the primary arguments play an important role because they determine the principal division of the matter of the entire discourse.

Structurally the whole argument is dominated by the arguments that stand logically next to the original proposition . . . for it is on the basis of these arguments that the first division of the matter is made. And these primary arguments must be deductive in the case of, literally, quite ninety-nine of every hundred subjects of public discussion or of academic debate. . . . In ninety-nine arguments out of a hundred, then, of the class we are considering, it is only after the primary arguments have divided the material that inductive arguments may appear. And even then, though often they are by no means less important than deductive arguments, they are in most debates less frequent. In nearly every discourse on a question of public discussion, then, the arguments that determine the main structural lines and most of those that determine subordinate structural lines are deductive.[1]

The "arguments that stand logically next to the original proposition" are almost always deductive for the very simple and practical reason that the questions which people ordinarily debate cannot be supported directly by inductive arguments. An inductive argument is one which draws its conclusion immediately from the facts. Suppose the proposition that capital punishment be abolished is under consideration. This proposition cannot possibly be inferred directly from the facts. It is necessary first to adduce reasons which can be inductively supported. One such reason might be the argument that capital punishment is not an effective deterrent to crime; another might be the argument that the lives of innocent people may be taken. The first argument might be supported inductively by citing statistics (examples) to show that capital crimes are increasing in states which employ the death penalty; the second might be given inductive support by citing examples of persons who suffered capital punishment and later were found to have been innocent.

In the illustration we are using, the two primary arguments cited are *deductive*. They may be stated in full as follows:

Capital punishment should be abolished, because

    i. Legal penalties which fail as a deterrent to crime should be abolished, and

    i'. Capital punishment fails as a deterrent to crime.

    ii. Any legal penalty which takes the lives of innocent people should be abolished, and

    ii'. Capital punishment takes the lives of innocent people.

A deductive argument is typically one which applies a generalization to a specific case (Chapter viii). Points i and ii in the foregoing illustration are generalizations, and points i' and ii' are the cases to which the generalizations are applied.

[1] C. G. Hoag, "The Logic of Argument," *Haverford Essays*, Haverford, Pa., 1909, p. 30.

Every deductive argument contains two premises and a conclusion. The premise which states the generalization is called the *major premise,* and the premise which relates a specific case to the generalization is called the *minor premise.* In most cases, the major premises are not expressed in general argumentation on the assumption that listeners will make the desired inferences without them. If the major premise is one which the listener has already formulated or one which patently comports with general experience, its omission in argument is a wise economy of time and energy. If there is question about it, however, the speaker will do well to state it explicitly, and he is under obligation to defend it if challenged by an opponent. It is always a vital part of the structure of argument. It can be assumed only tentatively. If questioned, it must be proved. Failure to recognize this, either by advocate or listeners, may result in the listener or reader thinking or saying, "I believe you are wrong, but I can't put my finger on your exact failure." In fact it may move the opposition or other listeners to use the always untenable remark, "Your argument is all right in theory, but it will not work." No theory that "won't work" is ever any good if it is a theory concerning something that is *supposed to work.*

A. The syllogism. The form in which deductive arguments are expressed has been called a *syllogism* for many centuries. "When two propositions are so formulated and laid down that a third proposition necessarily follows from these two propositions, we have a syllogism."[2]

The relationships involved in the syllogism are those between generalizations and cases (as explained above) or, stated differently, those between classes and members of these classes (class inclusion). Both of the arguments cited above to prove that capital punishment should be abolished may be taken as examples of syllogisms. Structurally, they are identical with the classical example of the syllogism:

> All men are mortal (major premise)
> Socrates is a man (minor premise)
> Therefore, Socrates is mortal (conclusion)

[2] Aristotle, *Prior Analytics,* I, 1.

Here again the major premise expresses a generalization, and the minor premise relates a particular case to the generalization or, stated differently, the major premise places *all* men in the class of *mortal beings*, and the minor premise classifies Socrates as a man. Since all A's are B's and C is an A, it follows that C is a B. When deductive arguments are explained as syllogisms, it is possible to examine the logical grounds upon which these arguments rest with considerably more precision than is otherwise possible. Students of argumentation and debate can profit greatly from a careful study of logic wherein the forms and regulations of the syllogism are examined in greater detail than is possible here.

1. Kinds of syllogisms. We shall discuss three kinds of syllogisms, the Categorical, the Disjunctive, and the Hypothetical.

a. The categorical syllogism. The categorical syllogism is the form in which categorical deductions are stated. It is characterized by the fact that its major premise is always a categorical or unqualified statement of either a relationship of causation or resemblance which admits of no conditions or exceptions. The following syllogism is categorical.

> a. Every school in the conference won a majority of its football games.
> b. Michigan is a school in the conference.
> c. Therefore: Michigan won a majority of its football games.

(I) *The categorical syllogism must contain three and only three terms.* The three terms to which this rule refers are the major term, the middle term, and the minor term. In the above illustration the major term is *the winning of a majority of its football games;* *the schools in the conference* is the middle term; and *Michigan,* the minor term. Every term is used twice in the syllogism. In composing a categorical syllogism, the terms should be arranged as follows:

> 1) Major premise: Middle term—Major term
> 2) Minor premise: Minor term—Middle term
> 3) Conclusion: Minor term—Major term

In ordinary speaking or writing, however, the terms do not appear in any definite order, and only a thorough understanding of the syllogism will enable the persuader to reduce an argument to the proper syllogistic form.

(II) *The middle term must be distributed in at least one of the premises.* By a distributed term is meant one that refers to a class of things in its entirety, as "all men" or "every law." A term is distributed when it includes all the members of any category, or all the parts of a whole; and it is undistributed when it is not universal or all-inclusive as "some men," "a part of the group," or "many animals." In many cases, terms are distributed or undistributed without such words as "all," "every," "some," or "many" appearing in the term. Generally speaking, the following rules obtain in such cases: (1) The subjects of statements are usually distributed; (2) the predicates of affirmative statements are usually undistributed; and (3) the predicates of negative statements are always distributed.

The fallacy in reasoning occasioned by the failure to distribute the middle term in at least one of the premises is illustrated in the following syllogism:

> a. Some college men belong to fraternities.
> b. John Smith is a college man.
> c. Therefore: John Smith belongs to a fraternity.

(III) *A term must not be distributed in the conclusion unless it is distributed in one of the premises.* Since the middle term does not appear in the conclusion, this rule applies only to the major and minor terms. The fallacies arising from violations of this rule are illustrated by the following syllogisms:

> a. Horses are animals.
> b. Cows are not horses.
> c. Therefore: Cows are not animals.

In the foregoing syllogism, the major term, "animals," is undistributed in the major premise, and distributed in the conclusion. The fallacy becomes more apparent when the major premise is stated, "Horses are (some) animals."

> a. All Senators are at least thirty years old.
> b. All Senators are voters.
> c. Therefore: All voters are at least thirty years old.

In this case, the minor term, "voters," is undistributed in the minor premise and distributed in the conclusion. Here also the fallacy becomes more apparent when the word, "some," is stated in the minor premise, "All Senators are (some) voters."

(IV) *A valid conclusion cannot be inferred from two negative premises.* The student can illustrate this rule for himself by taking any two negative premises. The precaution should be observed, however, that the mere occurrence of a negative particle in a statement does not necessarily make that statement negative. Thus the argument:

    a. What is not a compound is an element.
    b. Gold is not a compound.
    c. Therefore gold is an element.

contains negatives in both premises, but is nevertheless valid, because the negative in both cases affects the middle term which is really the negative term, "not-compound."

(V) *If one premise is negative the conclusion must be negative.* The student can also readily illustrate this rule to his own satisfaction. Here again, however, care must be taken to ascertain that the premise thought to be negative is actually a negative statement and not simply an affirmative statement containing the particles *no* or *not*, or the prefix *non*, as a part of one of the terms.

b. The disjunctive syllogism. The disjunctive syllogism is the form in which disjunctive deductions are stated. It is characterized by the fact that its major premise is always a disjunctive statement setting forth certain alternative possibilities. Whereas a categorical statement expresses an unconditional relationship of causation or sign, a disjunctive proposition states alternative relationships of causation or sign as follows: "Either a cyclone or earthquake caused the destruction of the city"; or "The books on this shelf are either biography or fiction." The following syllogism is disjunctive:

    a. A Federal Department of Education must be justified either on the basis of its ability to subsidize education, or its ability to conduct educational research more efficiently than the existing Office of Education.
    b. A Federal Department of Education cannot be justified on the basis of superior ability to conduct research.

c. Therefore: It must be justified on the basis of its ability to subsidize education.

(I) *The alternative possibilities enumerated in the major premise must be all-inclusive.* Failure to include all the possibilities in a disjunction destroys its validity. Any conclusion deduced from an incomplete disjunction can be seriously weakened by presenting possible causes or classifications not contemplated by the disjunction. The following syllogism illustrates this point:

a. Crop failures are caused either by drouth or excessive moisture.
b. This crop failure was not caused by excessive moisture.
c. Therefore: It was caused by drouth.

In this case, the inference could be destroyed and the conclusion opened to serious question by showing that insects, frost, hail, as well as other causes might have operated to produce the crop failure.

(II) *All the possibilities enumerated in the major premise must be mutually exclusive.* If the possibilities set forth in the disjunction overlap, the elimination of one alternative will seriously impair any others with which it may overlap. Consider the following case:

a. The American farmer must seek relief either through the provisions of the McNary-Haugen Farm Relief Bill, or through the control of surplus production.
b. It is impossible to control surplus production.
c. Therefore: The farmer must seek relief through the Mc-Nary-Haugen Bill.

Readers who remember the McNary-Haugen Bill will recall that it was a farm-relief measure which proposed to assist the farmer by an elaborate plan to control surplus production. In the foregoing syllogism, then, when the minor premise eliminates surplus control, it also eliminates the McNary-Haugen Bill insofar as it depends upon surplus control.

(III) *If the minor premise affirms one of the possibilities, the conclusion must deny the other.*

(IV) *If the minor premise denies one of the possibilities, the conclusion must affirm the other.*

c. The hypothetical syllogism. The hypothetical syllogism is the form in which hypothetical deductions are stated. It is characterized by the fact that its major premise always expresses a hypothetical or conditional relationship of causation or sign. We shall refer to the conditional or "if" clause in the major premise as the antecedent, and the clause to which the condition is applied as the consequent. Thus in the following syllogism, "if the drouth continues" is the antecedent and "the crop will be lost" is the consequent:

    a. If the drouth continues, the crop will be lost.
    b. The drouth continued.
    c. Therefore: The crop was lost.

(I) *If the minor premise affirms the antecedent, the conclusion must affirm the consequent.* This rule expresses the relationship between premises which obtains in most hypothetical reasoning, and is evident from the foregoing illustration.

(II) *If the minor premise denies the consequent, the conclusion must deny the antecedent.* In the following syllogism a valid conclusion is drawn by denying the consequent:

    a. If the United States will disarm, other nations will disarm.
    b. Other nations will not disarm.
    c. Therefore: The United States will not disarm.

The reasoning in this syllogism is sound because the disarmament of other nations is alleged to be an absolute consequent of disarmament by the United States. If other nations will not disarm, it can be deduced infallibly that the United States will not disarm, assuming, of course, that the major premise is true. The student should understand that we are making an assumption of this kind in all the illustrations used in this chapter. In actual argument any premise is open to attack if it is not properly evidenced. In this chapter, however, we are concerned with inferences and the forms in which they appear rather than evidence. So, assuming the premises to be sound, we narrow our discussion to the validity of inferences.

(III) *A conclusion drawn from a minor premise which denies the antecedent is not necessarily true.* Consider the following illustration:

a. If a Federal Department of Education is established, the Federal appropriation for education will be increased.
b. A Department of Education will not be established.
c. Therefore: The Federal appropriation for education will not be increased.

The conclusion in this syllogism is not necessarily sound because the minor premise denies the antecedent. While the major premise states that the appropriation will be increased if a Department of Education is established, so far as this hypothesis goes, there could be many causes other than the one stipulated which could operate to produce the same effect.

(IV) *A conclusion drawn from a minor premise which affirms the consequent is not necessarily true.* The following syllogism in which the minor premise affirms the consequent illustrates the weakness of a conclusion drawn from such hypothetical reasoning:

a. If a large crop is produced, prices will be low.
b. Prices are low.
c. Therefore: A large crop was produced.

Here again the conclusion does not follow from the condition stated in the major premise. Whereas high prices would prove beyond question that a small crop was produced, low prices would not necessarily prove that a large crop was produced. So far as the major premise in the syllogism goes, many other causes might have operated to produce low prices, but a large crop is alleged to be a certain cause. Thus, the existence of high prices must necessarily mean that a small crop was harvested, while the existence of low prices may or may not mean that a large crop was produced.

2. **The syllogism in argumentation and debate.** We have already explained how syllogisms enter into argumentative discourse. Each argument offered in support of the proposition can be expressed in full syllogistic form if so desired. While such fully stated syllogisms rarely occur in argumentative speaking or writing, the structure of this discourse is none the less syllogistic in character even if major premises are omitted and assumed or conclusions are stated first and premises follow. The essential rhetorical problem in the syllogism is in the fact that its rules and regulations contemplate a degree of certainty which can rarely be achieved in a rhetorical demonstration. The crucial test of the syllogism is that the middle term be

distributed in at least one of the premises.[3] The point here is that the middle terms in rhetorical syllogisms can rarely be distributed perfectly and completely. The things we talk about in most public and private debates are variable rather than discrete and categorical. The best we can say in most cases is "most," "the great majority," "the trend is in this direction," "in 60 per cent of the cases," "usually," "frequently," etc. A series of syllogisms whose middle terms are qualified in such manner might very well establish an exceedingly high degree of *probability;* and yet, *logically,* strictly speaking, they amount to exactly zero, because the middle terms are not distributed. This anomalous situation was recognized by none other than the Greek philosopher, Aristotle, the man who first described the syllogism over 2,000 years ago. In order, then, to accommodate his syllogistic doctrine to the kinds of proofs which speakers and writers must ordinarily use, he invented the "rhetorical syllogism" or the *enthymeme.*

B. The enthymeme. The enthymeme (as conceived by Aristotle) is a concept of great theoretical importance and practical utility to the practitioner of argumentation and debate.[4] It is almost universally defined today by rhetoricians and logicians alike as an elided or truncated syllogism; *i.e.,* as a syllogism with one of its premises or the conclusion omitted. Such an omission (usually the major premise) is characteristic of rhetorical discourse, as we have seen, but it is *not* the essential difference between the syllogism and the enthymeme as originally conceived and *as it should be conceived today.* The real difference is in the certainty of the matter and the form. The logical syllogism is built on premises which are "materially" true; it is tested by the rules of formal validity; the middle term *must* be distributed in at least one of the premises; and the conclusion either follows *certainly* from the premises or it does not follow at all. The rhetorical syllogism or the enthymeme is

---

[3] This, in effect, is just as true of the disjunctive and hypothetical syllogisms as it is of the categorical. They are simply linguistic variations of the categorical syllogism anyway, and, if valid, are always reducible to valid categorical syllogisms.

[4] See James H. McBurney, "The Place of the Enthymeme in Rhetorical Theory," *Speech Monographs,* Vol. III, 1936, pp. 49–74; *ibid.,* "Some Recent Interpretations of the Aristotelian Enthymeme," *Papers of the Michigan Academy of Science, Arts, and Letters,* Vol. XXI, 1935, pp. 489–500.

built on "probable" premises; it admits middle terms which are only "partially distributed"; and it limits its conclusions to probabilities. This accords with the nature of rhetorical discourse as we know it to be and as we have discussed it throughout this book (See Chapter II).

For the record, it should be said here that anyone who applies syllogistic logic to rhetorical discourse, without the qualifications which the enthymeme (as here defined) imposes, will be stopped before he gets well started; and anyone who criticizes the applications of the syllogistic doctrine to rhetorical discourse without benefit of an understanding of the enthymeme is almost certain to do an injustice to the syllogism. Both the textbooks and the critical literature are replete with these mistakes.

1. Kinds of enthymemes. Enthymemes can be classified in three ways: (1) on the basis of the omission of one or more parts of a complete argument; (2) on the basis of the character of the major premise; and (3) on the basis of the relation which the minor premise bears to the conclusion.

A fully expressed enthymeme, like a fully expressed syllogism, has two premises and a conclusion. If the major premise is omitted, the argument is an enthymeme of the "first order"; if the minor premise is omitted, it is one of the "second order"; and if the conclusion is omitted, it is one of the "third order." The full enthymeme is infrequent; the first order is typical; the second order is rare; and the third order is used occasionally for "rhetorical effect."

Enthymemes, like syllogisms, may also be classified as categorical, disjunctive, and hypothetical. These labels derive from the character of the major premise (expressed or implied). Since the major premises may be categorical, disjunctive, or hypothetical generalizations, the arguments applying such generalizations to particular cases may with some propriety be similarly labeled. The objection to this terminology in the case of the enthymeme is, of course, that the major premise is not "categorical" in the sense of being unqualified, and the generalizations typically assert something to be true of *most* of the *members* of a certain *class* rather than *all*. The objection is not critical, however, if these interpretations are understood.

Thirdly, enthymemes may be classified on the basis of the relation which the minor premise bears to the conclusion. So classified there are four types of enthymemes or four kinds of argument—cause, sign, example, and analogy. This we believe to be the most useful classification. It is explained in detail in Chapter VIII. In presenting arguments to support a proposition, as we have seen, we can present a reason which explains *why* the proposition is true (cause) or a reason which provides a basis for believing it *is true* (sign), or examples, or analogies. All arguments are reducible to these types.

The careful reader of this book will ask at this point: Can you properly list *example* and *analogy* as types of enthymemes since example and analogy are inductive arguments and the enthymeme is a deductive instrument? Historically, this is a moot question.[5] We raise the question here to avoid the appearance of an inconsistency and also because consideration of the question will help clarify our analysis. Arguments from cause and sign are clearly deductive as we have explained them. The following illustrations will help to make this clear.

(Conclusion) Antihistaminic drugs in proper dosages relieve the symptoms of allergic colds, because

(Minor premise) i. These drugs contain chemicals which combat the histamine generated by the body in allergic reaction, and

(Major premise) i′. If we can combat the histamine generated by the body in allergic reaction, we can expect relief from colds caused by allergy.

(Minor premise) ii. Clinical evidence indicates that such relief may be expected in most allergic colds where proper dosages are administered, and

(Major premise) ii′. If clinical evidence shows such results, we may conclude that the antihistaminics are helpful in the symptomatic relief of allergic colds.

We have here two fully expressed enthymemes (arguments) adduced to support the same conclusion. The first enthymeme is a causal argument because it attempts to explain why the antihistaminic drugs relieve allergic colds. The second enthymeme is an argument from sign because it attempts to show that antihistamines *actually do* relieve allergic colds. Both are "hypothetical" enthymemes as here expressed. All of the premises in these two

[5] Compare Aristotle's *Rhetoric* I.2 and II.25; see also *Prior Analytics* II.27.

arguments, with the exception of II′, would need to be expressed and proved inductively to make the case convincing to most people. Such inductive support would call for examples or analogies.

The major premise of the first enthymeme in the foregoing illustration expresses, of course, a causal generalization (in hypothetical form). In substance, it alleges that any drug which combats the histamine generated by the body in allergic reaction will usually *cause* the symptoms of the allergic cold to be so reduced as to give relief. This is the theory or hypothesis upon which antihistaminic medication rests. To prove it inductively, one would need to cite convincing experimental evidence. Such evidence might consist in, let us say, ten controlled experiments in ten different laboratories by ten different experimenters, each example supporting this causal relationship. Actually, in this kind of case, any *one* experiment might involve hundreds of subjects and thus hundreds of examples. In terms of our analysis here, the cases reported are the evidence, and the inference from the cases which permits the generalization is argument from example.

We still have the question: Can an *inductive* argument from example be cast in syllogistic or enthymematic form? The answer is "yes," but not in such a way as to add anything to the force of the argument. The assumed major premise in all inductive enthymemes is this: "If the examples cited are acceptable, the conclusion follows"; or "If examples 1, 2, 3, 4, etc. are reliable and representative, the relationship they exhibit may be generalized." Since such a major premise patently adds nothing to the argument, these inductive arguments are rarely thrown into syllogistic form.

2. The use of enthymemes in argumentative discourse. The syllogism and the enthymeme explain the structure of argument as it is exhibited in a properly drawn brief or logical outline and provide the structural basis, through such outlines, for the composition of the finished discourse. They also make it clear that all (deductive) reasoning proceeds by relating generalizations to particular cases through the mediation of middle terms which are common to both and provide tests which can be used to check the validity of deductive inferences.

John Quincy Adams discusses the rhetorical applications of the syllogism in these words:

A syllogism, as you well know, consists of three propositions, denominated the major and minor propositions, and the conclusion. From the two former, which are the premises, the latter is a necessary inference; because in them the subject and predicate of the conclusion, called by logicians the major and minor terms, or the extremes, are distinctly compared with a middle term, or particular common to them both. These propositions in the simple syllogism are all categorical or positive affirmations. And these propositions all belong alike to the *enthymeme*. The difference is that, as the domain of rhetorical argument is not certainty but probability, the propositions are not absolute but always in some degree problematical. The logician lays down his propositions as incontestable truths; and uses no words other than those which clothe the propositions themselves, to obtain the assent of his auditor to them. And as they must either be true or false, they can be opposed only in the same categorical manner in which they are asserted. The opposition admits of no degrees or modifications; it must either be received with implicit acquiescence, or express denial.

But the propositions of the orator are only given as probabilities. They do not exact unhesitating belief. The major or the minor proposition, from which he purposes to draw his conclusion, or both of them, may require reasons for their own support. . . .[6]

Mr. Adams, in a later passage, explains how the enthymeme usually appears in discourse.[7]

It is to be remembered that uniformity is the favorite character of logic, and variety is equally essential to rhetoric. The syllogism is confined to a very few modifications, and rejects every irregularity of arrangement. It has but one process, from which it inflexibly refuses to depart. Whether proceeding in affirmation or in negation, whether evolving particular or general conclusions, the order of march is eternally the same. The propositions are always categorical. The major advances in the van; the minor settles in the center; the middle term is common to them both; and the conclusion closes in the rear. In rhetoric, the syllogism, by sliding into the enthymem or spreading into the epichirema, seems to change its nature. It retains all its powers, but is emancipated from all its restrictions. It reverses at pleasure the order of its propositions. It gives alternate precedency to either of the premises, or posts the conclusion in front of both. It is not always arrayed in the dogmatism of unqualified assertion. Is it uncertain, it states its proposition in the dif-

[6] John Quincy Adams, *Lectures on Rhetoric and Oratory*, Vol. II (Cambridge: Hilliard and Metcalf, 1810), pp. 38–39. The term "enthymeme" has been substituted for "epichirema" in this quotation. [7] *Ibid.*, pp. 42–43.

fidence of the potential mood. Is it emphatically certain, it bids defiance to the opponent by challenging denial in the shape of interrogation. Is it humble, it may convey its idea in the form of conjecture. Is it conscious of authority, it may assume the language of command. It adapts itself to every gradation of intellect. It suits itself to every variety of disposition. But under all its metamorphoses the primary matter of the syllogism, the major, minor, and middle terms, must substantially remain, or the reasoning will be imperfect.

Aristotle has this advice to offer on the use of enthymemes:

We have already stated that the Enthymeme is a syllogism, and in what sense it is so. And we have noted how enthymemes differ from the syllogisms of Dialectic: (when you wish to persuade,) you must not begin the chain of reasoning too far back, or its length will render the argument obscure; and you must not put in every single link, or the statement of what is obvious will render it prolix. . . . Our speaker, accordingly, must start out, not from any and every premise that may be regarded as true, but from opinions of a definite sort—the (actual) opinions of the judges (audience), or else the opinions of persons whose authority they accept. And the speaker must make sure that his premises do appear in this light to most, if not all, of his audience. And he must argue not only from necessary truths, but from probable truths as well.[8]

II. INDUCTIVE REASONING IN ARGUMENT

Inductive reasoning consists in drawing inferences from the facts, from experience, from evidence. It is the means by which we attempt to make true statements about the phenomena with which we are concerned. "Inductively given" statements are statements which presumably meet the tests of "material" validity; they are true to life, true to the existential world. Whereas deductive inferences deal with the relationships among *given* propositions for the purpose of interpreting these propositions and deriving new propositions from *given* propositions, induction is the logical process by which we "get" the propositions in the first place.

As we have seen, inductive arguments usually appear as the *last* arguments in the chains of reasoning supporting the proposition. If the proposition can be supported directly by inductive arguments, so much the better, but this is rarely possible. More fre-

[8] *Rhetoric* II.22.

quently, the primary arguments are deductive. Each primary argument (if deductive) potentially involves two premises which must be supported. If these premises can be supported inductively, so much the better. If not, they become the conclusions of secondary arguments, each of which potentially involves two premises. The premises of the secondary arguments become the conclusions of tertiary arguments, etc. In other words, each chain of reasoning is refined to a point where the "last" premises can be supported inductively. The evidence always lies next to the inductive argument, hence "below" (in a written brief) or "in support of" the last premises.

When we say that the inductive arguments appear "last" in a chain of reasoning, we, of course, make the assumption that the advocate begins with his proposition, as is usually the case. To be entirely correct in this matter, we should say that the deductive argument (if any) lies *between* the proposition and the inductive arguments. Actually, the speaker may begin with his evidence and inductive arguments, and then proceed to his proposition via such deductive arguments as may be required. This approach withholds the proposition until the groundwork in evidence and argument has been laid. It simply reverses the usual sequence in presenting a case, and the outline, of course, is inverted. Changing the sequence of arguments, however, does *not* change the arguments. Since some writers refer to this inverted sequence as the "inductive approach," and the sequence which begins with the proposition as the "deductive approach," it should be emphasized that the terms "inductive" and "deductive" in this context are used differently from the way we have used them. If labels are necessary, we prefer to avoid this confusion by referring to the so-called "inductive approach" as the indirect approach and the so-called "deductive approach" as the direct approach. Aristotle has an interesting comment on the matter we are discussing here:

In the absence of Enthymemes, the speaker must make Examples serve the ends of logical proofs, since it is proofs that carry conviction in the audience. If, however, he has Enthymemes, he must use Examples for the ends of confirmation, subsequent and complementary to the Enthymemes. The Examples should not precede, for then the argument will seem like an induction; but [anything like a scientific] induction is not appropriate in Rhetoric, save in rare cases only. When they follow the Enthymemes, Examples function like witnesses—and there is always a tendency to believe a witness. Accordingly, when the speaker puts the Examples before, he must use a good many of them; if he puts them after, one may suffice—on the principle that a single witness, if you have a good one, will serve the purpose.[9]

It might be inferred from what has been said in this chapter that all "basic" or final premises must be supported inductively. This *is* the logical responsibility of the speaker wherever such support is demanded and it can be given. Actually, many of the premises entering into an argument will be accepted without proof because the listener already believes them; in such cases, for rhetorical purposes, the inductive proof is redundant. And in other cases, especially where speculative or philosophical matters are involved, inductive proof may be impossible; here the speaker can do no better than rest his argument on deductive interpretations.

III. FORMAL VALIDITY AND MATERIAL TRUTH

So far as it is possible, the speaker should attempt to make his arguments both formally valid and materially true. This amounts to saying that the deductions from his premises should be carefully drawn and his premises should be inductively sound. The rules of the syllogism are designed to give formal validity and the rules of inductive reasoning are designed to secure material truth. In dealing with probabilities, we approximate these conditions as closely as possible.

The distinction between formal validity and material truth has been implicit throughout our discussion. We make it explicit here for purposes of further clarification and also for the purpose of answering an important objection.

In the following syllogism, the conclusion is formally valid, the major premise, at least, is materially false, and the conclusion may or may not be materially true.

        a. All cats have five legs.
        b. Our neighbor's pet is a cat.
        c. Therefore, this pet has five legs.

[9] *Rhetoric* II.20.

In the argument below, the premises are materially true, and the conclusion happens to be true, but it in no way follows from the premises. The argument, therefore, is not formally valid.

    a. All normal horses have four legs.
    b. All normal dogs have four legs.
    c. Therefore, all normal cats have four legs.

A formally valid argument is one in which care is taken to relate the premises in such a way that the conclusion follows. The conclusion of such a formally valid argument will be materially true if the premises are inductively derived (existentially sound) or reliably deduced from premises which are existentially sound.

The concept of formal validity in logic rests upon what have been called the laws of thought: the law of identity ($A = A$); the law of contradiction (every A has its non-A); and the law of excluded middle (B is either A or non-A). These laws make the assumption that it is possible to define terms categorically, thereby setting up classes which include or do not include other terms. Thus one may define a "horse" with sufficient accuracy to make it possible to say of any animal (or any conceivable thing) that it either is a horse or it is not a horse. Similarly one may define "sanity" with sufficient accuracy to be able to say of any man that he is either sane or not sane (insane).

Some writers have objected to these laws of thought (and the logic based on them) on the grounds that the phenomenal world, the existential world, the real world of people and things, seldom, if ever, exhibits these discrete, classifiable, categorical characteristics. They argue, in substance, that people and things are infinitely variable, or, at least, that variability is more characteristic than constancy. As a result, they deplore a logic or "defiant" argumentation which appears to generalize and classifies without regard to individual differences. This objection is fundamental and requires an answer.

In the first place, forgetting the real, existential world for the moment, it is perfectly possible to *postulate* the laws of thought, define terms *arbitrarily* on the basis of these laws, and relate these terms in such ways as to draw formally valid conclusions. Such definitions and such relationships may not have any resemblance to the real world, but they can be made just as definite, immutable, internally consistent, and reliable as a game of chess or a set of mathematical inferences.

In the second place, to return to the real world of objects and things, anyone who is at all observant must concede variability and change. It is, of course, much more apparent in some areas than others. No one would wish to say, for instance, that all "insane" people are equally insane at any given moment, or that their degrees of insanity are precisely the same at the next moment. And yet, we have found it wise in civilized society to define what we mean by insanity and to place the insane in "classes" which are as definite as the walls of an asylum. As a matter of fact, life could not go on if we were not to make all sorts of classifications and generalizations. As I write, I assume my chair will not collapse, that the walls will not fall in on me, that the furnace will not explode under me, etc. These objects are sufficiently constant to warrant such generalizations. In other words, in the presence of variability and change, there are "working" classifications which can and *must* be recognized if life is to go on—if decisions are going to be made and action taken.

Thirdly, it should be pointed out that in reflective deliberation (inquiry, discovery, investigation) every possible precaution should be taken to recognize variability and individual differences. Generalizations should be made with great care and always properly qualified. Discussion (as distinguished from debate) performs this role in public deliberation. But if a problem is being discussed which must, by the nature of the circumstances, be brought to a conclusion, it is often necessary to make motions and conduct debate. In other words, if you are in a group situation where you cannot reach a consensus through discussion and you cannot agree to disagree for practical reasons, debate is the only reasonable alternative to force.

As we know, all argumentation and debate begin with a proposition. This proposition presumably represents your best judgment, all things considered. It has been, or should be, arrived at by processes which give full consideration to variability and change. Having made the decision, in all sorts of practical situations, you are called upon to convince others of its truth, justice, and wisdom as you see it, and to defend it against the opposition of others who, for reasons of their own, disagree with you. This is the realm of argumentation and debate.

In advancing your arguments, you normally begin by stating your proposition, defining your terms, and stating the issues. You then offer deductive and inductive arguments supported by evidence to show that your proposition is true, just, or wise. These arguments, of course, should be as formally conclusive and as materially sound as you can make them.

In a world of variability and change, any decision, any proposition, any action is "brutal" and "hazardous" in the sense that it may do injustice to some of the variables. But we must make decisions and take action—conduct our lives—on the best available evidence and argument. The advocate, and after him the administrator, have the responsible tasks of defending and executing decisions which appear to reduce the "brutalities" and the "hazards" to a minimum.

Exercises

1. Outline the constructive speeches in one of the debates in the Appendix of this book. Having made this outline, use it to assist you in identifying the kinds of argument employed. State all the deductive arguments in full syllogistic form.
2. Prepare a careful outline in support of a proposition. Identify marginally the kinds of argument used and be prepared to state these arguments in syllogistic and enthymematic form.
3. Prepare four good examples of argument from sign and four of causal argument. State these in syllogistic form and present one or more inductive arguments in support of the premises involved.
4. Present six-minute argumentative speeches in class in which special attention is given to the organization of the speech and the structure of the argument.

Chapter **X** · EXPLANATION AS ARGUMENT

The four principal forms of discourse are description, narration, exposition, and argumentation. In Chapters VIII and IX, we discussed the kinds of argument and the structure of argument in speaking and writing. This is the doctrine of argumentation in the traditional and restricted meaning of the term. Actually, however, there are many circumstances under which description, narration, and exposition may be used to serve the ends of argumentation, to influence belief and action. We use the term "explanation" to cover description, narration, and exposition when they are used for argumentative purposes. In this chapter we use the term "confirmation" to describe argument in its traditional syllogistic and enthymematic forms.

I. THE NATURE OF EXPLANATION

A. Explanation defined. Explanation is that form of support in which belief and action are sought by explaining the data connected with any proposition in such a way as to cause the audience to accept the proposition by implication. It is a process of argument in which the speaker analyzes and synthesizes the materials bearing on the proposition, thereby leading the audience to imply its truth. The method has been described as follows:

Its plan [that of support by explanation] is simply to portray a situation which gradually, of itself, without compulsion or contention on the part of the speaker, through the compelling power of a developing situation, makes evident to the mind of the hearer the necessity of one certain solution. The method is not in the orthodox and generally accepted sense argumentative; rather it is that of exposition with a goodly dash of narration and description. It does not appear to argue; it merely sets forth—yet slowly, definitely, as it proceeds, the lines of descriptive development begin to converge and it becomes compellingly evident to each thinking mind that such a set of conditions implies, necessitates,

130

one thing, the conclusion toward which an approach has been made from the beginning. It is argument in a very true sense, its aim is to convince and persuade, yet it is argument of which exposition, narration, and description are handmaidens.[1]

B. Explanation and confirmation distinguished. The distinction between confirmation and explanation as forms of argument must be sought (1) in the methods of procedure employed, and (2) in the nature of the inferences involved. We have seen in the two preceding chapters that the method of confirmation is essentially that of arranging a chain of syllogisms or enthymemes in a logical progression and supporting their premises where necessary by examples (generalization) or by a comparison of cases (analogy) which prove or tend to prove these premises. This method is argumentation in the old and generally accepted sense. Now the methods of explanation are essentially those of description, narration, and exposition, intended to convince and actuate, and thereby made to subserve the ends of argument. Thus the explanatory development abandons the syllogistic approach characteristic of confirmation and relies upon a systematic exhibition of the data connected with the subject to imply the proposition, the acceptance of which is being sought.

That the methods of confirmation and those of explanation are quite different is readily apparent. The question now to be considered is whether the difference between these two forms of argument is one of method only. Are there any differences in the nature of the inferences involved? The inferences employed in confirmation are frequently referred to as "linear inference."[2] This linear conception of inference, which is that of the syllogism and generalization from recurrent particulars, we wish now to distinguish from a theory of inference known as "implication."[3] Implication has been defined as "the connection between terms or sets of terms in virtue of a common nature which binds them into parts within a continuous system such that you can tell from one or more parts of

[1] Gladys Murphy Graham, "The Natural Procedure in Argument," *Quarterly Journal of Speech*, Vol. XI, No. 4, p. 321. Copyright 1925. Used by permission of the Speech Association of America.

[2] Bernard Bosanquet, *Implication and Linear Inference*, London, Macmillan and Company, 1920. See Chapter II, "The Linear Conception of Inference," especially pp. 21–30.   [3] *Ibid.*, pp. 1–21.

it what the other parts of it, or some of them, are and how they are behaving."[4] This, we feel, is the essence of the inferences in explanation. It consists of a juxtaposition of the original data connected with the proposition, and out of the necessities which impose themselves when these data are thus arranged and exhibited to the audience arises a datum—a premise which partakes of the nature of a conclusion and is so accepted by the hearers.[5] Bosanquet, who speaks of this as "the natural procedure in argument," states, "I believe that the natural method of opening the case descriptively, and placing the reader or hearer within the system which is the development of our subject, not merely follows an instinct of common sense, but is a well grounded logical procedure and ultimately fundamental."[6]

The theory of implication in relation to argument will be discussed in this chapter. The thought has been expressed previously that "a clear explanation of a subject will often constitute a wholly persuasive treatment of it."[7] This is exactly the thesis we wish to develop.

C. The persuasive values of explanation. The following are certain advantages of explanation as a method of argument.

1. It dispels unfamiliarity. Support by explanation has special value as a means of persuading an audience which is inadequately informed on the proposition. What argument could be more persuasive to a person who is indifferent or opposed to a proposition because he is not informed regarding it, than one which supplies him with this information? Almost invariably when the opposition has its basis in unfamiliarity, the speaker has but to explain the proposition in order to dispel this opposition and secure the desired action.

2. The audience is prepared for the conclusion by its own thinking. That you cannot pour conclusions into the heads of people as you would pour water into a receptacle is a matter of common knowledge. Only as the listener is stirred to "purposeful activity" can you expect to influence his thinking or overt conduct. Conclusions arrived at by one's own thinking are thus infinitely stronger

[4] *Ibid.*, p. 14.   [5] *Ibid.*, p. 116.   [6] *Ibid.*, p. 113.
[7] J. M. O'Neill and A. T. Weaver, *The Elements of Speech*, Boston, Longmans, Green and Company, 1926, p. 434.

than those imposed by others, so far as the individual is concerned. In the explanatory method the persuader does not simply recite his own conclusions before the audience. Rather, he sets forth those facts and opinions which led him to conclude as he did, in such a way that the hearers will be led to go through the same reasoning process.

3. It avoids the "contrarient idea." This method also avoids what some writers have called the "contrarient idea."[8] When a speaker starts his presentation with certain conclusions, the very announcement of these conclusions invariably sets off inhibitions which might never otherwise occur. Some people seem to resist other people's conclusions. They question at the slightest opportunity. They immediately begin a mental argument with the speaker and fight him from the first word to the last. In many situations these obstacles can be avoided or at least greatly minimized by the method of explanation.

II. THE THEORY OF THE IMPLICATIVE SYSTEM

Really to understand explanation as a method of argument, it is necessary that we bring another logical concept into our study. That concept is the implicative system.

A. What the implicative system is. The implicative system may be defined as a logical thought-whole consisting of a set of propositions so related (by implication) that the truth of one is implied by the truth of the others. A proposition may be looked upon as a part of this whole or system. In argument by explanation, the proposition for discussion is always one of the propositions of an implicative system. It is the task of the persuader to present the other related propositions in such a way that the truth of the proposition under discussion will be implied. The accompanying figure illustrates the point we are making.

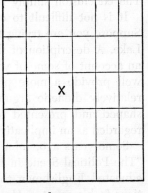

[8] William MacPherson, *The Psychology of Persuasion*, New York, E. P. Dutton and Company, 1920, p. 161.

Let us say that the larger square represents an implicative system and each of the smaller squares a proposition. If we let the square marked by the x indicate the proposition for argument, we suggest that its truth may be implied as we explain the propositions or data represented by the other squares. The more of these related propositions we explain, the more evident will become the proposition under discussion. The whole process is comparable to a picture puzzle which is unintelligible until its various parts are assembled. As the fragments are pieced together, the place of each remaining part becomes increasingly evident from the nature of the picture which is beginning to take form. Propositions, like the pieces of the puzzle, are not intelligible as isolated entities. Their identity as true or false statements, so far as any individual is concerned, is determined by many relationships. It is the task of the speaker to bring these relationships to light. If the proposition under discussion can be identified with a group of other propositions which cannot be logically denied or which are accepted by the audience, the truth of the proposition is thereby implied. A proposition is thus related to a system as a part is related to the whole. It is the speaker's task to make it clear that the proposition he is defending is a part of a system which the listener cannot safely or logically deny. When that system has been explained, the truth or falsity of the proposition can be implied by it. In most cases the implication is perfectly obvious if the speaker's work has been well done. The conclusion simply rushes ahead of the argument.

It is not difficult to cite examples of explanation as argument. Suppose you are trying to persuade a group to vacation at Clarke Lake. A description of the lake and the surrounding territory and an account of some of your own good times at the lake might very well provide a more persuasive treatment of the matter than a relatively didactic argument. If this description and narration is shaped and presented to imply a specific conclusion, it may be regarded as an implicative system.

Some years ago, John Langdon Davies spoke in this country on "The Political Scene in England." In this case, the speaker was an educated Englishman thoroughly conversant with political conditions in his country. He contrasted conditions in the United States and England where those conditions had a bearing on the English political situation. He related sketches of English party history in

almost narrative form. He described the types of people composing
the different parties in England. He explained England's greatest
needs as a nation. He built up an implicative system which permitted but one conclusion, and that conclusion was that the Labor
Party then in power in England should be continued in power.
It is interesting to note that this proposition was never once enun-
ciated in so many words, and yet such was clearly the implication
of the system the speaker constructed. It was an excellent illustration of a case in which a controversial objective was gained without a struggle.

B. The "this-or-nothing" disjunction. When a speaker builds an
implicative system such as we have just discussed, he leads his
audience to infer the truth of the proposition under discussion by
confronting them with a rough disjunction, "This or nothing."[9]
That is, the audience must either accept the proposition under discussion or reject the propositions which imply its truth. The "this"
in the disjunction refers to the speaker's proposition, and the "nothing" refers to those related propositions whose truth is so evident
that their rejection is well-nigh impossible. The "nothing" in the
disjunction implies the absence of all logical grounds, the denial
of truth as we know it and commonly accept it. For instance, in
the illustrations cited in the preceding section, the argument in
each case can be reduced to a "this-or-nothing" disjunction. In the
Clarke Lake example, the speaker should explain the vacation
possibilities in such a way that to refuse to accept the proposition
would mean (or appear to mean) a denial of facts and interpretations which are beyond reasonable question. Likewise, the speech
of John Langdon Davies explained the English political situation
in such a way that the audience was persuaded to accept the conclusion that the Labor Party should be continued in power, because
a refusal to accept this proposition, it seemed, would mean an
abrogation of many principles which are unquestionably sound
and a denial of many conditions which unquestionably existed.

In supporting a proposition by explanation, it is the objective of
the speaker, then, to set up an implicative system, or, in other

[9] "The Essence of the Inference in Implication, then, would be in showing
of any suggested proposition, that unless we accepted it, our province of truth
would as a whole be taken from us." Bernard Bosanquet, *Implication and
Linear Inference*, p. 3.

words, to confront the audience with such data as will cause the implication of the proposition in question. To make certain that the proper implication will be made, the speaker needs to present a case which will compel the audience either to accept his proposition or adopt the questionable alternative of rejecting the data he has presented. This disjunction with which the audience is confronted may be tersely phrased, as we have explained, as "this or nothing."

We now wish to set forth three rules which need to be observed in arguing by explanation in order to make certain that the implicative system constructed by the speaker will confront the audience with the "this-or-nothing" disjunction.

1. **It must be all-inclusive.** In the first place, the disjunction must be all-inclusive. That is, the speaker must be certain that the listener will not reason to himself, "I will accept neither 'this' nor 'nothing.' I will not accept your proposition nor will I deny the facts you have submitted. I can consistently imply another proposition from these same facts. I will take another course of action which you have not contemplated." Here would be a case in which the audience implied a conclusion from the system presented which had not been considered by the speaker.

This mistake was recently made by a speaker who addressed a state teachers' association on the proposition that a Federal Department of Education should be established. His explanatory development built up a system which compelled an implication all right; but the difficulty was that the wrong proposition could easily be implied. And that was exactly what happened. Most people were persuaded that the Federal Government should do more for education than it was then doing, but a need for a department was not at all apparent. He lost his cause to many listeners because his disjunction was not complete. Instead of concluding that a department of education should be established, the listeners concluded variously that the existing Office of Education should be given an improved status, that more money should be appropriated, etc.

To be conclusive argument, the system developed must imply the proposition defended by the speaker to the exclusion of all other propositions. The listeners must be confronted truly with the necessity of either accepting the proposition at hand ("this"), or rejecting their province of truth as a whole ("nothing").

2. It must be mutually exclusive. Secondly, the two members of the disjunction must be mutually exclusive. Unless this precaution is taken, the audience is likely to reason, "Accepting 'this' means accepting 'nothing.' To accept your proposition is to deny many truths and facts which are beyond question. Therefore, I am opposed to your proposition."

The most complete violation of this rule would be the instance in which the system built up by the speaker implied the exact opposite of what he was trying to prove; that is, where the system implied the negative of the proposition rather than the affirmative, or the affirmative rather than the negative. Here the speaker's proposition, or the "this" in the disjunction, would be exactly equivalent to the "nothing," and would, of course, be entirely rejected. Had the advocate of a department of education mentioned in the preceding section so completely bungled the situation as to have led his audience to conclude that it was the acceptance of his proposition rather than the rejection which would necessitate a denial of their province of truth, we would have an illustration of this point.

While it is true that such complete failures rarely take place, it is also true that this error occurs very frequently in lesser degrees with results almost as damaging. For instance, failure to dismiss any salient objections to the proposition to that extent identifies the proposition with the "nothing" in the disjunction. If your chief objection to a department of education lies in your belief that it will lead to federal domination of education, quite obviously no system will imply that proposition to your satisfaction until it removes your fears in that direction.

It is clear, then, that in direct proportion as the speaker fails to make the proposition and the "nothing" in the disjunction mutually exclusive, his proposition becomes less and less evident from the system presented.

3. It must avoid possibility of wrong choice. Finally, the speaker must beware lest the audience accept the "nothing" in the disjunction in preference to the "this." In such case, the listener would reason, "You have presented me with two alternatives, 'this' or 'nothing.' I think you are right in saying that I must either accept your proposition or deny certain facts and truths. However, I prefer to make this denial rather than accept your proposition." To avoid a choice of this kind, the speaker must make the alternative to acceptance of his proposition so completely undesirable that the possibility of such a choice will be entirely removed, or at least made exceedingly remote. The following case illustrates an argument in which the speaker did not take sufficient care to avoid a wrong choice.

In a recent mayoralty campaign, a speaker arguing in behalf of one of the candidates before a certain fraternal organization to which the candidate belonged, built up an implicative system which made it evident that the audience must either vote for this candidate or sacrifice both party and fraternal loyalty. His argument very apparently failed with most of the audience, because, granting the truth of his disjunction, they preferred the alternative to casting their vote for the candidate in question.

A choice of the "nothing" in the disjunction in preference to the "this" most frequently occurs in highly controversial matters in which the listener is very much opposed to the speaker's proposition. In the case of the proposal that a department of education be created, for instance, the question is sufficiently controversial to make it necessary that the speaker show the denial of a great province of truth to be coincident with its rejection. To impel an opponent of this proposition to imply its adoption, the speaker would need to build a system which tied his cause by descriptive, narrative, and expository relationships to beliefs, principles, and facts which could hardly be denied. Anything less than this would lead the listener to reject the beliefs, principles and facts rather than accept the proposition.

III. TYPES OF EXPLANATION

We have already said that the principal methods of explanation are description, narration, and exposition. These familiar forms of discourse achieve argumentative significance when they are advanced as an implicative system.

A. Description. "Description is that process or form of Explanation which exhibits the properties, attributes, and relations of *spatial* objects in their proper order."[10]

To illustrate description as a factor in argument, let us consider the salesman's proposition. The orderly description of the commodity for sale is a vital part of most sales talks. Such a description should do exactly the things suggested by the foregoing definition. It should point out the properties and attributes of the article for sale and relate it to the customer's needs and demands in such a way as to lead the customer to infer the advisability of its purchase. In this manner the salesman can build up an implicative system which will avoid many of the objections and inhibitions which might occur through the use of other forms of support.

A very persuasive talk recently given was an argument for the leasing of a tract of land to be used as a Boy Scout camp. The speaker proceeded descriptively almost altogether, telling of the woods, the lake, and other available factors which argued for a good camp-site. This speech, while almost wholly descriptive, proved to be a winning argument. The description implied the advisability of favorable action on the lease, and in that way supported the proposition, probably better than any other form of support could have done.

B. Narration. "Narration is that process or form of Explanation which presents a proposition in its *time* relations, or which exhibits events in their proper order."[11]

The value of narration as a factor in argument is particularly well illustrated with any proposition of policy. In arguing for or against a policy of any kind, it is highly persuasive to place it in a historical setting which implies its adoption. It should be made apparent that the policy advocated is the logical next step, that all that has gone before points to the adoption of this policy. Listeners will draw such conclusions from the argument without compulsion if these narrative lines are effectively drawn.

In a debate on the proposition that a lake-to-ocean canal be constructed via the St. Lawrence which would accommodate ocean-going vessels, the affirmative team abandoned the usual confirmatory method of support, and proceeded to build its case through

[10] James H. Hyslop, *Logic and Argument,* New York, Charles Scribner's Sons, 1899, p. 66. [11] *Ibid.,* p. 68.

an explanation consisting mainly of narration and description. The history of the canal was told with the aid of a chart, pointing out that huge sums of money had already been expended on portions of the canal to make it navigable for ocean-going vessels, that appropriations had already been made for other sections of the canal, and that there was an increasing demand for the use of the canal. These facts, along with others, were presented in a simple and straightforward explanation of the situation which permitted but one implication, and that was that funds should be provided so that the remaining sections of the canal could be made navigable for ocean vessels.

C. Exposition. "Exposition is that process or form of Explanation which exhibits a proposition as a logical thought whole independent of time or space relations."[12]

From this definition it can be seen that exposition deals largely with abstract and general conceptions, while pure description and narration are generally occupied with concrete things. Whereas description and narration deal with things seen, heard, depicted, as matters of observation, exposition is concerned with things conceived, identified, classified, as matters of penetrative and systematic thinking. Description and narration consider traits and acts that distinguish objects as individuals; expositions looks for the traits and acts that unite individuals into classes. Assume, for instance, that you have occasion to explain some controversial religious doctrine or scientific principle. Neither narration nor description would suffice, because such a subject cannot usually be exhibited in relations of time or space. It is an abstract concept which can be adequately explained only by an exposition of its logical relations to other known concepts. These logical relationships are usually those of causation and classification or resemblance, and are expounded by *analyses, comparisons, and examples.* Thus to persuade an audience by exposition that socialism is a sound theory of government would require a statement of all causal and resembling relationships which would tend to establish the point. Socialism could be analyzed, compared with other forms of government, and examples cited. In this way, an implicative system could be built which would imply the proposition.

[12] *Ibid.,* p. 69.

Of the various types of explanation, it can be seen that exposition most nearly approximates confirmation. It displays essentially the same relationships as are used in confirmation, but they are approached from the explanatory point of view, that of the implicative system, rather than being stated in the usual inductive or deductive forms.

IV. CONCRETE HELPS IN EXPLANATION

A. Charts. Charts, diagrams, and maps are frequently helpful in explaining a subject. Wherever it seems that these devices can be used more effectively than a purely verbal explanation, and the occasion is propitious for their use, the speaker should by all means use such devices. If they are to be used in public address, however, ready visibility is a problem which needs to be carefully considered.

B. Models and samples. Models and samples are also aids to explanation on certain occasions. Probably no single class of persuasive speakers uses these devices more than salesmen. Such devices can be displayed before the audience or passed around for individual inspection. The precaution should be observed, however, that these devices are introduced only at the time when the speaker wishes the attention of the audience directed to them. A speaker who fails to do this is apt to find himself talking to a group which is busily engaged in attending to his models or samples, with the result that the argument falls on deaf ears.

C. Demonstrations. Perhaps the most persuasive concrete help to an explanation is a demonstration of the object under explanation. For example, if a salesman is selling an automobile, he invariably demonstrates the machine to the prospective buyer. A demonstration should be carefully planned before it is undertaken to make certain that it coordinates well with the arguments and proceeds smoothly.

V. THE USE OF EXPLANATION

In this chapter we have developed the relatively simple and essentially commonplace observation that "a clear explanation of a subject will often constitute a wholly persuasive treatment of it." The doctrine of the implicative system has been introduced to explain the circumstances under which description, narration, and exposition can be made to serve the ends of argument. It is a rare argumentative discourse indeed in which descriptive, narrative, and expository elements do not enter to supplement an essentially syllogistic structure, and in many cases the primary approach may well be implicative in nature. The important things are to realize that belief and action can be influenced by these forms of discourse ordinarily associated with informative speaking (rather than argumentative speaking), and to know how to use them purposefully and effectively in argument.

Exercises

1. Write a 300-word explanation on one of the following subjects. Have a definite proposition in mind and make your treatment as persuasive as possible.
   a. A book to read
   b. A place to go for a vacation
   c. An athletic event to attend
   d. A play or movie to see
2. Prepare a five-minute, argumentative speech on some proposition of local, state, or national policy in which you use the explanatory method. Hand in an outline of this speech and an explanation of the implicative system you have tried to construct.
3. Present a five-minute, explanatory argument in which you make use of charts, diagrams, maps, models, samples, or demonstrations.
4. Divide the class into groups of two and assign a proposition to each group. Let one member of each group support the assigned proposition with a confirmatory argument and the other member support the same proposition with an explanatory argument. Compare methods and results.

Chapter **XI** · MOTIVATION IN 'ARGUMENT

I. THE PLACE OF MOTIVATION IN ARGUMENT

A. Explanations of motivation. Motivation may be defined generally as the process of stimulating inner urges or desires which prompt persons to action. For practical purposes, the student of persuasion needs a more specific definition which indicates the workings of that complex process. There is no exact synonym for "motivation." It is a general term which covers the direction, control, or influencing of behavior. The word "motive" is likewise difficult to define. While it is true that behavior can be motivated, it is incorrect to refer to a motive as a thing. Motives are inferred from the observation of behavior.

Seashore[1] offers an operational definition to which we subscribe. He says that motivation is the *selective reinforcement* or *inhibition* of stimuli or sets (preparatory responses) evoking any given type of response in competition with stimuli or sets leading to other behavior. Motivation is *selective* in the sense of (1) orienting an organism in a position for maximal (or optimal) sensory stimulation, and (2) sensitizing the person by lowering thresholds of stimulation for one set while raising them for others. Motivation is *reinforcing* (positive motivation) or *inhibiting* (negative motivation) in the sense of adding to or subtracting from the intensity of stimulation leading to any given response, or in inducing a set or habit which will facilitate or inhibit the given response.

Suppose that a political debater seeks, as the desired audience response, the support of candidate Jones as opposed to that of candidate Smith. He might place his audience in a position for optimal stimulation by means of stage setting, music, "spontaneous" demonstrations, seating arrangement, lighting effects, and the "build-up" by an enthusiastic chairman. These devices, possibly coupled with an offer of free refreshments, would aid in sensitizing

[1] Robert H. Seashore, "Introduction to Motivation," unpublished lecture, Northwestern University, 1949.

the listeners by making it easier for them to get favorable impressions of Jones than of Smith. In addition, there would be no mention, or at least no favorable mention, of the rival. All pictures, posters, banners, leaflets, balloons, and the personal references in the speech would call attention to Jones. The motivation might be mostly positive, *i.e.*, to urge the election of Jones. However, negative motivation in the form of an attack upon Smith could operate reciprocally. The speaker would arouse strong and somewhat relevant desires, interests, or values, use affective (emotionally-toned) language, associate Jones's election with the satisfaction of those aroused desires, and deliver his speech with some vigor. By this means he would intensify the stimulation and hope to arouse some habitual response, such as favoring a "100 per cent red-blooded American," which presumably would win votes for Jones.

Motivation usually has an affective "core" of feeling tone, such as likes, dislikes, etc. The typical patterns in which motivation occurs may be classified in many ways, and, like all affective processes, these are not discrete; rather, they represent overlapping patterns of partly differentiated concepts. However, any one pattern of response may be evoked by some stimulus situation. Thus we may speak of positive-negative, pleasant-unpleasant, intensity, relation-to-cultures, and other aspects of motivation. Positive motivation facilitates a type of behavior, while negative motivation inhibits it. The pleasant-unpleasant feeling tones involve likes, dislikes, preferences, interests, etc. The intensity factor is related to the strength of some drive in a person. Finally, the relation of motivations to cultural ideals, customs, ethics, aesthetics, law, and the like should be recognized as a facet of the problem. Many motives are not universal or capable of being taken for granted; they vary among cultures. For instance, note the different motives at work in capitalistic and socialistic countries.

Tiffin, Knight, and Asher[2] say that when things matter to us, we have feelings about them; but when they matter very much, we experience strong emotional reactions. Thus our emotional behavior appraises the worth of things to us. There is scientific justification for saying that much of our thinking is in the service of our feelings and our emotional reactions. In fact, some writers

[2] See J. Tiffin, F. Knight, and E. Asher, *The Psychology of Normal People*, Boston, D. C. Heath, 1946.

argue that our affective states get us into and out of difficulty more often than our logical analysis does. Whether our affective states get us into or out of trouble depends upon the kind of adjustments we make. We may say, according to Van Dusen,[3] that adjustment is a continual struggle to satisfy needs and thereby to maintain an equilibrium. In this connection it is well to note three points: differences among persons are largely a function of the methods used in gaining satisfaction of needs; most of our needs must be satisfied through relationships with other persons; we learn to control our relationships with others as methods for the satisfaction of our needs. Useful emotional adjustments include preparations for physical danger, gestures and other expressions which aid us in meeting situations, mental stimulation resulting from excitement, and relief from inhibitions. Unsatisfactory emotional adjustments may cause adults to act like children, impair fine coordinations, prolong emotional responses such as fear, and harm our general efficiency. Thus we believe that emotional behavior *per se* is not something to be decried; rather, immaturity of adjustment in emotional behavior should be avoided.

Emotional behavior can be explained further in terms of what it involves, what affects it, and the nature of its observable manifestations. Emotional behavior involves values which are about to be attained or lost, bodily disturbances, and impulses to act. This behavior is affected by physiological states, external conditions, and an accumulation of experience. We can observe its manifestations in facial expressions, voice patterns, postures, breathing ratios, and some subtle changes which can be detected only by laboratory equipment.

B. Relation of motivation to other forms of support. Although we distinguish between motivation and the kinds of argument, we do not regard these categories as being mutually exclusive or discrete. The reason-emotion dichotomy, for example, is considered unsound as a psychological classification. The ways of reacting which we call thoughtful and emotional are not distinct units motivating particular instances of behavior but exist in varying proportions in the different situations. We have shown that emotional behavior comes increasingly into play when goals are sought with

[3] A. C. Van Dusen, "Working Principles," unpublished lecture, Northwestern University, 1949.

unusual tenacity and vigor. In fact, it is obvious that all behavior has its motives, be they strong or weak. Thus an argument may have logical validity *and* emotional appeal. In other words, an advocate who stirs up desires and associates them with his proposition is not inevitably illogical.

Ought every effective argument to enlist the desire of the audience in the cause for which the appeal is being advanced? This question brings up the dual problem of logical adequacy and audience acceptability. In the first place, we feel that there are occasions when the speaker's first concern should be with logical unity, continuity, and completeness, irrespective of the desires of the audience. In the second place, we feel that it is possible at times, even when audience acceptability is taken as the primary test, to premise the argument on existing beliefs of the audience and to reason both persuasively and convincingly without giving special attention to the desires of the listeners. While desire is the important factor in motivation, it is also true that persons can sometimes be persuaded to act in opposition to a desire which has been dominant.

This is not to say that the persuasive force of desire is insignificant. Argument often must take account of this factor; and in our analysis, that kind of appeal which is designed to stimulate desire and associate it with the proposition is called motivation. It is true that narration, exposition, and the kinds of argument may focus desire on a proposition; but since this function is not a vital part of these methods, and since there are special problems in utilizing desire which have nothing to do with them, we have seen fit to treat motivation as a separate method of support.

C. Persuasive values of motivation. An outstanding advantage of motivation is that it utilizes the reaction tendencies, otherwise known as drives, desires, tensions, etc., which are characteristic of human beings. Desires may be said to be dynamic, conative (striving) impulses which demand gratification. A person is likely to resolve his tensions into equilibrium, either through goal-attainment or compensation. It is also likely that he will accept an idea which a persuader has alleged to be inherently involved in that resolution of tension. The effective utilization of reaction tendencies or emotional behavior in the process of motivation can be seen in three typical experiments. Remmers and Knight[4] administered tests to ten college freshmen at ten o'clock at night after a week of "hazing" during which each man had slept only two hours per night. Their test scores were compared with those made by ten juniors of equal ability who were tested at eight o'clock in the morning after a normal amount of rest. The freshmen were motivated by the fraternity president who told them that their scores would determine their final acceptance or rejection by the fraternity. The juniors were given no special motivation. As a result, the freshmen did twice as much work per unit of time, and their accuracy was equal to that of the juniors. Lefford's[5] report of psychological tests which have been used in recent years to measure partiality of reasoning, the influence of wishes, and fair-mindedness and inference also shows the effect of emotional involvement upon thinking. In dealing with subject matter which arouses an emotional reaction, the person does not retain his capacity for the correct reasoning required for the successful solution of syllogistic problems. In fact, there is little relationship between ability to reason accurately in nonemotional and in emotional situations. Several studies show that there is a high correlation among inferences, attitudes, and wishes. Hartman's[6] study of the comparative effectiveness of "emotional" and "rational" political leaflets shows a plainly greater impressive and retentive effect of the sentimental appeal.

Another advantage of motivation lies in the fact that it commands the attention of the reactor. In some respects, this is simply a corollary of the preceding point concerning the utilization of reaction tendencies. Since persuasion is more likely when the interest and attention of the reactor are continuously and exclusively held, it follows that the advocate should use material which is high in attention values. It is known that we attend to things that *matter* to us, and that keen interest is one of the main driving forces in life. There is probably no more effective material than that which appeals to desires, drives, or emotional reactions, as

[4] See R. H. Wheeler, *Readings in Psychology*, New York, T. Y. Crowell Co., 1930, p. 261.

[5] See A. Lefford, "Influence of Emotional Subject Matter on Logical Reasoning," *Journal of General Psychology*, XXXIV, April, 1946.

[6] See G. W. Hartman, "Experiment on Comparative Effectiveness of 'Emotional' and 'Rational' Political Leaflets," *Journal of Abnormal and Social Psychology*, XXI, 1936, pp. 99–114.

they are variously named. This method of support tends to avoid the questioning, inhibiting, and objecting attitudes which frequently accompany disagreement.

II. CLASSIFICATIONS OF MOTIVE APPEALS

A. Impossibility of definitive classification. Although it would be convenient and helpful to have a definitive classification of motive appeals, such a statement cannot be formulated at this time. Some of the difficulties include the interrelationships between primary and secondary drives, the factor of individual differences among persons, varying degrees of dependability among motives, and the limitations of a simple, mechanistic view of stimulus-response phenomena. The primary drives are usually innate and primarily physiological, while the secondary drives are socially conditioned. The latter differ considerably among persons according to age, sex, race, social status, and vocation. It is obvious that not all persons can be motivated by the same appeal at the same time. Because of the exceptions or the lack of universality among motives, it is clear that their degrees of dependability vary. Furthermore, the primary and secondary drives may alternate in influencing one's behavior, and whichever one is operating may be concealed or disguised by rationalization. For instance, in the "Chimpomat" experiment, in which chimpanzees used a coin-operated food dispensing machine, the secondary drive (to accumulate tokens) became practically equivalent to the primary drive (to get food). The fact that the acquisition of tokens eventually became an autonomous activity (independent of the hunger drive), indicates by inference that another drive became active. The means became the end. When persons do this, they rationalize their hoarding by saying that they are saving only what they need for the purchase of necessities in the future. Finally, a simple, mechanistic view of behavior is invalid. A person does not come equipped with an electrical-control panel consisting of numerous push-buttons labeled "love," "fear," "hate," and the like. The behavior patterns so named are not "pushes" or "pulls"; they are tensions. Furthermore, most behavior patterns are complex and variable. Even though successful motivation may be difficult to achieve, a high level of skill in that activity is one requisite of leadership.

B. Some typical lists of appeals. How, then, can an advocate stir up desires which he can associate with his proposition? We shall select some items from the lists and classifications of appeals in an attempt to offer some usable advice. Wheeler[7] lists six "human demands": to be active, to achieve, to gain position or power, to command respect, to be recognized for something, and to gain security. In his discussion of emotional behavior he uses four examples: fear tension, anger tension, love tension, and distress tension. Carroll[8] refers to four basic needs: for emotional security, for achievement or mastery, for recognition or status, and for physical satisfactions. He emphasizes the great variability in the desires for mastery, status, friends, acquisition, affection, attention, and approval. The lesser drives include curiosity, self-abasement, and imitativeness. Klineberg[9] offers four categories of "dependable motives" which, he states, are "tentatively presented." In the first category he lists the universal, primarily physiological motives based upon hunger, thirst, need for rest, organic needs, desire for activity, and aesthetic appreciation. The second category includes the basically physiological motives which exist in all societies, are socially modified, and have individual exceptions: sex, post-maternal behavior, and self-preservation. Those having an indirect physiological basis, frequent occurrence, and occasional exceptions, such as aggressiveness, flight, and self-assertiveness, are in a third category. Those in the fourth category have a social basis: they are gregariousness, paternal motive, pre-maternal motive, filial motive, self-submission, and acquisitiveness.

It is possible to give illustrations of emotional behavior and to indicate general categories of motives. The illustrations of emotional behavior usually include anger, fear, love, remorse, pleasure, envy, jealousy, generosity, pride, hate, courage, kindliness, elation, honor, disgust, bewilderment, and dismay. Muenzinger[10] suggests a few, broad categories of physiological and social deficiencies or

---

[7] See R. H. Wheeler, *The Laws of Human Nature*, p. 2; also *Readings . . .* , p. 149.

[8] See H. A. Carroll, *Mental Hygiene*, New York, Prentice-Hall, 1947, pp. 19-28.

[9] See Otto Klineberg, *Social Psychology*, New York, Henry Holt and Co., 1940, pp. 160-162.

[10] See K. F. Muenzinger, *Psychology: The Science of Behavior*, New York, Harper's, 1942, pp. 33, 215.

discomforts which produce felt needs. To these he adds so-called impositions such as verbal instructions, hypnotic suggestions, routine, and custom. Wickert's[11] "Goal-Values Blank" for experimental purposes lists nine motive categories or general attitudes; namely, personal freedom, helpfulness, new experience, power and influence, recognition, response, security and stability, submission, and workmanship. Van Dusen[12] classifies as psychological the need for feelings of security (affection, attention, belongingness, sensory satisfaction) and the need for feelings of adequacy (achievement and recognition). Eisenson[13] lists and explains six fundamental, unlearned drives which we identify tersely as desire for physical well-being, desire for success, desire for social approval, desire for affection, desire for peace of mind, and desire for zestful living. Human beings tend, of course, to avoid the opposites of these. Related to these unlearned drives are the interests and attitudes which are learned. Landis[14] broadens our purview by showing that certain values which are defined by a given society become motivators of human behavior in that society. We are familiar with such examples as religion, family, wealth, the state, individual worth, size, speed, power, novelty, competition, progress, and epicureanism. These social values, he says, are counterparts of personal attitudes.

We have stated that an advocate ought to arouse and associate with his proposition one or more desires which he deems to be relevant and strong. Some of these may prove to be: (1) gregariousness, group approval, desire for response, love, friendship, attention, belongingness, and respect; (2) self-preservation and physical well-being; (3) sensory satisfactions and aesthetic appreciation; (4) acquisitiveness, property, and wealth; (5) religious tenets, hope, faith, and moral codes; (6) family loyalty; (7) secondary-group loyalties, such as patriotism and school spirit; (8) new experience, zestful living, and novelty; (9) stability, security, and peace of mind; (10) courage and self-reliance; (11) competition, power, mastery, status, and achievement as opposed to sub-

[11] See *Journal of Social Psychology*, XI (1940), pp. 259–302.
[12] A. C. Van Dusen, *ibid.*
[13] See J. Eisenson, *The Psychology of Speech*, New York, F. S. Crofts and Co., 1940, Chapter 17.
[14] See P. H. Landis, *Social Control*, Chicago, J. B. Lippincott Co., 1939, Chapter 8.

mission; (12) generosity, good will, kindliness, helpfulness, pity, justice, and fair play; (13) curiosity; (14) group or individual activity; (15) pride of workmanship; (16) social values such as size, speed, power, progress, value of the individual, and freedom. The strength of these appeals usually depends upon their arousal of emotional components known as anger, fear, hate, elation, disgust, remorse, pride, shame, envy dismay, and the like.

III. ASSOCIATING DESIRE WITH THE PROPOSITION

A. General methods. One cannot state a set of rules or a precise system for doing this, but there are three distinct methods available to an advocate who wishes to associate motive appeals with his proposition; namely, suggestion, rationalization, and forthright statement.

1. **Suggestion.** This method involves the offering of a stimulus in such a way as to produce a response unchecked by critical thought. When it is intentionally used, this technique of indirect influence is a process in which the advocate's main idea works in the fringes of the listener's attention while a related idea occupies the center of attention. Thus a defense attorney might focus upon each juror's center of attention the facts of the case in narrative form, but his selection of facts, his choice of language, and his delivery might lodge in the fringes of attention a strong emotional reaction of pity for the accused. This is subtle persuasion.

The effectiveness of suggestion varies greatly among individuals and situations. For this reason a brief consideration of the factors influencing the efficacy of suggestion in advocacy will be helpful. One factor certainly is the prestige of the source. This being true, the advocate should either cite the authority of others or try to establish his own authority on the subject in question. Another factor is the vividness of imagery and the forcefulness of presentation. Listeners must be made to see and feel the idea. Specific details coupled with appropriate delivery are obviously called for. Thirdly, a positive slant coupled with an implied reward for acquiescence is often effective. Thus it is better to call for the acceptance of the desired idea than the rejection of the unwanted one, and this acceptance should be related to the achievement of a pleasant outcome. A fourth factor is the polarization and unification of the audience. It is helpful to secure undivided attention to a single source of stimulation, and it is likewise useful to secure unified responses. Some practical procedures in effecting these conditions include the seating of persons in a compact group; the calling for unison activities such as applauding, singing, raising hands, etc.; the provision for the comfort of the audience; the use of respected symbols; and the placing of the speaker in a dominant position. The use of repetition is a fifth factor. The recurrence of an idea seems to have a cumulative effect in the fringes of attention, and listeners are often unaware of the influence of that reinforcement. A sixth factor is the superiority of indirect suggestion in many instances. A suggested idea is more likely to be accepted if the listeners can be made to think that it was their idea. Herein lies the suggestive force of argument by implication. Finally, it is well to avoid any suggestion of a rival idea. It was for this reason that the Office of War Information advised us not to repeat a wartime rumor, even for the purpose of denying its validity.

2. **Rationalization.** A second general method of associating desire with the proposition is by rationalization. Although audiences are more likely to be influenced by appeals to emotional tendencies and drives than by intellectual appeals, they prefer to believe that they are acting logically. In this situation, resourceful speakers, including demagogues, give their listeners a rationalization, which is an emotionally-aroused conclusion that is rendered plausible on pseudo-logical grounds. Persons often do what they desire to do, and then they seek reasons for doing it. We do not suggest that a student speaker adopt the ethics as well as the devices of rabble-rousers. However, there are times when an audience can be moved to accept an ethically sound proposition by emotional means only, but it wants some seemingly logical justification for its action. However unfortunate the fact may be, it is certain that most audience decisions are influenced more by desires than by evidence. A speaker can satisfy his audience and justify himself by determining the motives in his audience, associating them with his proposition, and then presenting his logical support.

One who wishes to be a critical thinker must be able to detect the use of rationalization in communication. This pseudo-logical thinking has several characteristics: it centers attention on materials that *seem* to be relevant; its apparently definite ideas are vaguely outlined; it masks suggestion as deliberation; "good" reasons are presented as "real" ones; subjective ideas are disguised as objective ones; it thwarts careful scrutiny while seeming to encourage it; it utilizes the fallacies and stratagems which we describe in Chapter xvi.

3. Forthright statement. This method of associating desire with the proposition makes that association by means of a frank and open explanation or demonstration. Rather than using suggestion or rationalization, the arguer proceeds directly to establish the connection between certain desires and his proposition. He may explain how the acceptance of his proposition will lead to certain satisfactions, he may demonstrate or give a sample, or he may do both. This doctrine is consistent with that principle of learning which states that the proffered motive should be logically relevant to the goal.

B. Specific techniques for speakers. The control of behavior through motivation may be exerted positively or negatively, and it may be speaker-centered or listener-centered. A positive approach facilitates the response which the speaker desires, while a negative approach inhibits the response which the speaker opposes. A speaker-centered approach seeks to influence others to favor the speaker's notion of the listeners' needs. A listener-centered approach considers the listeners' conceptions of their needs. For example, a listener-centered, positive approach facilitates a response by having the listener analyze his needs or interests, by helping him to analyze them so as to be able to design solutions to his needs, or by associating the stimuli represented by his needs with those essential to the speaker's desired response instead of "high-pressuring" him to fit the speaker's idea of his needs.

Those effective speakers and writers who associate desires with their propositions have been known to utilize some specific techniques which we report. They bring into the focus of consciousness some important value and show how it can be realized or how it is jeopardized. Often they appeal to the common values, such as patriotism, love of family, truth, desire for justice, fair play, and the like. They bring such values vividly or dramatically into play by suggestion or one of the other general methods, proceed to show that these values are in danger, and arouse the audience to put down the threat. Among the popular, vivid narratives are those of cruelty to children, exploitation of the underdog, etc. When the reactors have been shown how the evil can be removed, they will be, at least for a short time, in favor of the action expressed in the proposition. Seeking to capitalize on this impulse, advocates aim to secure quick, overt action in the form of a show of hands, the signing of a petition, or the nomination of a committee. An overt expression of a new enthusiasm for a cause serves to prolong it and assists in leading to an effective expression. "Strike while the iron is hot."

Sometimes an advocate wishes to dissipate harmful emotional behavior or divert it into constructive channels. His appeal may aim at prejudice and fear, for instance, and tie them to loftier motives such as love of justice and fair play.

Delivery, which we discuss in some detail in Chapter xv, is closely related to the specific techniques in associating desires with propositions. Displayed emotional behavior tends to influence other persons. An impassioned orator is more likely to move a large audience. Within limits, of course, zeal is a part of effective salesmanship.

IV. EXAMPLES OF MOTIVATION

A. In contemporary mass persuasion. Appeals which seek emotional responses are made by speakers, advertisers, demagogues, and others who reach publics. The mass media of modern communication have increased the size and number of publics and have thereby widened the field of emotional appeals. Some familiar examples of motivated mass action include religious revivals, mass inoculations after a smallpox "scare," panic resulting from the "Invasion by Mars" broadcast, some war-bond drives, nation-wide strikes, and the deluge of protests which followed President F. D. Roosevelt's proposal to alter the Supreme Court in 1937.

Psychological warfare is an example of mass persuasion. It is intended to bolster civilian and military morale on one side and to undermine it on the other. It is also used to influence the neutrals. Tactical propaganda for enemy soldiers presents an alternative to the risk of death in battle. Large numbers of "safe-conduct" leaflets which are dropped behind enemy lines from military aircraft urge enemy soldiers to come forward bearing these leaflets so that they may receive food, medical attention, and transportation from the danger zone. Strategic propaganda aims for subversive action of the enemy population against their leaders. Appeals for subversion must maximize the motivations for self-sacrificial action, *i.e.*, they must try to inspire belief in ideas that are worth the possible sacrifice which detection of subversion by the enemy police is sure to entail.

There is an interesting case study of mass persuasion by radio during a "war-bond drive" in the United States.[15] Kate Smith, a radio entertainer, spoke sixty-five times, for one or two minutes each, at intervals of fifteen minutes during a period of eighteen hours. Pledges to buy a total of thirty-nine million dollars' worth of bonds were telephoned to network stations during that marathon. The speaker's appeals, in the order of their importance, referred to servicemen's sacrifices, civilians' sacrifices, desire to participate in a mass action, competition between cities, family ties, facilitation (easy to 'phone a pledge), and Kate's personal sacrifice. Specifically, she spoke of neighbor boys who were facing danger and death in foreign lands. She asserted that the purchase of a bond would shorten the war, bring the boys home sooner, and thereby save lives. The emotional appeals were based upon love, hate, hope, fear, honor, and shame (if one did not buy a bond). Her voice suggested deep emotion, according to many listeners who were subsequently interviewed. She used repetition with variation. No counter-persuasion was allowed to appear. There were no economic arguments about the accrual of interest or the prevention of inflation. The bonds were treated as something sacred, not secular.

Another case study[16] illustrates the use of high-pressure epithets as motivators of mob action. On October 26, 1947, a Communist was to address a public meeting in a rented hall at Trenton, New Jersey. However, the attempt was abandoned as a result of mob action. The leaders of the disruptive element called for mob action in harangues containing these terms referring to their own purposes: "The Constitution," "our way of life," "Bill of Rights," De-

[15] See R. K. Merton, *Mass Persuasion: The Social Psychology of a War Bond Drive*, New York, Harper's, 1946.
[16] See R. C. Myers, "Anti-Communist Mob Action: A Case Study," *Public Opinion Quarterly*, Spring, 1948, pp. 57–67.

mocracy," "what we stand for," "what we fought for," "red-blooded Americans," and "the American Way." However, with reference to the Communists these symbols were used: "Commies," "rats," "bastards," "Stalin-lovers," "dirty," "lousy," "stinking," and some less printable expressions. The leaders might well have concluded in the words of Shakespeare, "Now let it work. Mischief, thou art afoot, Take thou what course thou wilt."

B. In American public address. Examples of the association of re-action tendencies with propositions would fill many volumes if we were to survey the literature of public address from Pericles to the present time. In the interest of brevity we shall cite only one short excerpt from each of nine eminent American speakers whom we have selected to represent various fields of activity in the span of two centuries.

Beginning with Jonathan Edwards, an eighteenth-century Calvinist preacher, we find arguments for repentance and conversion associated with fear motivation in vivid, suggestive language:

> O sinner! Consider the fearful danger you are in: It is a great furnace of wrath, a wide and bottomless pit, full of the fire of wrath, that you are held over in the hand of that God, whose wrath is provoked . . . against you . . . You hang by a slender thread, with the flames of divine wrath flashing about it, and ready every moment to singe it, and burn it asunder . . .

Theodore Parker, the preacher who became a leading reform lecturer and prominent Abolitionist, associated his argument against slavery with his listeners' historical pride in New England. In his speech, "The Slave Power," he appealed to the pride of Massachusetts people in their state:

> Will Massachusetts conquer her prejudices in favor of the "inalienable rights of man"? . . . she will have to forget two hundred years of history. She must efface Lexington and Bunker Hill from her memory, and tear the old rock of Plymouth out from her bosom.

Speaking in Faneuil Hall, Boston, in 1842, Wendell Phillips, who was another great Abolitionist, sought to gain from an extremely hostile audience a hearing for a Negro speaker. His introduction drove at liberty, family, fair play, and sympathy for the unfortunate:

Fellow-citizens, I will ask your attention but a single moment. I wish only to bear my testimony in favor of liberty. [Uproar.] There are husbands, brothers, and sons before me. I ask, in the name of humanity that you will hear me speak for a son and a husband. [Great confusion.] No generous man will try to drown my voice, when I plead the cause of one not allowed to speak for himself.

Henry W. Grady's main topics in "The New South" dealt with the accomplishments of his region, the Southern treatment of the Negro, and the loyalty of the South. He linked these with the common desire for friendship and good will and the emotional attitudes of his audience toward Grant, Lee, and Webster:

Now, what answer has New England to this message? Will she permit the prejudice of war to remain in the hearts of the conquerors, when it has died in the hearts of the conquered? [Cries of "No! No!"] Will she transmit this prejudice to the next generation, that in their hearts, which never felt the generous ardor of conflict, it may perpetuate itself ["No! No!"] Will she withhold, save in strained courtesy, the hand which straight from his soldier's heart Grant offered to Lee at Appomatox? Will she make the vision of a restored and happy people, while gathered above the couch of your dying captain, filling his heart with grace, touching his lips with praise and glorifying his path to the grave; will she make this vision on which the last sigh of his expiring soul breathed a benediction, a cheat and delusion? [Tumultuous cheering and shouts of "No! No!"]

When Booker T. Washington spoke in the North to gain support for Tuskegee Institute and to improve intersectional relations, he identified his program with emotionally-tinged social values, such as respect for property, self-reliance, industry, religion, and humanitarianism. On race relations he urged the use of the golden rule:

If you want to know how to solve the race problem, place your hands upon your hearts and then, with a prayer to God, ask Him how you, today, were you placed in the position that the black man occupies, how you would desire the white man to treat you, and whenever you have answered that question in the sight of God and man, this problem in a large degree will have been solved.

To an audience of businessmen in 1914, Samuel Gompers of the American Federation of Labor expressed his agreement with their view that the United States should arm to protect itself. To this self-interest motivation he tied his proposition that laborers should receive adequate wages:

> All we ask is that you who are not workers realize that for war you need strong bodies and you can't get them if you give your workers starvation wages. That for war you need fever-resisting men, and that that kind of man doesn't come from the slums. The sledge-hammer will make such a man if he works with it, but only if the worker has ample food and clean surroundings. So more on your own account than on ours you have a reason to pay the American worker a liberal wage, give him reasonably short hours, and enable him to be an efficient human being.

Robert M. LaFollette, as governor of Wisconsin, spoke for state regulation of railroads in 1903. In one of those speeches we note his skill in vitalizing statistics and identifying his proposition with his listeners' desire to make money:

> In 1900 Langlade county had 6,357 acres seeded to oats and harvested 198,580 bushels of oats. This is an average of 31 bushels to each acre. As it costs you 1.23 cents per bushel more to produce and market your oats here, on account of exorbitant freight rates, than it does in Iowa, your loss from this source amounts to over 38 cents per acre. Now, what do these 38 cents per acre mean? It means, first, that your net profits from your efforts are reduced by this amount. It means that this extra reduction in your profits reduces in turn the value of your land . . . For the purpose of raising oats, therefore, your land, under your present freight rates, is worth $6.33 per acre less than if you had as low rates as the Iowa farmers are enjoying. Had you enjoyed the benefit of the same rate for the same service as the Iowa farmers, it would mean that the 6,357 acres seeded to oats in this county last year would be worth $40,239 more than they are at present. Would not that addition to the value of the land of this county mean something to you?

The peroration of Daniel Webster's "Defence of Judge James Prescott" in 1821 contains an appeal to pity which was addressed to the Massachusetts Senate during impeachment proceedings:

> If you send away the respondent, condemned and sentenced, from your bar, you are yet to meet him in the world on which you cast him out. You will be called upon to behold him a disgrace to his family, a sorrow and shame to his children, a living fountain of grief and agony to himself.

In his "First Inaugural Address" of 1933, President Franklin D. Roosevelt recommended confidence, cooperation, and hard work by appealing to "social values more noble than mere monetary profit":

Tho measure of the restoration (of our civilization) lies in the extent to which we apply social values more noble than mere monetary profit.

Happiness lies not in the mere possession of money; it lies in the joy of achievement, in the thrill of creative effort.

The joy and moral stimulation of work no longer must be forgotten in the mad chase of evanescent profits. These dark days will be worth all they cost us if they teach us that our true destiny is not to be ministered unto but to minister to ourselves and to our fellow-men.

Exercises

1. Select five advertisements and identify the motive appeals used in each.
2. Identify the instances of motivation in a printed speech or a long editorial.
3. Prepare and deliver a five-minute persuasive speech in which some kinds of logical argument are supplemented by motivation. Label the persuasive techniques in the outline, and be prepared to state why you think your motive appeals are relevant and strong in terms of the audience and the proposition.
4. Discussion question: Is it ethical to persuade others through the use of motive appeals?
5. Point out and analyze instances in which one or more of the three methods of associating desires with a proposition have been used.

Chapter **XII** · THE CASE

I. THE CASE DEFINED

A. General meaning. The word "case" is used to designate the position or stand which either affirmative or negative advocates take on the proposition. It is the complete statement which an advocate or a team of advocates presents to the listeners or readers. This statement embodies the evidence, reasoning, exposition, narration, description, and motivation upon which one side chooses to rest its cause and upon which it must win or lose. It is not merely the case outline; it is the completely composed discourse.

B. The concept of a prima facie case. A case is said to be prima-facie when it is logically adequate to establish a reasonably high degree of probable truth in its favor. In other words, such a case has probative force. In fact, the presentation of a logically adequate case is the only way to prove a given side of a proposition. For this reason we urge the advocate to present a case which logically supports his position. The degree in which it does so can be determined in relation to the presumption and the burden of proof, the issues, and the burden of rebuttal. These will be discussed below.

There are relatively few situations in which the presentation of a prima facie case is not required or at least expected. For instance, in the arguments in which only one side is represented, some advocates present cases which fall short of prima facie proof of their propositions. A time limit may be the guiding factor in some cases. It is certainly more effective to treat thoroughly a limited aspect of the proposition in the alloted time than to attempt a complete prima facie case which cannot be developed adequately. Furthermore, there are situations in which only certain phases of the proposition are important. For instance, in the case of an argument for a new building on the campus, one audience might be primarily interested in the financing of the project, while another might be concerned with the uses to which the structure was to be put.

In class speeches or other similar situations with respect to time limits, it is advisable to partition the whole case in the introduction, and then state the point or points which are to be developed in the speech. This enables the audience to get a perspective of the whole case, even though it is argued only in part. Closely related to this method of saving time is the expedient of narrowing the proposition. Instead of establishing the whole proposition, the advocate substitutes a sub-proposition or issue for the original proposition. His points in partition will then answer only one issue instead of all of them.

Quite apart from these situations, however, there are occasions on which persuasive discourses are given without proving the propositions. We see evidence of this in political campaign speeches, sermons, sales talks, and argumentative conversations, especially those in which only one side is represented, or at least only one side is represented by an advocate who is prepared to meet the situation. The effectiveness of these logically inadequate cases can be attributed to the failure of listeners and readers to think critically, because such cases are easily refuted.

For this reason we repeatedly point out that the presentation of a logically adequate case is the only way to prove the proposition, and in many situations it is the best way to secure belief. Certainly there are circumstances in which this is the only legitimate method. Thus we urge the advocate to present a case which logically supports his position on the proposition, at least insofar as the circumstances make it feasible.

It is important that both sides present prima facie cases in formal arguments that are regulated with respect to the division of time and the order of speeches. In fact, the presence of an opponent should serve to warn an advocate that his case must be prima facie, regardless of its persuasiveness, or the logical shortcomings will be pointed out. Theoretically, the negative is not called upon to reply until the affirmative has set out a prima facie case. If such an affirmative case is made out, the affirmative may rest until the negative submits a prima facie rejoinder. In actual practice, however, both sides attempt to break down the opposing case before it is completed, and the argument becomes a give-and-take affair throughout. In short, it is safer to present a prima facie case in arguments in which both sides are represented. One exception to this rule is the affirmative case which omits a vital point because the negative has admitted it.

II. RELATIONSHIPS IN A PRIMA FACIE CASE

A. Prima facie case, presumption, and burden of proof. The theory of argument is that the affirmative, upon whom the burden of proof always rests is a correctly phrased proposition, can discharge this burden only by presenting a prima facie case which establishes a presumption in favor of the proposition. At the outset of the argument, as we have said, the affirmative is under obligation to present proof of the proposition before the negative should be expected to reply. The presumption favors the negative at the outset of the debate, and this advantage can be overcome only by the presentation of a prima facie affirmative case. If such a case is presented, the negative must make a rejoinder which will block it and thereby overcome the presumption which has been raised against the negative case. Thus it is imperative that the affirmative present a prima facie constructive or opening case and that the negative present a prima facie rejoinder, otherwise a good argument cannot ensue.

B. Prima facie case and the issues. In Chapter IV we defined issues as the inherently vital points or subpropositions, stated in question form, which are affirmed by the affirmative and denied by the negative, upon the establishment of which depends the establishment of the main proposition. Thus any affirmative case which is used in an attempt to prove the proposition must contain evidence and reasoning which will logically support affirmative answers to each contested (actual) issue. Likewise, any negative case which is used in an attempt to disprove the proposition must contain evidence and reasoning which will logically support a negative answer to one or more of the issues. Thus if the case treats the issues in the manner explained here, it meets the proof requirement which was stated in the preceding paragraph. At this point one should recall that each of the three kinds of propositions has its characteristic type of issues which should be sought in the process of analysis.

In this process of building a case which answers the issues, one is concerned with points in partition or "talking points." The main points of a case, which are labeled with Roman numerals in a case outline, are known as points in partition. They are not necessarily issues. The wording and the grouping of these points may differ somewhat from the statement of the issues. The considerations of effective composition sometimes require this distinction. For instance, an issue might be expressed in this fashion: "Are the financial conditions of Lilliput in a serious plight?" An affirmative point in partition might say: "Lilliput is broke."

C. Prima facie case and the burden of rebuttal. When we pointed out the obligation of the negative to reply to the prima facie case of the affirmative, we were dealing with the burden of rebuttal which the negative had at that stage in the proceedings. When the negative makes a prima facie rejoinder, the burden of rebuttal is shifted to the affirmative. Following this, a successful affirmative counter-rejoinder shifts the burden of rebuttal back to the negative. Thus it is that the burden of rebuttal, not the burden of proof, can and often does shift from one side to the other in a debate. The presentation of a prima facie case for one side places the burden of rebuttal on the opposing side.

III. STEPS IN DEVELOPING A CASE

The following diagram and the numbered statements which fit into it are designed to illustrate the steps which an advocate might take in the process of building the framework of his case for the affirmative on a proposition of policy. Items 6 to 13 would be worded negatively for the opposite side. The number of issues, contentions, and points in partition will vary among propositions.

1. General problem: What should be done about child labor?
2. Proposition: *Resolved, That the proposed amendment to the Constitution in reference to child labor should be adopted.*
3. Issue: Is child labor a national menace?
4. Issue: Does this require a national remedy?
5. Issue: Would the proposed amendment most effectively resolve the problem?
6. Affirmative contention: Child labor is more than a local problem.
7. Affirmative contention: It is increasing in amount.
8. Affirmative contention: It is a menace to our future citizenry.

9. Affirmative contention: States have failed to remedy the matter.
10. Affirmative contention: A national remedy would be most effective.
11. Affirmative contention: This proposal would give Congress effective power.
12. Affirmative point in partition: A national program for dealing with child labor is needed.
13. Affirmative point in partition: The proposed amendment is the best solution to the problem of child labor.

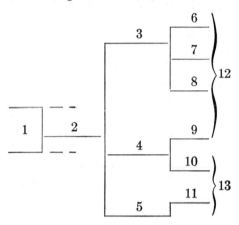

IV. DIVISIONS OF THE CASE

As we shall explain in the next chapter, there are three divisions of a case outline. Consequently, the case itself is likewise divided into introduction, body, and conclusion. Since the processes of outlining, composing, and presenting these divisions of the case are treated in detail in other chapters, we shall briefly mention the divisions of the case at this time.

A. The introduction. This has some elements in common with the introductions of other types of speeches and essays. In general, it appears at the beginning of the argument and prepares the audience for the development which is to follow in the body. The material in the introduction is more likely to be noncontroversial. It is intended to gain attention, arouse interest, provide a setting for the present argument, define terms, set out the issues, partition the case, and provide a smooth transition to the body.

B. The body. This is the part of the case which presents the argument proper. It constitutes the main support of the proposition. The materials which are noted in the body of the case outline are fully developed in the body of the case. In other words, the points in partition for one side are fully supported and developed in this section. The materials for this purpose are discussed at length in Chapters VII, VIII, X, XI, and XIV.

C. The conclusion. The final portion of the case is relatively short. It strives for a lasting, favorable impression of the case and its proponent. Like the introduction, it does not develop an argument which belongs in the body. As Aristotle[1] pointed out many centuries ago, the functions of an advocate's conclusion are: (1) to render the audience well-disposed to his side and otherwise to the other side; (2) to magnify his points and depreciate those of the other side; (3) to put the audience in a favorable emotional state toward his case; (4) to refresh the memories by recapitulating the major clashes of argument. In effect, the advocate says, "I have done; you all have heard; you have the facts; give your judgment."

V. TYPES OF CASES

A. The affirmative case. Except in those special situations which were noted in our discussion of "the concept of a prima facie case" earlier in this chapter, the affirmative case is required to discharge the burden of proof by affirming the issues in a logically adequate fashion. The case thus made should be of sufficient merit to win if not refuted. Any case which is intended to have such probative force should be based upon a sound interpretation of the proposition and should be organized as simply and clearly as is feasible. In this connection it is well to realize that an affirmative case should not assume more burden of proof than the proposition requires. If the proposition calls for the installation of parking meters in specified city blocks, the affirmative case does not urge such

[1] Aristotle, *Rhetoric*, 3.19.

installation throughout the city. In general, it is better to limit the affirmative case to a firm support of the objective as stated in the proposition and to concentrate the support of that position upon as few arguments as will constitute an adequate case for the purpose. Extreme affirmative cases, or those based upon freakish or strained interpretations, or those whose support is scattered over a wide variety of points, are seldom effective.

B. The negative case. Any case for this side must constitute a vital objection to the acceptance of the proposition. As in the case of the affirmative, it is usually better to take a fundamentally sound position and to concentrate upon a few decisive arguments. For instance, some negatives on propositions of policy have stood on one point: "It won't work." In terms of the *logical* aspect of the situation, as we have explained several times, the negative case needs only to block the affirmative on *one issue*. However, this may require the refutation of more than a single affirmative point in partition.

1. Pure refutation. This is one of four kinds of negative cases. Its basic strategy involves the logically adequate denial of one or more issues without the presentation of a preconceived constructive case. Since the burden of proof is on the affirmative, the negative can win by successfully refuting the vital arguments of the affirmative, insofar as the logic of the situation is concerned. In other words, this is one way to prevent the affirmative from establishing and maintaining a prima facie case. However, there are logical and psychological weaknesses in this strategy. Pure refutation is likely to be safe only when the affirmative case is weak. In addition, a purely destructive negative approach may give the affirmative a psychological advantage with the audience. The negative in a legal situation with a judge presiding can win by pointing out that the affirmative (plaintiff or prosecution) has not proved its case, but public audiences generally prefer that an advocate stand *for* something.

2. Defense of the present, at least in principle. This is a strong negative stand if the present situation is defensible. The presentation of this preconceived case, plus the adaptation of it to the affirmative case, results in the refutation of the affirmative. The difference between this strategy and pure refutation is that a defense of the present is not only *against* the affirmative; it stands *for* something.

Even if the present situation (status quo) is not entirely defensible, the negative is usually well advised to minimize the grievances as stated by the affirmative. This removes much of the force of the affirmative case. For instance, if the affirmative case calls for the passage of a certain piece of legislation to regulate labor-management relations, the negative could argue that existing legislation is sufficient.

3. Adjustment or repair of the present situation. This involves an admission by the negative that the present situation has some faults, plus the recommendation of certain reforms, changes, or repairs which are intended to remedy these admitted faults without going so far as the affirmative does in departing from the status quo. This is a popular kind of negative case, and it is usually strong. It concedes the existence of shortcomings in the present state of affairs, argues that these faults are not inherent, and contends that they can be corrected by changes that are easier, less expensive, more expedient, etc., than the "drastic" change supported by the affirmative. If the affirmative contends that our school should erect a new classroom building, the negative could urge instead the remodeling or the enlargement of an existing building.

4. A counter-proposition. This is usually the most radical kind of negative case. It admits the affirmative indictment of the present situation, but it offers a solution which is vitally inconsistent with the affirmative remedy. As we have explained earlier, each side must prove its own case in this strategic situation. The contest is between plan A and plan B as rival solutions to an admitted need for *some* solution which is essentially unlike the present situation. For example, if the affirmative case demands statehood for Hawaii, a negative proposal of Hawaiian independence as a nation is a counter-proposition.

There are two principles which must be observed in the use of this kind of negative case. In the first place, the counter-proposition must be stated with the utmost clearness. Since the negative must assume a burden of proof on its alternative, it is imperative in terms of safety and clearness that the counter-proposition be carefully conceived and phrased. In the second place, the counter-proposition must be truly counter to the affirmative proposal. It is not enough that the counter-proposition be different; it must be vitally inconsistent with the affirmative plan. If an affirmative case demands the nationalization of *several* industries, and if the negative counters with a proposal to nationalize only *one* industry, the affirmative may adopt the negative plan as a means to its own end. Thus, the negative loses. But suppose an affirmative case which calls for the construction of a memorial shaft in the public square of a city. A negative proposal calling for a similar investment in scholarships for the children of the commemorated heroes could be a legitimate counter-proposition. In other words, a negative case of whatever type must *clash* with the affirmative case on some vital issue, other-wise the negative loses.

Exercises

1. Read a long, printed argument in which both sides are represented, such as an intercollegiate debate in the *University Debater's Annual, Intercollegiate Debates,* or a similar collection. On the basis of the selected debate, prepare a diagram and a list of items such as you read in Section III, "Steps in the Development of a Case."

2. In preparation for your own argumentative speech, prepare a chart and a list of items as explained above, using the ideas which you will employ in that speech.

3. Phrase a policy proposition of current interest, state the issues, and sketch briefly the major points which a negative advocate might make in terms of each of the four kinds of negative cases.

4. Phrase a proposition, state the issues, and sketch briefly the main lines of argument which would be needed in a prima facie affirmative case.

5. Analyze the Dewey-Stassen debate which is printed in the Appendix. State the proposition, set out the actual issue or issues, list the main ideas which are developed, identify the type of negative case used, and classify the main ideas of each case under "introduction," "body," and "conclusion."

6. Conduct class debates using the following plan: affirmative constructive case, 6 minutes; negative rejoinder, 9 minutes; affirmative rebuttal, 3 minutes. Pay particular attention to the affirmative and negative cases.

Chapter **XIII** · BRIEFING AND OUTLINING

I. THE PURPOSES OF OUTLINING ARGUMENT

A. To aid in preparing the case. The purposes of outlining are to aid in preparing the case and in presenting it. Making an outline is an indispensable step in the preparation of a case. This process typically follows that of listing the points which one might make. An outline differs from a simple list in these respects. (1) An outline deals with only those points which seem most useful; (2) it is divided into an introduction, body, and conclusion; (3) it is supported by evidence; and (4) the points in the outline are organized in a systematic manner.

A preparation outline is useful in that it organizes the evidence and argument in an orderly fashion. It becomes a storehouse of information. When it is carefully drawn, the speaker can observe in perspective the main lines of argument, the relation of the several parts, the adequacy of his evidence, and the logical adequacy of the thing as a whole.

B. To aid in presenting the case. An outline is equally necessary as an aid in presenting the case to listeners or readers. Its orderly arrangement assists the advocate in maintaining his line of thought, and it likewise enables others to follow the argument. Clear organization is basic to effective communication.

II. KINDS OF OUTLINING

A. Logical outlining. In a logical outline, there is a necessary relationship among the ideas. Each subpoint must stand as a reason for the validity of the point to which it is immediately subordinated. The following sequence of ideas illustrates this principle:

I. The regulation of child labor by the Federal Government is impractical, for

A. The states are the proper agencies to cope with the problem, for
  1. The child-labor problems differ widely among states, and
  2. Existing state laws evidence the competence of the states to deal with the problem.

The relationships which obtain in this type of outlining should always be indicated by the preposition "for" or "because." In fact, the logical adequacy of the outline can be tested by reading it from top to bottom and stressing the connectives. Then the points can be read in inverse order, substituting "therefore" in place of "for" or "because." If both readings make sense, the outline is probably sound. The reliabilty of this test depends upon the use of complete sentences in all points and subpoints.

A chain of reasoning as in a logical outline is well adapted to the inferences used in confirmation or proof. Such an outline usually consists of a series of enthymemes whose premises are supported by one or more of the four modes of reasoning. This may be seen in the specimen brief and case outlines which appear later in this chapter. The student should work with logical outlining until he can readily reduce all confirmatory inferences to such a framework, and until he can readily discern in a logical outline the confirmatory inferences which are involved.

B. Topical outlining. Topical outlining is peculiarly adapted to expository, descriptive, or narrative speaking and writing. In the topical outline each subtopic stands as an *explanation* of the point to which it is immediately subordinated. The relation between any given topic and the subtopics listed under it is that of whole to part. Depending upon the nature of the composition, the subpoints, then, may be nonargumentative parts of the idea expressed in the main heading.

It is possible, but not essential, to use complete sentences; words or phrases will often suffice. Then, too, the connectives, if any are used, differ from those of logical outlining. Some common expository connectives are "as follows," "namely," "for instance," and "in that." The following samples illustrate the use of description, narration, and exposition in topical outlining:

Description of Mr. X

I. His discipline
  A. Reasonably firm

B. Gives students benefit of doubt
   1. Assumes the best until a student proves himself untrustworthy
II. His humanness
  A. Attends games and parties
  B. Appreciates jokes on himself
III. His appearance
  A. Height
  B. Weight
  C. Dress, etc.

Narration of An Incident

I. Tourist arrives in strange city
  A. Alights from train
  B. Looks for a taxi
  C. Finds and enters one
II. Takes short ride to hotel
  A. Observes new sights
  B. Wonders what the fare will be
III. Incident at end of trip
  A. Driver announces the charge
  B. Passenger believes it excessive
  C. Indignantly refuses to pay
  D. Driver threatens to call policeman
  E. The compromise

Exposition of a Writing Technique

I. Typical characteristics to incorporate in familiar essay
  A. Use free and easy style
  B. Make it plausible
  C. Employ specificity
  D. Choose from wide range of subjects
  E. Achieve freshness
  F. Avoid conclusiveness

III. GENERAL PRINCIPLES OF ALL OUTLINING

A. Coordination. There are five fundamental principles which must be observed in both types of outlining, either logical or topical. The first of these is coordination. This means a series of generically related points, all of which have one or more important elements in common. This principle is violated when foreign or unrelated ideas are placed in an otherwise homogeneous list. Note the error in point "C":

I. Political parties in national politics
   A. Democratic
   B. Republican
   C. Norman Thomas
   D. Prohibition

B. Subordination. This means that topics or reasons should be subordinated or placed in inferior order to others on the basis of some significant relation which obtains between or among them. This rule is violated when subtopics are introduced which bear no significant relation to the topic to which they are subordinated. Note that point "C" does not prove, explain, or illustrate "I":

I. Values of the gyropilot
   A. Increased comfort for passengers
   B. Relieves pilot of physical burden
   C. First used in planes in 1909

C. Discreteness. Each point in the outline should represent a separate and distinct idea in its own right. This principle is violated when points overlap, merge, or are otherwise indistinct and confused, one with another. Note that point "C" overlaps "A" and "B":

I. How to choose a camp site
   A. Locate near a source of drinking water
   B. Be sure of proper drainage in case of rain
   C. Avoid a swamp

D. Sequence. Effort should be made to arrange the points in each coordinate list in some kind of significant order or progression. The common sequences are those of time, place, magnitude, or such order as may be dictated by the proof requirements of a thesis. In the following specimen, point "C" deviates from the time order:

I. Development of football
   A. Rugby developed in English boys' schools
   B. First college game in U.S. in 1869
   C. Early Spartans and Romans played harpaston

E. Symbolization. Every point in the outline should be marked by a symbol which at once designates the degree of subordination and also its place in a coordinate list. Moreover, it is wise for a speaker to adopt some set of symbols and to use them consistently in all of his outlines. The common practice is to use Roman numerals for main points, capital letters for the first series of subpoints, and then Arabic numerals and lower case letters. The following arrangement of symbols illustrates this practice:

I. First main talking point
  A. First support of "I"
    1. Proves, explains, or illustrates "A"
      a. Supports "1"

The careful observance of these principles will improve the unity, coherence, and emphasis of one's composition. In fact, unity, coherence, and emphasis are very largely functions of these principles.

IV. THE BRIEF

A. What it is. The brief of a nonlegal case is a complete, logical outline which organizes and records all the available material on one side of a proposition. It is not intended to serve as a case outline or a speaker's outline; it is strictly a preparation outline. Some consequences of this distinction will be elaborated in the discussion of "The Case Outline" later in this chapter. As we have said above, a brief is a storehouse of material. In addition, it serves as a device to test the logical adequacy of one's intended proof.

Briefing as we know it in general argumentation is an offspring of the legal brief. Although there are points of similarity, there are also some noteworthy differences in purpose and structure. Both kinds of briefs are finished, logical arrangements of the evidence and argument on one side of a proposition. They are impersonal; neither is designed to persuade a popular audience. The legal brief is not a preliminary outline for a speech or an essay. It may be presented to judges without additional comment of any kind, or it may be presented preliminary to oral argument. The general argumentative brief is a complete, logical statement of one side so that the debaters will understand the whole argument. It may be used as the basis of a number of case outlines, and it serves to record and test the results of preparation. In terms of form, the general argumentative brief is a detailed outline including quotations and the like, while the legal brief is likely to have some solid paragraphs and to appear unlike an outline as we know it.

B. Is it indispensable? Is the brief an indispensable preparatory step? The affirmative answer is that the brief should constitute a step in the preparation of every *comprehensive argument*. It is designed to compel the speaker to think the proposition through logically and completely, carefully scrutinizing the evidence and argument needed to confirm the proposition. Failure to draw a brief may result in a lack of insight into the proposition, and leads to unwise choices of supporting materials.

Briefing is sometimes criticized on literary and logical grounds, but these objections do not invalidate the foregoing argument in defense of briefing. Strict adherence to the brief in composing a speech will probably produce a wooden style. It is a mistake, therefore, to think that the language, or even the specific order of ideas, of the brief must appear in the finished speech. It is also true that a brief is not well adapted to explanation and, to some extent, motivation. However, there is a useful logical discipline involved in reducing arguments to a linear statement as in a brief, even though the subsequent presentation outline assumes a quite different form.

Let us apply a pragmatic test. Do debaters and their directors find briefing to be an indispensable preparatory step? Many of them do not, and some of these have been consistently successful in terms of critics' decisions, shift-of-opinion ballots, and other measuring devices. They do, however, prepare case outlines with great care. The extra steps involved in briefing are probably done informally and are not committed to writing.

C. Rules governing the brief. There are numerous rules or principles governing the brief. Some of them are specific applications of the five general principles of all outlining which we have discussed previously.

1. General rules

(a) The brief should bear a title. See the specimen brief for the application of this and other rules.

(b) There should be three main parts, the introduction, the discussion, and the conclusion. Each of these three parts should be labeled with its name and should be treated as a separate unit. The various steps in each part should be numbered independently. That is, if there are four main divisions in the introduction, they should be labeled "I," "II," "III," and "IV," respectively. The main points of the discussion start with "I" again.

(c) Complete sentences are used in the major portion of the brief which is a logical outline. The possible exceptions are the introduction, in which topical outlining is often used, and the statement of statistics or similar lists of data in the discussion. These statistics or lists should appear in the lowest-order subpoints under a major point which they support.

(d) A definite set of symbols should be used consistently. Refer to the explanation of this rule under "symbolization" in section III of this chapter.

(e) Use only one symbol per heading or subheading. Symbols and indentions indicate the relation of ideas. Each statement is either a heading or a subheading. A person is likely to err in using two symbols for one statement when he cannot invent a heading which will cover the subheadings. Note this example of the error:

I. A. Free trade will result in national economic dependence.
    B. Existing international relations make such dependence dangerous.
    C. A protective tariff is sound in principle.

One of two actions must be taken in this case. Either a main point must be found to include the three subpoints, or the list must be reorganized under headings which will stand as conclusions. In this example, point "C" is the disturbing items. Discard it or use it elsewhere, and brief the remainder as follows:

I. The removal of the protective tariff is dangerous under existing international political conditions, for
    A. Free trade will result in national economic dependence, and
    B. Existing international relations make such a condition dangerous.

(f) All subpoints should be given a wider left-hand margin than the points to which they are subordinated. We have seen that symbols and indentions indicate the relative rank of ideas.

(g) All coordinate lists of points should be indented uniformly. All Roman numerals should be equidistant from the left edge of the paper, and all capitals should be uniformly indented but farther from the edge than the Roman numerals, and so on.

(h) Each heading and subheading should contain only a single idea. It may be necessary at times to use more than one sentence per point in the introduction, in quotations of opinion evidence, or in the development of a complex idea. Even so, a single sentence should be used in most cases.

(i) If the statement of any point requires more than one line, indent all of those lines equally. This prevents the obscuring of the symbols.

(j) The brief should be an impersonal statement of evidence and inference. It should not include the personal touches of the speaker's notes or the final persuasive composition. Expressions such as "Let me read to you," "We contend," etc., are to be avoided.

2. Rules governing the introduction

(a) Include *only* as many of the following eight items as are essential to an understanding of the discussion or body of the brief: a statement of the proposition, the origin and history of the problem, the immediate cause for discussion (present timeliness), a definition of terms, a statement of irrelevant matter, a statement of admitted or waived matter, a statement of issues, and a statement of the points in partition. Make a separate heading for each item used.

There is a distinction between issues and points in partition which beginning students of argumentation frequently find troublesome. The points in partition are the main points in the discussion section of the brief and the case outline. Their symbols are Roman numerals. They *may* correspond with the issues only when the outline encompasses all of one side of a proposition. An important difference is that issues are stated as questions, while points in partition are stated as declarative sentences. The issues are the logically complete and irreducible questions upon which the truth or falsity of the proposition turns, but the partition simply states the topics which will be developed as answers to the selected issues. For instance, an arguer who is preparing to speak in favor of establishing a federal world government might begin with the stock issue, "Is there a need for a change?" In his introduction he might phrase the issue, "Can any confederation-type of world government succeed?" His point in partition might become, "The

United Nations is bound to fail," or he might use two or three points in partition as answers to one issue.

(b) Present only noncontroversial material in the introduction. Do not argue; merely explain or illustrate. The introduction is designed to make way for the support of one's stand on the proposition, and not to set forth that support.

(c) Finally, use topical outlining. Complete sentences need not be used. The subpoints explain or illustrate their superior points. Refer to our treatment of topical outlining in section II of this chapter.

3. Rules governing the discussion

(a) As we stated above, the points in partition should appear as the main points in the discussion or body of the brief. Each point in partition should be supported by evidence and reasoning.

(b) Logical outlining must be used throughout the discussion. This kind of outlining was explained in section II of this chapter.

(c) The outlining should begin with an accurate statement of the proposition, and be refined through the level of evidence. The question "Why?" is answered by developing all the evidence and arguments on one side of the proposition. Therefore, in order to test each point in the discussion section of the brief, ask that question and see whether the evidence is sufficient to answer it.

(d) Carefully document each item of evidence. Adopt one of three methods and use it consistently. The exact source may be stated in one of three places: (1) in a footnote, (2) in the margin at the left of the evidence being documented, or (3) in parentheses at the end of the citation. The third place is used in our specimen brief.

(e) The points in each coordinate series of topics should be mutually exclusive. As we stated in section III under "Discreteness," there must be no overlapping of points. It is well to avoid broad terms such as "undesirable" and "unnecessary."

(f) The points in each coordinate series of topics should be all-inclusive. The subpoints should constitute a logically adequate support for the point to which they are subordinated. As we stated in discussing subordination as a general principle of outlining, the Arabic numerals support the capital letters, and the latter support the Roman numerals. If every series of subpoints is to constitute logically adequate support for its superior point, the brief must include all the significant evidence and argument on one side of the proposition.

(g) Objections to be refuted should be dealt with as they arise. While drawing a brief one may have occasion to include refutation of opposing points. Such refutation should not be segregated; it should be inserted wherever the point naturally arises.

(h) In phrasing refutation, the heading should state clearly the argument to be answered and the character of that answer. Refutation should be clearly indicated in a brief. In order to make refutation effective, it is necessary that the attention of the audience be first directed toward the exact point in controversy, in order that they may see the contrast between the sides and so feel the destructive force of the answer. State the point and answer it as in this illustration:

A. The charge that a world federation would cause more and worse wars is false, because
    1. ...., **and**
    2. ...., because
        a. ...., **and**
        b. ....

(i) Finally, whenever a concession (admitted matter) is to be stated in connection with a point, it should be written as a subordinate clause attached to that heading or subheading. Note this example: "Although it is true that confederations have a record of failures in national and international governments, yet that system is not inherently unsound."

4. Rules governing the conclusion

(a) The conclusion should be a summary of the essential points of the discussion. Usually it is a list of the points in partition.

(b) Close with a statement of the proposition to be established. We suggest the following form which exemplifies the two preceding principles:

Therefore, since:
    I. Any international confederation cannot succeed, and
    II. There is a workable plan for world federation, and
    III. This federation will best further international peace and progress.

It is to be concluded that a federal world government should be established.

D. A specimen brief. The following brief is a specimen prepared by students in Northwestern University.[1]

AN AFFIRMATIVE BRIEF

on the proposition

Resolved, That a federal world government should be established.

INTRODUCTION

I. *Immediate cause of discussion.* The question of an international organization with federal powers has arisen recently as a result of world tension and the threat of a third world war.
   A. Controversy as to the ability of the United Nations to maintain peace has furthered talk of world union.
      1. The actions of many nations lead us to believe they have little desire to cooperate within the United Nations.
      2. The inability of the major powers to establish a basis of agreement on questions of atomic control or an international police force within the structure of the U.N. raises serious doubt as to its functional value.
   B. The inability of Russia and the Western powers to resolve their day-to-day conflicts has brought an armament race and renewed fears of a third world war.
      1. Unofficial Russian occupation of Czechoslovakia, through underground agents, has increased tension between the United States and Russia.
      2. The inability of the United States and Russia to agree on policies for the control of Korea or Germany is a further sign of mutual noncooperation.
   C. The vast destruction wrought by the second world war has led to many economic and social maladjustments which demand unified action and effort for their solution. This condition has furthered the talk of federation.
      1. In Europe, Churchill and many other prominent men have publicly campaigned for an economic and military union of Western Europe.
      2. The leaders of most of Asia met at New Delhi to discuss the problems of the continent in an attempt at unified effort for security.
II. *The history and origin* of the movement for a federal world government.

[1] Dean Olds and Arthur Davis, undergraduates in the School of Speech.

A. In the struggle against Catholic domination in 1313, Dante proposed ending European strife through the establishment of a universal empire.

B. Emeric Cruce, in his volume *The New Cyness* (1623), argued a possible need for a central world authority to enforce peace.

C. Duc de Sully's "Grand Design of Henry IV" planned a Christian Republic for Europe. This was to operate through a central authority which could negotiate, make, and enforce decrees.

D. William Penn, in 1688, proposed as the only means of ensuring peace, an immediate organization of the European parliaments to legislate "rules of justice for sovereign princes."

E. In 1713, the Abbé de Saint-Pierre's "Project de paix perpetuelle" was actually only an elaborate draft for a world constitution. This, he hoped, would interest peace-makers at Utrecht.

F. The first proposal of a true federation of states of all the peoples of the world was made by Immanuel Kant.

G. The proposed League of Nations, although not a plan for world federation, was a large step toward international cooperation.

H. At the time of the League of Nations debate, the Lepart plan for world federation was presented to the French League for the Society of Nations.

I. Belgian's Paul Otlet suggested, almost simultaneously, a democratic people's world parliament.

J. The present United Nations is not a federal world government, but it *is* the largest step yet taken toward world cooperation.

K. Today there is a movement for federal world government.

III. *Definition.* The definition of a federal world government is flexible in that no specific details of the functions and limitations of the government can be given on the individual level without making the debate question hopelessly involved. However, certain basic principles can be set up for the operation of a federal world government. (Sources for definition of federal powers found in Bouvier's *Law Dictionary.*)

A. The federal world government would have the collective power to vote and enforce limitation or abolition of armaments by national governments.

   1. Certain military forces necessary for the maintenance of internal peace would be allowed the several nations.

   2. On the question of control of atomic energy or any other weapon with peaceful uses, the world government would have the power of inspection, subject to the limitations of majority rule.

B. The federal world government would have the power, upon

majority vote, to require belligerents to submit their disputes to an international court, whose decision would be binding and enforceable.

1. In cases of violation of a court decision, the police force of the world government would be used if affirmed by a two-thirds vote of the members.
2. The international court would be a body separate from all other units of the world government and would have certain of its own powers.
    a. The court would have the power of making recommendations in the fields outside aggression or war.
    b. The court would have the power of calling a temporary truce between belligerents while engaged in arbitrating the dispute.
    c. The court would have the power of enforcing its decisions upon the individuals of nations should they be found guilty of aggression or international crimes such as those outlined at Nuremberg.

c. The federal world government would have the power to set up other councils and branches in such fields as immigration, international trade, world health, and taxes. These councils would not have power vested in them and could receive their specific power only by an amendment to the federal world government constitution. While such fields as are listed above are certainly vital to the long-range success of any government, they are not so important as the immediate cessation of wars. Also it might be added that such problems as trade can be more readily resolved after effective peace instruments have been established.

1. The power of amendment would be by two-thirds vote of all member nations.
2. There would be specific provision for the investigation of an International Trade Council similar to the one at present in the United Nations.

    (*Draft Charter for the International Trade Council,* Department of State Bulletin, Publication 2027, Commercial Policy Series 106.)

IV. *Admitted, waived, and irrelevant matter: none.*
V. *The following major issues present themselves:*
    A. Is the United Nations inherently inadequate to cope with the dangers to world peace?
    B. Is a federal world government capable of preserving peace?
    C. Would a federal world government be the most desirable plan for world peace?

vi. *Points in partition.*
  A. The present system of international affairs under the United Nations is not satisfactory.
  B. A federal world government would avoid the inherent weaknesses of the United Nations confederation.
  C. The plan of federal world government is the most desirable framework for international relations.

DISCUSSION

i. The present system of international affairs is not satisfactory, for
A. The United Nations is failing to keep the peace, for
  1. It is not resolving present international armed conflicts, for
    a. "The very existence of the Greek state is today threatened by the terrorist activities of several thousand armed men, led by Communists, who defy the government's authority at a number of points, particularly along the northern boundaries." (Speech by Harry S. Truman before the Congress of the United States, March 12, 1947, *The Turkish Aid Program*, Department of State publication 3014, Economic Cooperation Series 1, p. 13.) And
    b. In Palestine the lack of effective action that exists today has been brought about by the Anglo-American fear that the Arabs might turn to Russia if they were not allowed to continue supreme in the Middle East. (T. Das, *Human Rights and the United Nations, Annals of the American Academy,* July, 1947, p. 59.) And
    c. In China the differences between the forces of the National government and the Communists appear to be incapable of solution as long as the present basic differences of ideals and goals exist. "Involved are differences as basic as those between the North and the South over slavery."
    (David Rowe, "American Policy Toward China," *Annals of the American Academy,* January, 1948, p. 140.)
  2. It does not guarantee the political integrity of nations, for
    a. In the case of Czechoslovakia: "After a week-end of sustained governmental crisis, Gottwald acted. Police of Communist Nosek's interior ministry, armed with tommy guns and bayoneted rifles surrounded most government offices and the Prague radio station. Equally ominous was the act of General Ludvik Suvboda, Minister of National Defense . . .

his advice to the troops read: 'The army must seek a stronger brotherhood with the Soviet Union.'"

(*Time,* March 1, 1948, p. 18.) And

b. In the case of Finland: "Finland was forced against its will to sign a mutual aid treaty with Soviet Russia. The treaty tucked Finland even more snugly into the Soviet orbit."

(*Time,* April 19, 1948, p. 30.) And

c. In the case of Italy: "Both the United States and Russia have actively attempted to influence the Italian election; the former by sending food, coal, and by enlisting the support of the various factions; the latter by a campaign of propaganda demanding social reforms through the agents of the Italian Communist party."

(*Time,* April 19, 1948, pp. 27, 28, 29.) And

d. In the case of Korea: "For about two years the United States government has been trying to reach agreement with the Soviet government about the independence of Korea. Korean people, not former enemies, but a people liberated from forty years of Japanese oppression, are still not free. They have been deprived of the right of free elections and have suffered great economic losses as a result of the failure to agree on terms for Korea."

(Excerpt from the address by the Secretary of State delivered before the General Assembly of the United Nations, September 17, 1947, *Korea's Independence,* Department of State publication 2933, Far Eastern Series 18, p. 15.)

B. A fundamental code of international law which is capable of punishing aggressors is impossible in a confederation of sovereign states, for

1. Majority decisions cannot be enforced because of the veto power, for

a. "Decisions of the Security Council on all other matters shall be made by an affirmative vote of seven members including the concurring votes of the permanent members."

(*United Nations Charter,* Article 27, Section 3.)

2. The method of reaching decisions under the United Nations makes any code of international law impossible, for

a. Each decision is made according to the political alignments and power blocks of the day, for

(1) " . . . the behavior of the United Nations stems from the stresses between the Western world and Soviet

Russia. The occurrence of this trend confirms that the United Nations is an instrument of its members. In spite of its corporate personality . . . the United Nations is basically not an agency with a will of its own." (E. N. van Kleffens, "The United Nations and Some Main Trends of Our Times," *Annals of the American Academy,* July 1947, p. 74.)

3. The World Court fails to meet the fundamental premise of law—the power to enforce decisions, for

    a. "The jurisdiction of the Court comprises all cases that the parties refer to it and all measures specially provided for in the Charter of the United Nations or in treaties or conventions in force. The states parties to the present Statute may at any time declare that they recognize as compulsory the jurisdiction of the Court." (The *Charter of the International Court.* Article 36, Section 1 and 2.) And

    b. If a nation fails to abide by the decision of the World Court, appeal to the Security Council for enforcement is still blocked by the veto.

c. It perpetuates war by forcing the nations into competitive armaments, for

    1. The structure of the United Nations puts the burden of security on the individual nations, for

        a. The United Nations has failed to establish a workable system of atomic control, thus perpetuating an atomic armament race, for

            (1) "I shall content myself with the comments as to the imperative necessity for speed. I beg you to remember that to delay may be to die. I beg you to believe that the United States seeks no special advantage . . . there must be no more delay in the setting up of an atomic control program. Already the atomic armament race has begun."

            (Address by Bernard Baruch, United States Representative to the Atomic Energy Commission, December 5, 1946, *Report by the President to the Congress,* Department of State publication 2735, report series 7, pp. 179–180.)

        b. The United Nations has failed to establish an international police force, thus forcing individual nations into an armament race, for

(1) "The work expected of the military staff committee on the building up of the United Nations police force was unfortunately obstructed during the whole of last year and nothing was accomplished."

(Alexander Cadogan, "Disarmament and Security," *Annals of the American Academy,* July, 1947, pp. 88–89.)

2. The United Nations has allowed the growth of a "cold war" between the United States and Russia, for

a. The "cold war" is a part of the vicious circle of fear, distrust, and insecurity that perpetuates competitive armaments, for

(1) The declarations of a "cold war" have been so numerous that there is little point in a formal listing of them here. One of the chief outgrowths of this has been the proposal of universal military training in the United States.

II. A federal world government would avoid the inherent weaknesses of the United Nations confederation. (In this section we shall content ourselves with the logic behind federal world government. Since the proposition of world government has not been proposed to the world by any nation, it is impossible to state definitely that all of the nations will accept it. However, federal world government does offer the solution to the problems which all the nations face today. Therefore, logically, it should be adopted.) For

A. The institution of federal world government would bring a solution to the present political and military threats to world peace, for

1. It would be capable of resolving present armed conflicts such as those in Greece, Palestine, and China, for

a. Federal world government would establish an investigating committee, and

b. An enforced truce would be effected, and

c. Enforcement of the decisions of either the World Court or the Assembly would be necessary, and

d. The prestige of a world organization with force behind it would in itself tend to prevent the outbreak of armed conflicts.

2. It would guarantee the political integrity of all nations. (Unlike armed conflict, political coercion is not easy to see. It is difficult, therefore, to set down procedures; instead, a general system of principles is necessary.) For

  a. Every nation should have the right of free election without fear of coercion from neighboring states, and
  b. No nation shall be forced into agreements against its will by a single nation by either economic, military, or political pressure.

B. The institution of federal world government would bring enforceable law into all fields of international affairs, for
  1. There would be no veto power in either the Assembly or the World Court, and
  2. Majority decisions would tend to produce a greater long-range consistency in reaching international decisions, for
    a. In the present system, under the United Nations, a change of policy of a single major nation can completely alter the course of the United Nations action, and
    b. Under a world government a change of attitude on the part of many nations is necessary to alter the course of action, thus tending to produce long-range consistency.

C. The establishment of a federal world government would tend to lessen those strains which lead to war, for
  1. Under a system of federal world government the burden of security preparation would be taken off the individual nation, for
    a. The federal world government would establish control of atomic energy as recommended by the United Nations Atomic Energy Commission, and
    b. The federal world government would set up an international police force sufficiently powerful to enforce decisions on any nation.
  2. The federal world government would alleviate the "cold war" between the United States and Russia, for
    a. It would bring the conflict out into the open and allow frank appraisal of the factors in the tension, and
    b. World government control of atomic energy would guarantee to all nations that they need not arm for individual security.

III. The plan of federal world government is the most desirable framework for international relations, for
  A. All other attempts at maintaining permanent peace in the past have failed, for
    1. Attempts to create permanent peace by conquest have failed in every instance, for
      a. The peace of Rome lasted for three hundred, revolution-racked years and finally disintegrated, and
      b. Ghenghis Khan's attempt to wipe out all opposition by con-

quering the world ended in the total destruction of his plans and the continuance of war, and

   c. Adolph Hitler's failure to subdue conquered nations or the world is another example of conquest failing to bring permanent peace.

2. Attempts to bring permanent peace by power alliances has failed in every instance, for

   a. The Holy Alliance of Austria, Russia, and Prussia failed to maintain peace either between the members of the alliance or in Europe. (Hall and Davis, *The Course of Europe Since Waterloo*, p. 27.) And

   b. The Quadruple Alliance of England, Prussia, Russia, and Austria which, upon the entrance of France, became the Quintuple Alliance to guarantee territorial integrity for Europe, failed to keep the peace. (*Ibid.*, p. 29.) And

   c. Alliances before the First World War such as the Franco-British and Franco-Italian alliances failed to prevent the growing armament race which led to the Second World War. (*Ibid.*, Chap. 27.)

3. Attempts to bring permanent peace by confederate organizations have always failed, for

   a. The confederation of the Congress of Vienna failed to maintain either the status quo or the peace of Europe. (*Ibid.*, p. 29.) And

   b. The League of Nations failed to maintain security for the nations, prevent armament races, and thus by its inaction brought on the Second World War.
    (*Ibid.*, p. 658.) And

   c. The United Nations, as was pointed out above, is failing today to bring about peace.

B. The federal type of government has always been used to resolve intergroup conflicts and has thus far had the best record in this field, for

1. In the consolidation of the German states the power of any one of the small states to veto action of the confederation of Germany brought strife and ultimately federation as the solution to the problem. The German state has had relative internal peace since then. (*Ibid.*, p. 187.) And

2. In the Italian states strife and war were rampant until the unification of the Italian duchies into the federation of Italy. (*Ibid.*, pp. 180–182.) And

3. In the United States the many faults of the Articles of Confederation were remedied and the situation was improved by

the adoption of federal powers in the national government.
(Commanger and Morrison, *The Growth of the American
Republic,* Vol. 1, pp. 350–370.)

c. World federation would solve international problems constructively, for

1. Resources, energy, and time formerly devoted to war will be
channeled into the paths of peace, and

2. The federal world government can be kept democratic by a
system of checks and balances similar to those of the United
States, for

   a. The limited field of the federal government's jurisdiction
   in questions of aggression, armament control, and international relief would simplify the problem of limiting the
   powers of the federal government, and

   b. The existence of widely differing groups would provide
   the element of active opposition to any steps toward
   dictatorship.

3. The present frictions between nations could be overcome to
bring those nations together in a world government, for

   a. The overwhelming desire of the peoples of the world for
   peace would be a powerful factor in forcing the national
   governments to consider world government, for

   (1) Public opinion surveys show the following percentages
   of people to be in favor of world government:

U.S.	56%
Holland	44%
Sweden	47%

   and in addition in Canada and England over 50% of
   the people have shown their willingness and desire to
   turn over the atomic bomb to a world government.
   (Gallup Poll, December 23, 1947.)

   b. The increased economic dependency of devastated nations
   upon international trade would be a further stimulus to the
   acceptance of a trade-stimulating world government, for

   (1) "The Soviet Union considers it imperative to the welfare of the peoples of the world that free world trade
   be immediately resumed and that reconstruction of
   devastated areas be carried on without delay. At the
   same time the general disarmament of the world is
   essential in order to reduce military budgets without
   which it is impossible to lighten the burdens of taxa-

tion borne by the people, who will be unable to carry this load for long without complaint."
(Speech by V. M. Molotov at the United Nations General Assembly, Nov.–Dec., 1946, Publication of the Embassy of the Soviet Union, pp. 4, 10, 15.)

CONCLUSION

Because

1. The present system of international affairs under the United Nations is not satisfactory;
2. A federal world government would avoid the inherent weaknesses of the United Nations confederation;
3. The plan of federal world government is the most desirable framework for international relations;

therefore, a federal world government should be established.

V. THE CASE OUTLINE

A. Distinguished from the brief. The case has been defined as the argument which the speaker plans to take before a specific audience. Hence, the case outline is an outline of that argument. Doubtless we can define the case outline more clearly by distinguishing it from the brief.

First, let us consider the general differences. After the impersonal brief is finished, a case outline should be drawn up for the speech or speeches to be presented. The case outline and the speaker's outline based upon it should be drawn with the considerations of audience adaptation and persuasion in mind. Thus the arrangement of ideas and the rhetorical style of their statement in a presentation outline should differ from those in a brief.

There are four specific differences between the brief and the case outline. One is that the case outline is for presentation, whereas the brief is a preparation outline. The audience is not considered in brief-drawing. The writer is solely concerned with completeness and logical adequacy. A second difference is that the discussion section of the case outline may include either logical or topical outlining or some combination of the two, depending upon the type of support used. The presentation outline tempers logical adequacy with audience psychology. Thirdly, the case outline is more selective in coverage than the brief in that only the materials required by a given occasion are presented. The scope of the brief is not required by most audiences, and there is seldom enough time anyway. Finally, the sequence and arrangement of materials in a case outline are adjusted to persuade a particular audience. The brief would be less persuasive than the case because it proceeds from genus to species, from conclusion to premise, and from main points to supporting materials. The brief would be tiresome to listen to, and its form is not in the typical mode of thought. The sequence of ideas in a brief is particularly unsuited to a doubtful or a hostile audience.

In summary of these four points of difference, we see that the case outline is adapted to take cognizance of the reaction tendencies of an audience, whereas the brief is a complete, logical survey of proof which takes no account of specific reactors. The case outline is a psychological variable; the brief, a logical constant.

B. Drawing the case outline from the brief. We have said that the case outline is drawn from the brief. This process necessitates two steps, selection and arrangement. The persuader selects from the brief the materials of proof which a specific audience seems to require. He then arranges his materials in a psychological order and determines the proportion or amplification of each minor point. His decisions in these matters should be governed by considerations of time, audience attitude and information, and presence or absence of other speakers.

C. The divisions of a case outline. The case outline, like the brief, has three divisions, the introduction, the discussion, and the conclusion. However, each serves a somewhat different function here from that which it serves in the brief. This matter will be treated at length in the next chapter, "The Composition of Argument." Suffice it to say here that the purely expository introduction, the strictly linear development, and the formal summary, which characterize the brief, are rarely the best rhetorical forms in which to state a finished argument. The case outline and the speech or essay based upon it are more likely to provide for the problems of attention, interest, desire, and the like.

Thus a case outline includes evidence, reasoning, and possibly narration, description, exposition, and motive appeals. These may be arranged to develop a linear argument as in a brief, or they may be organized so that the argument seems to unfold into "this-or-nothing" logic by the implicative process. The case outline, then, must be a form which is capable of expressing any or all of these forms of support.

D. A specimen case outline. The following case outline is a specimen prepared by the students who wrote the brief. It is included to show the distinctive features of this type of outline.

AFFIRMATIVE CASE OUTLINE

on

Resolved, That a federal world government should be established.

INTRODUCTION

(Use selected introductory items from the brief, or invent other statements which will serve the functions of an introduction.)

DISCUSSION

I. Today the world is headed toward a third world war, for
   A. The first barometer of war, national propaganda against the "enemy," is rising, for
      1. Since the war, East and West have renewed and intensified their propaganda against each other, and
      2. Comparative opinion polls show that more and more people are becoming convinced of the inevitability of another war.
   B. The second barometer of war, an international armament race, is rising, for
      1. In the United States, Russia, and other major nations, increased allocations for armaments, military conscription, and research activities give indication of the race for military supremacy, and
      2. Widespread anxiety about each country's status in the atomic and hydrogen bomb rivalry both indicates and intensifies this race.
II. There are two causes for this snow-balling toward war, for

A. We are dealing with an aggressor nation—Russia, for

1. The deliberate weakening of peace organizations is the first aggressive characteristic, for

a. The Axis states put every possible hindrance in the path of the League of Nations, and

b. Today Russia is evidencing the same tactics in the United Nations.

2. The building up of a strong army is the second characteristic, for

a. The Axis powers followed this policy just before the Second World War, and

b. Today Russia is gearing her whole economy to the task of producing for war.

3. Russia is propagandizing at home for the necessity of a war to save the nation from attack by the "enemy," for

a. The Axis powers all had propaganda lines pointing out the necessity for living-room, or natural boundaries, etc., and

b. Today the Russian leaders are talking about the encirclement of Russia by aggressors and of the necessity of war.

4. The forced submission of neighboring states is the next characteristic, for

a. The Axis powers began their careers with the conquest of small states, and

b. The Russian pressure which forced Northern Korea, Czechoslovakia, and Hungary into her fold is but an underground method of aggression.

B. The United Nations is so hopelessly inadequate that by its very inadequacy it is forcing the nations into unilateral action, for

1. The United Nations has no method of punishing international aggression and thus is forcing the nations into individual security preparation, for

a. The veto prevents the use of any United Nations police force in the event of a major war.

2. The United Nations is not dealing with the causes of war which exist in the world today, such as famine, disease, lack of housing, for

a. The United Nations budget of barely $40,000,000 is totally inadequate for the huge job.

III. Federal world government should be adopted now as the best remedy to the foregoing problem, for

A. It could succeed even if Russia would take a very hostile attitude toward the organization, for

1. The proposal and imminent adoption of world government would show up Russia as an aggressor and thus unify the nations in time to save themselves, and
2. Now is the time, before Russia is ready to start a war, to discover whether she wants effective peace enforcement or whether she is just stalling until ready to strike.

B. If Russia did not actively oppose the discussion of world government, then great progress could be made, for
   1. Even if not adopted, the discussion of the problems under the stimulus of a proposed world government would help the present tense situation, and
   2. If world government were seriously proposed before the world, it is probable that many defects in the United Nations would be brought out and remedied.

CONCLUSION

Thus we say that the present system of international affairs is not satisfactory. Furthermore, our only hope of survival lies in the immediate adoption of this proposition.

VI. THE SPEAKER'S OUTLINE

A. Distinguished from the case outline. Every speech should be delivered from an outline, although the notes need not be taken to the platform. Whether written or memorized, however, the speaker's outline should consist of such notes as will most readily recall the *ideas* which have been carefully worked out in the longer outlines and selected for presentation. It differs from the case outline, from which it is derived, in these respects: it is more condensed; it is for the speaker's use only; it serves to recall ideas during presentation rather than to organize the composition of the case; it may be based upon a direct or an indirect order of argument. The direct or so-called "deductive" order of argument may be seen in the brief and the case outline. The indirect order of argument may involve the same materials, but the sequence of main points and subpoints is inverted. This process of beginning with evidence, illustrations, and lesser points and leading up to main points is thought to be more effective in the presence of an unfavorable audience.

The following speaker's outline is a specimen prepared by the students who wrote the brief and the case outline.

B. A specimen speaker's outline:

First Affirmative Speaker's Notes

I. Two Barometers Indicate Third World War
  A. Propaganda
    Gallup poll—Roper poll
  B. Armaments
    N.Y. Times quote—Bonn quote
II. Two Causes
  A. Russia
    1. Weak peace organization
      Byrnes quote—give statistics
    2. Strong army
      Tribune—AP dispatch
    3. Propaganda
      Osborne
    4. Neighboring states
      Time—Newsweek
  B. United Nations
    1. Veto
      Quote charter
    2. Money
      Budget quote
  Conclude

VII. ORGANIZATION OF INFORMAL ARGUMENT

It is erroneous to believe that organization is not important in arguments for which there has been little specific preparation. The need for organization is just as great in those forms of argument for which carefully written outlines cannot be prepared as in those types which may be so outlined. There is little persuasive force in disorganized, rambling speaking or writing. The person who wishes to become effective in arguments on short notice must learn to organize his thinking and speaking as the argument proceeds. He must have an outline, but it must suggest itself at the time of speaking and unfold during the argument. The best way to learn the basic techniques of organization is to prepare and deliver arguments which do permit the deliberate preparation of written outlines. Exercises for the development of facility may be used later.

Exercises

1. Prepare a short sample of topical outlining on some familiar subject which lends itself to this kind of treatment. The subtopics are to be descriptive parts, narrative parts, and expository parts of the main topics.
2. Prepare a short sample of logical outlining. It may be wise to use one proposition in all the assigned chapter exercises. Restate the argument thus outlined in as many syllogisms as are necessary to state this argument correctly. Revise the outline until it can be stated in a series of syllogisms.
3. Prepare a long specimen brief. Avoid the mistakes made in the short outlines.
4. Draw from the brief a case outline.
5. Prepare speaker's notes based upon a portion of the case outline.
6. Hand in an outline of a speech or an essay you have read, or a speech or a debate which you have heard.

Chapter XIV · THE COMPOSITION OF ARGUMENT

I. A BASIC REQUIREMENT

While it is a commonplace among teachers of speech that language in speech properly differs in certain respects from language in writing, it is generally true that the language of written argument should approximate as closely as possible the effective language in spoken argument. It is obvious that in reading certain documents the reader may have an opportunity to pause and look up the meaning of words or even consult an encyclopedia for a complete understanding of certain doctrines or principles mentioned in the document, and that no such opportunities are ever available to the listener to spoken argument. In other words, that which is spoken must be instantly intelligible or something of attention is undeniably lost. If the hearer tries to turn over in his own mind what the speaker has said in order to get the exact meaning, or if a hearer asks the person next to him exactly what the speaker meant, the speaker loses the attention of one or more hearers while something in his speech is *perhaps* being clarified for certain of his listeners.

We believe that the necessity of instant intelligibility which applies to all speech should pretty generally apply to all argumentative writing. Something is lost when the reader of an argument has to stop reading to investigate to learn just what the writer is saying at a given point. It is obviously true that one can never speak effectively to an audience in any language other than the language of the audience, regardless of what the speaker's language may be. Communication, to be effective, must use symbols that have common meaning to the person using the language and the person receiving it. It follows that something is lost when the writer or the speaker tries to exhibit a wide and learned vocabulary rather than tries to make the most effective immediate communication to gain his purpose.

Some suggestions for the effective use of language in argument follow. They should be taken seriously by all advocates using either written or spoken language if they want to have the language used most helpful in accomplishing specific purposes with specific audionoo or reader groups.

II. DESIRABLE QUALITIES

A. Sincerity or earnestness. Among the definite qualities that may be mentioned as particularly desirable in argumentative composition, the first is sincerity or earnestness. No man will be persuaded by any one who he thinks is trying to deceive him or play with his convictions for personal ends. A suspicious reader or listener is the hardest kind to handle, and undoubtedly an *audience* does not require much to make it suspicious. Lyman Abbott gave all advocates some excellent advice years ago as follows: "When he rises to speak he must forget himself, pray to be delivered from the ambition to be eloquent by an ambition to win a result; be careless of admiration and covetous of practical fruits in his auditors' lives. Without this moral preparation he will be a mere declaimer: with it he may be an effective speaker. And whether he is what men call an orator or not is a matter of no consequence." Ernest conviction is begotten only by a belief in the earnestness of him who persuades. The quality of sincerity or earnestness should be evident in the *composition*—the *language* used. One has only to examine the great speeches from Demosthenes to Webster to see how thoroughly the orators have in all parts of their work impressed their sincerity on their audiences. One has but to study the wrecked careers among orators to realize that insincerity is the chief obstacle to persuasion. Without sincerity all else, in the long run, goes for naught. Consequently the effective speaker or writer should be certain that his words, as well as his manner, help to make the audience or the readers believe that he is sincere.

The following exordium is an example of one of the most common methods of introduction. It is taken from the speech of Sir James McIntosh in behalf of Jean Peltier before the Court of the King's Bench, February, 1803, and shows how necessary a man, of even so great eloquence, thought it to be that his audence believe in his sincerity.

I must begin with observing that, though I know myself too well to ascribe to anything but to the kindness and good nature of my learned friend, the attorney-general, the unmerited praises which he has been pleased to bestow on me, yet, I will venture to say, he has done me no more than justice in supposing that in this place and on this occasion, where I exercise the functions of an inferior minister of justice, an inferior minister, indeed, but a minister of justice still, I am incapable of lending myself to the passions of any client, and that I will not make the proceedings of this court subservient to any political purpose.

B. Modesty. Another quality in the speaker or writer that should be evident in his composition is modesty. Modesty, in this connection, does not mean an attitude of subservience or self-suspicion. Indeed, the advocate should feel and (with modesty) exhibit the feeling that he is competent, prepared, knows what he is talking about. Self-respect, self-confidence, authority, and leadership are perfectly consistent with true modesty. Proper modesty does not require that a speaker apologize for his poor abilities, his "inadequacy to the task before him," etc. A good rule to follow in public speaking of any kind is "never apologize, never offer excuses." If it is true that you are "totally unprepared" and know nothing about the subject, do not attempt to make a speech—if it is not true, do not lie about it.

There is such a thing—even in public discussion—as false modesty, and it is a detriment to him who exhibits it. Self-confidence and manly courage are perfectly consistent with every attribute of real modesty. *True modesty requires simply that the man should be made secondary to the subject.*

C. Brevity. Appropriate brevity is attained, not by leaving out material that should be used, but by omitting all unnecessary remarks. It is a relative rather than an absolute quality. The proper length for any given speech will depend upon many circumstances. Brevity is violated when one talks simply to fill up time, or because he does not know how to quit, or because he cannot drop one point when he has said enough on it. The use of unnecessary words or sentences constitutes a breach of the law of brevity. The shortest explanation that will explain, the shortest allusion that will awaken the desired memories or associations, is the most persuasive. Wasting time with unnecessary talk irritates an audience and greatly hinders persuasion. Herbert Spencer after commenting on numerous maxims of rhetoric goes on as follows (italics not in the original):

On seeking for some clue to the law underlying these current maxims, we may see shadowed forth in many of them, *the importance of economizing the reader's or hearer's attention.* To so present ideas that they may *be apprehended with the least possible mental effort,* is the desideratum towards which most of the rules above quoted point. When we condemn writing or speaking that is wordy, or confused, or intricate—when we praise this style as easy, and blame that as fatiguing, we consciously or unconsciously assume this desideratum as our standard of judgment. Regarding language as an apparatus of symbols for the conveyance of thought, we may say that, as in a mechanical apparatus, the more simple and the better arranged in its parts, the greater will be the effect produced. In either case, whatever force is absorbed by the machine is deducted from the result. A reader or listener has at each moment but a limited amount of mental power available. To recognize and interpret the symbols presented to him, requires part of this power; to arrange and combine the images suggested, requires a further part; and only that part which remains can be used for realizing the thought conveyed. Hence, the more time and attention it takes to receive and understand each sentence, the less time and attention can be given to the contained idea, and the less vividly will that idea be conceived.

How truly language must be regarded as a hindrance to thought, though the necessary instrument of it, we shall clearly perceive on remembering the comparative force with which simple ideas are communicated by signs. To say "Leave the room" is less expressive than to point to the door. Placing a finger on the lips is more forcible than whispering "Do not speak." A beck of the hand is better than "Come here." No phrase can convey the idea of surprise so vividly as opening the eyes and raising the eyebrows. A shrug of the shoulders would lose much by translation into words. Again, it may be remarked that when oral language is employed, *the strongest effects are produced by interjections, which condense entire sentences into syllables.* And in other cases, where custom allows us to express thoughts by single words, as in *Beware, Heigho, Fudge,* much force would be lost by expanding them into specific propositions. Hence, carrying out the metaphor that language is the vehicle of thought, there seems reason to think that in all cases the friction and inertia of the vehicle deduct from its efficiency; and that in composition, the chief, if not the sole thing to be done, is to reduce this friction and inertia to the smallest possible amount. Let us then inquire whether *economy of the recipient's attention* is not the secret of effect, alike in the right choice and collocation of words, in the best arrangement of clauses in a sentence, in the proper order of its principal and subordinate propositions, in the judicious use of simile, metaphor and other figures of speech, and even in the rhythmical sequence of syllables.

D. Simplicity. The first five definitions of simplicity given in Webster's dictionary show how in practically every shade of meaning of the word, simplicity as a rhetorical quality must aid communication by economizing attention. The definitions are: "1. The quality or state of being simple, unmixed, or uncompounded. 2. The quality or state of being not complex or of consisting of few parts. 3. Artlessness of mind; freedom from cunning or duplicity. 4. Freedom from artificial ornament, pretentious style or luxury; plainness. 5. Freedom from subtlety or abstruseness; clearness." Simplicity in rhetoric means all these things: unmixed, not complex, free from cunning, duplicity, artificial ornament, pretentiousness, subtlety, and abstruseness. The absence of such simplicity both in composition and delivery lies at the bottom of the greatest fault known in public speaking, *i.e.*, an artificial, ornate, bombastic style resulting in a speech that is an *exhibition* and not a *communication*. This indirectness which is a sort of parading of voice and vocabulary—ringing, long-drawn, emotionally false cadences in voice, and high-flowing, ponderous periods in language, is absolutely inconsistent with clear *thought*. A mentality that is alive and active *at the moment of utterance* cannot use this sort of medium. So this fault is most common in declamation or in the speech of those who have learned to speak largely by declamatory practice. The common custom of choosing only the perorations of great speeches (the parts in which emotion was at its height with the audience prepared for it—a tense, emotional passage) for declamatory practice, in a flat, uninteresting, absolutely unemotional atmosphere, by a boy who often cannot grasp the mighty thoughts of the orator is a fruitful source of this kind of hollow, declamatory, meaningless speaking. The result is a *show* rather than a conversation. Such speakers display their powerful voices and teeming vocabularies *before* an audience. They do not present *live* thoughts *to* an audience. They do not reason *with* an audience. There is no contact. It is all detached, impersonal, indirect; literally "sound and fury signifying nothing." After such an experience the listeners may say (if their taste is low), "What a fine speech!" They will not say, "Let us march against Phillip!"

Simplicity is akin to sincerity. The speaker or writer who is really sincere usually treats his subject with simplicity. In fact, having any one good quality aids us in getting the others. False ornament, the ringing, alliterative adjectives, and trite figures of speech, which always hinder communication of thought, are usually the specific offenses against simplicity. Such hollow rhetoric should be eliminated, whatever the cost. There can be no speech or manuscript that will not be improved by such cutting—regardless of the nature of what is left.

E. Vividness. This is an essential quality of all good communication, either oral or written. Vivid means strong, bright, animated, *lifelike*. To get vividness we must have material capable of vivid presentation; so we must keep this quality in mind when choosing facts, evidence, anecdotes, etc. Of course only that can be vivid which is understood by reader or hearer. A reference to anything with which your audience is unfamiliar, instead of enforcing your case by calling up a vivid image, only hinders your case by distracting the hearer's *attention*. While the man in the audience is wondering whom you meant, or trying to recall the historical fact to which you refer, he is paying *no* attention to what you are saying. The reference must be instantly intelligible or nothing is gained and much may be lost by distracting attention.

The concrete and specific is always more vivid than the abstract and general. Note the increasing vividness in the following series: vegetation, vegetable, radish, white radish, long white radish, big long white radish, a white radish four inches long, a withered white radish four inches long; flower, rose, yellow rose. Consumption is more specific than disease; disease than indisposition; drunkenness than dissipation.

Do not write "quite a distance" when you can just as well write "twelve miles," nor "rude habitations" when you mean "adobe huts," nor "intoxicating liquor" when you mean "Kentucky bourbon." Let your trees be maples or sycamores or live-oaks, and your birds towhees or blue-jays or vireos. Give your characters a name, your incidents a date, and even your sunsets a geographical location. Macaulay understood well the value of this device. The *Spectator* is "served up every morning with the bohea and rolls." When young men of rank went into the navy, "Mulgrave, Dorset, Rochester, and many others, left the playhouses and the Mall for hammocks and salt pork." Another man might have written: "Whenever the Mahrattas threatened an incursion, the inhabitants fled for their lives." But Macaulay writes: "Wherever their kettledrums were heard, the peasant threw his bag of rice on his shoulder, hid his small savings in his girdle, and fled with his wife and children to the mountains or the jungles—to the milder neighborhood of the hyena and the tiger."[1]

F. Variety is the life of speech. "Deadly monotony" is a familiar term that is full of meaning. Monotony always tends to put a reader or an audience to sleep; it dulls interest and kills attention. Monotony of voice, of rhythm, of sentence structure, of paragraph organization, in words, in the use of evidence and illustration—in fact, monotony of any kind tires and alienates and makes persuasion difficult or impossible. Avoid monotony by securing, first, variety of material; secondly, variety of phrase, sentence, paragraph, etc. Such material spoken with the mind alert, with a "lively sense of communication," will necessarily insure a varied delivery. Seek ye first a variety of thought, and variety of delivery may be added unto you. The different qualities of good style, as has been said, are of course intermingled. Having some of them helps one to get the others. It is a universal law. "To him that hath shall be given." He who has simplicity and vividness will usually have variety also without taking special thought to obtain it.

Comparison and climax are two closely associated rhetorical devices that aid in securing the quality of variety (as well as the quality of vividness). The thoroughness of Whately's paragraphs is still well worth attention.

Comparison is one powerful means of exciting or heightening any emotion: *viz.*: by presenting a parallel between the case in hand and some other that is calculated to call forth such emotions; taking care of course to represent the present case as stronger than the one it is compared with, and such as ought to affect us more powerfully.

When several successive steps of this kind are employed to raise the feelings gradually to the highest pitch (which is the principal employment of what Rhetoricians call the Climax), a far stronger effect is produced than by the mere presentation of the most striking object at

---

[1] A. G. Newcomer, *Elements of Rhetoric,* p. 238. Copyright 1898. Used by permission of Henry Holt and Company.

once. It is observed by all travellers who have visited the Alps, or other stupendous mountains, that they form a very inadequate notion of the vastness of the greater ones, till they ascend some of the less elevated (which yet are huge mountains), and thence view the others still towering above them. And the mind, no less than the eye, cannot so well take in and do justice to any vast object at a single glance, as by several successive approaches and repeated comparisons. Thus in the well-known Climax of Cicero in the Oration against Verres, shocked as the Romans were likely to be at the bare mention of the crucifixion of one of their citizens, the successive steps by which he brings them to the contemplation of such an event, were calculated to work up their feelings to a much higher pitch: "It is an outrage to bind a Roman citizen; to scourge him is an atrocious crime; to put him to death is almost parricide; but to *crucify* him—what shall I call it?"

It is observed, accordingly, by Aristotle, in speaking of Panegyric, that the person whom we would hold up to admiration, should always be compared, and advantageously compared, if possible, with those that are already illustrious, but if not, at least with *some* person whom he excels: to *excel*, being in itself, he says, a ground of admiration. The same rule will apply, as has been said, to all other feelings as well as to Admiration: Anger, or Pity, for instance, are more effectually excited if we produce cases such as would call forth those passions, and which, though similar to those before us, are not so strong; and so with respect to the rest.[2]

G. Tact. Another quality that lies at the base of effective argument is tact. The tactful person easily adapts his remarks to his readers or his audience. Do not misunderstand what is meant by tact. It does not mean hypocrisy, flattery, servility, obsequiousness. There is nothing underhanded or deceitful about it. It is nearer to politeness, consideration for the feelings of others, good manners. Your despiser of tact uses a sledge hammer for all purposes, whether the task at hand properly requires a tack hammer or a pile driver. He is usually as incapable of great force as he is of delicate touch. He is an unskilled workman—a bungler who tries to make up for his lack of intelligence and politeness by ill-bred boasting of his honesty and good intentions. Of course tact is no proper *substitute* for careful preparation and honest convictions, but it is the most powerful *ally* of preparation and purpose. To decry tact because some clever people rely on it to the exclusion of other means is

[2] Whately, R., *Elements of Rhetoric*, p. 142.

silly. It is like decrying education because educated criminals are more dangerous than others. Intelligence is, of course, a more dangerous adversary than stupidity—it is also a more effective champion.

In the following extract, *talent* means practically that which is covered in argumentation by the word "conviction"—evidence, logic, fact—the general worth and truth of your case; *tact* means persuasion, the power of making your case effective, of finding a way to get your truth accepted by those to whom you present it.

Talent is something, but tact is everything. Talent is serious, sober, grave, and respectable; tact is all that, and more too. It is not a sixth sense, but it is the life of all the five. It is the open eye, the quick ear, the judging taste, the keen smell, and the lively touch; it is the interpreter of all riddles, the surmounter of all difficulties, the remover of all obstacles. It is useful in all places, and at all times; it is useful in solitude, for it shows a man his way into the world; it is useful in society, for it shows him his way through the world.

Talent is power, tact is skill; talent is weight, tact is momentum; *talent knows what to do, tact knows how to do it:* talent makes a man respectable, tact will make him respected; talent is wealth, tact is ready money. . . .

Take them to the bar, and let them shake their learned curls at each other in legal rivalry. Talent sees its way clearly, but tact is first at its journey's end. Talent has many a compliment from the bench, but tact touches fees from attorneys and clients. *Talent speaks learnedly and logically, tact triumphantly.* Talent makes the world wonder that it gets on no faster, tact excites astonishment that it gets on so fast. And the secret is, that tact has no weight to carry; it makes no false steps; it hits the right nail on the head; it loses no time, it takes all hints; and, by keeping its eye on the weathercock, is ready to take advantage of every wind that blows.

Take them into the church. Talent has always something worth hearing, tact is sure of abundance of hearers; . . . *talent convinces, tact converts.* . . .

Talent has the ear of the house, but tact wins its heart and has its votes: talent is fit for employment, but tact is fitted for it. . . . It has served an invisible and extemporary apprenticeship: it wants no drilling; it never ranks in the awkward squad; it has no left hand, no deaf ear, no blind side. It puts on no looks of wondrous wisdom, it has no air of profundity, but plays with details of place as dexterously as a well-taught hand flourishes over the keys of the pianoforte. It has all the air of commonplace, and all the force and power of genius.[3]

III. MISCELLANEOUS RHETORICAL DEVICES

A few simple rhetorical devices are generally considered of particular importance in all public speaking, and are valuable, we believe, to the advocate both in speech and in writing.

A. Use short sentences. "Short" is, of course, a relative word. But a number of short sentences will generally be more instantly effective to the reader or hearer in an argumentative situation than a few long or involved sentences. The ear or the eye grasps the total import of the short sentence without straining attention or taking time to reread or figure out the proper relation of the various clauses.

B. Repetitive effect. Repetitions which might be held to mar the perfection of artistic writing may be very effective in enforcing key ideas, either in written or spoken argument. It is probably substantially true to say that all argumentative language, either spoken or written, belongs under the category of the "prose of use" rather than the "prose of art." And the usefulness may well be enhanced by the judicious use of repetition if the result helps the advocate to accomplish his purpose with specific readers or hearers. That is sufficient justification for the repetition.

C. Pronouns. The advocate should use frankly the pronouns "I," "you," and "we," and not refer to himself in the third person as the speaker or the writer. He should openly take responsibility for what he is saying. Frankness, directness, and intimacy between the speaker and his audience, or the writer and the reader, is promoted by such a use of pronouns. Regardless of the propriety of avoiding the personal pronoun "I" in other types of writing, we are emphatically of the opinion that the advocate would do well to use it whenever its use would seem natural if he were saying substantially the same thing *in private conversation.*

[3] "Tact and Talent," *The London Atlas.* Quoted by Clark and Blanchard, *Practical Public Speaking,* pp. 110, 111.

D. Sharp questions. Questions either of the rhetorical type which are to be answered in the mind of the hearer or reader or answers to which are clearly implied in the questions themselves, or questions which the speaker asks and then immediately answers himself, add vividness and clearness. They sharpen the communication of the speaker's ideas to those with whom he is trying to communicate. It is frequently said that question marks are grappling hooks which draw the speaker and hearer or the reader and writer closer together than a simple declarative mode of expressing the same ideas.

Exercises

1. Comment upon the instant intelligibility of two speeches in Appendix A or B.
2. Evaluate one of the printed speeches in terms of the seven desirable qualities which are discussed in section II of this chapter.
3. Point out some instances of the use of the four miscellaneous rhetorical devices in the speeches of Dewey, Stassen, Gould, and Lucas.
4. Referring again to the appendices, how would you characterize each man's style of composition?
5. Compose the manuscript of a five-minute argumentative speech based upon one point in partition from either an affirmative or a negative case outline. This may be presented for written criticism or read aloud in class for evaluation.

Chapter XV · THE ADVOCATE AS SPEAKER

I. THE ROLE OF THE SPEAKER

A. **Range of activities.** The advocate appears as a speaker wherever oral argument takes place. His activities range from formal public debate to the most informal conversations. In considering the role of speaking in advocacy, it is important to recognize that much of this speaking is conducted in conversation with others on controversial issues of every kind and variety. Competence in "public speaking" is an asset to any advocate and indispensable to success in many situations, but not all arguments by any means are presented from a public platform. In this chapter we are mainly concerned with the qualities of good speaking, public or private, which affect *all* oral argument wherever it is conducted.

B. **Personal identification.** The advocate is usually identified with his subject in a more personal way than are other speakers. This factor, more than anything else, distinguishes the speaking of the advocate. He always recommends a position, point of view, or course of action to others, and in this capacity he stands as a sponsor of a cause. Indifference or detachment on his part is usually interpreted to mean a lack of conviction. He is asking his listeners to accept the proposition which *he* represents. Unless his presentation is such as to convey personal enthusiasm, interest, and conviction, his proposition may suffer an undeserved fate. By the same token, we must confess, a weak position may often be given an acceptance which it does not merit, because of the force of the personality supporting it. Psychologically, the advocate and his cause are one, at least while he is speaking. They are likely to stand or fall together.

This phenomenon is peculiarly associated with advocacy. It applies in all speaking, but speakers who seek primarily to entertain or inform are much less intimately associated with their ideas. The speaking advocate, more than any other speaker, must concern himself with those personal qualities which recommend him *and* his cause to his listeners.

II. THE ETHOS OF THE ADVOCATE

For more than twenty centuries the kind of persuasion which is produced by the listeners' impression of the speaker has been known as "ethos." The term, as a rhetorical concept, apparently originates in Aristotle's *Rhetoric*. He says of it:

The character [ethos] of the speaker is a cause of persuasion when the speech is so uttered as to make him worthy of belief; for as a rule we trust men of probity more, and more quickly, about things in general, while on points outside the realm of exact knowledge, where opinion is divided, we trust them absolutely. . . . We might almost affirm that the speaker's character [ethos] is the most potent of all the means to persuasion.[1]

In another place, Aristotle gives us his analysis of ethos:

As for the speakers themselves, the sources of our trust in them are three, for apart from the arguments (in a speech) there are three things that gain our belief, namely, intelligence, character, and good will. Speakers are untrustworthy in what they say or advise from one or more of the following causes. Either through want of intelligence they form wrong opinions; or, while they form correct opinions, their rascality leads them to say what they do not think; or, while intelligent and honest enough, they are not well-disposed (to the hearer, audience), and so perchance will fail to advise the best course, though they see it. That is a complete list of the possibilities. It necessarily follows that the speaker who is thought to have all these qualities (intelligence, character, and good will) has the confidence of his hearers.[2]

There can be no question that the impressions which listeners get of the speaking advocate, consciously or otherwise, constitute a persuasive element of great importance. We say "consciously or otherwise" because many of our reactions to persons are based upon stimuli of which we are not aware. Many persons have been heard to say, "I don't know why, but I don't think I'm going to like him." Listeners inevitably form impressions of a speaker's in-

---

[1] Aristotle, *Rhetoric*, 1.2 (Lane Cooper's translation). [2] *Ibid.*, II.1.

trinsic merits or flaws on the basis of his voice, appearance, language, topics, reasoning, and many other clues. These impressions affect audience reactions which are rooted in basic attitudes and habits. An experimental study has found positive correlations between successful persuasion and the factors of likeableness, attractiveness, sincerity, and general competence.[3]

From the speaker's point of view, the use or non-use of some kind of ethos is scarcely a matter of choice; he will be judged on the basis of whatever he says or does. Therefore, he should strive to make this factor of ethos work in his favor instead of against him.

The records of the characters and the utterances of many eminent American speakers reveal pertinent instances of ethical persuasion. When Theodore Roosevelt, who was known as an "Eastern goldbug," spoke in "free-silver" Colorado in 1900, the audience expected him to make an embarrassed retreat from his position. Instead, he shouted, "We stand on a *gold* platform. . . . We stand for the same thing in Colorado that we stand for in New York!" His audience "stopped the show" with their cheers for his courage, honesty, and seeming defiance of political expediency. Woodrow Wilson's ethical appeal stemmed from his academic status, his analytical ability, his language skill, and the high, moral quality of his principles. Ralph Waldo Emerson's earnestness and simplicity on the lecture platform bespoke sympathy and respect, particularly on the part of the more intellectual audiences. As a spokesman for organized labor, Samuel Gompers inspired trust because of his honesty and courage. To his followers he proved his devotion to the labor cause by refusing bribes, resisting intimidation, and declining salaries from businessmen. He not only sensed and expressed the prevailing spirit of labor, but also adapted his tactics to the conservatism of business audiences. Among the spokesmen for the farmers, perhaps no one was more sensational than Benjamin "Pitchfork" Tillman of South Carolina. He achieved his position of authority and leadership by virtue of his honesty, courage, sincerity, intelligence, and devotion to the welfare of his constituents. These are but a few of the many illustrations of ethical persuasion which could be cited.

[3] Franklyn S. Haiman, "An Experimental Study of the Effects of Ethos in Public Speaking," *Speech Monographs*, XVI (1949), 190–202.

III. FACTORS CONTRIBUTING TO THE ETHOS OF THE ADVOCATE

The ethos of the speaker is ultimately determined by the *choices* he makes—by the kind of propositions he elects to defend, by the materials he uses, by his attitudes toward persons and things, by the emotions he displays, by the language he uses—indeed by all the factors which enter into the speech situation, all the cues or signs available to the listener for interpretation. The speaker is likely to succeed as an advocate in the degree that his listeners interpret these choices, cues, and signs to mean that he is a man of intelligence, character, and good will.

The best way to make a listener think you are a man of intelligence, character, and good will is to *be* such a person! No artifice is a satisfactory substitute for long with very many people! The best we can do here is to suggest factors which will enable the advocate to put his best self forward. No speaker will do his cause full justice with less.

A. Assurance. When an advocate speaks with reasonable assurance, his apparent confidence and poise exert a positive suggestion in his favor. His voice and general manner bespeak sincerity and conscientious preparation. We advocate *reasonable* assurance because excessive self-confidence or "cockiness" exerts negative suggestion. The fact is that an audience is more receptive when the speaker seems to be in a good emotional state with respect to the proposition, the audience, and himself.

Although there are some advocates who seem to have too much confidence in themselves, it is generally true that students of this activity need some bolstering in this respect. Their psychological weakness may stem from a fear of failure, a dread of the unfamiliar, the memory of an embarrassing experience, or a complex of other causes. The symptoms of anxiety, such as oral dryness, trembling, moist palms, mental blockage, and the like, affect both the speaker and his audience. No one needs to be reminded of the effects upon the speaker. However, when the listeners notice the signs of nervous tension, the process of communication is hampered still more.

An advocate should, therefore, strive to bring his confidence level up to a point of efficient behavior. This requires perserverance, an understanding of the situation, proper attitudes toward the job, thorough preparation, practice, and intelligent criticism. One ought to realize that some tension is normal and necessary for efficient operation. Since it must be present, the wise procedure is to keep it under control and make it work *for* rather than against the speaker. In fact, a reasonable amount of tension tends to stimulate one to greater efforts in thought and delivery. Some speakers are helped by the thought that others are in the same state, and that most listeners are considerate. Another attitude is one of eagerness to share an enthusiasm with the audience. Still another is that of losing oneself in a cause to the extent that he forgets to be afraid; of this situation we might say that the proposition chose the speaker. In a teacher-pupil situation, the lessons should be arranged in the order of gradually increasing difficulty, one fault should be corrected at a time, the directions should be explicit, and the criticism should be constructive and not embarrassing.

B. Preparation. Intellectual competence is apparent in the speaker's grasp of the proposition. Listeners are more likely to be convinced or persuaded by a speaker who knows what he is talking about. The thoroughness of preparation is observable in the speaker's statement of his proposition, his analysis, his evidence, his reasoning, his organization of ideas, his oral composition, and other processes of which argumentation consists.

C. Intensity. Any advocate whose proposition really means a great deal to him will speak with intensity unless it is inhibited by fear. His intensity expresses itself in his voice, bodily action, and language. He leaves no doubt that he "means business." Some speakers who are skillful in a technical sense can simulate intensity more or less successfully, but their impact would undoubtedly be greater if they spoke from real conviction. In short, the intensity of the advocate's speaking gives the audience his appraisal of the significance of the proposition and his position with respect to it.

D. Flexibility. Another contributing factor to the ethical persuasion of an advocate is his flexibility or adaptability. This ability can be seen in his freedom from "canned" speeches, his adaptation of evidence and reasoning to the specific audience, his skill in refutation when the occasion calls for it, his method of dealing with questions from the floor, etc. A speaker who does not seem to be able or willing to adapt his demeanor and his remarks to the nature of the situation at hand generally loses some of his potential effectiveness. In extreme cases such inflexible speakers have been known to lose more by speaking than they would have by remaining silent.

E. Sincerity. This contributing factor includes the personal qualities which are known as genuineness, honesty, fairness, and sympathy. An advocate should reveal his true worth in the way he behaves. If his true worth will not bear revelation, he had better work on self-improvement. Sincerity, rather than artifice, should characterize a speaker's attitude. Artifice and simulation are poor substitutes for sound mastery of the subject, for honest conviction from which sincerity springs, and for the personal warmth which prompts one to respond to the needs of others. There is wisdom in the saying, "What you are speaks so loudly that I cannot hear what you say."

Honesty and fairness should be apparent in one's handling of arguments, both his own and those of an opponent. This can be accomplished by avoiding the sophistry which makes the worse appear the better reason. It can be accomplished also by distinguishing between probable truth and absolute truth. Finally, it can be achieved through sincerity and reasonable modesty. In this connection, an advocate should not allow his enthusiasm or competitive spirit to lead him into overstatements or extravagant claims.

Sympathy and good will can be revealed in the manner of a speaker's adaptation to his audience. He should show his awareness of their problems, express genuinely friendly sentiments, refer to current affairs, advise the best course as he sees it, and use language which is suited to the audience without indulging in stereotyped phrases and shallow platitudes.

F. Directness. This factor of ethical persuasion is usually considered to be a matter of delivery, but it is more than that. Directness stems from a compelling eagerness to communicate with others. It is revealed in the advocate's physical behavior, voice, ideas, composition, and whatever makes for conversational presentation.

Physical, mental, and vocal indirectness can be discovered quite simply. If, when a speaker is interrupted by a questioner, he changes his manner of delivery or perhaps his style of composition, it is likely that he was indirect. This fault may be manifested in elocutionary delivery, lack of eye contact because of note-reading or staring blankly at something, an uninterested attitude, and many other mannerisms.

Indirectness reduces a speaker's effectiveness, possibly in a serious degree. Persons prefer to be looked at by a speaker, and they will not become enthusiastic about a proposition if the advocate seems indifferent. A speaker should watch his audience for signs of approval, doubt, disagreement, or boredom. In addition, he should adjust to these conditions as he would in a conversation. The most effective modern speaking, according to our values, is that which has been characterized as enlarged conversation.

G. References to oneself. When a speaker makes references to himself for the purpose of enhancing his ethos, he is said to be using direct ethical persuasion. To be sure, many such attempts are obvious, negatively suggestive, and therefore ineffective, but some personal references have been used successfully. For instance, an advocate might refer to his associations with persons, places, institutions, and the like which have prestige value to the audience, provided that he does so with a sense of appropriateness. Similarly, he might mention his experiences and his sincerity for the purpose of establishing his authority to speak. John M. Thurston's "A Plea for Cuba" (1898) is a case in point:

Mr. President—I am here by command of silent lips to speak once and for all upon the Cuban situation. I trust that no one has expected anything sensational from me. God forbid that the bitterness of a personal loss should induce me to color in the slightest degree the statement that I feel it my duty to make. I shall endeavor to be honest, conservative, and just. I have no purpose to stir the public passion to any action not necessary and imperative to meet the duties and necessities of American responsibility, Christian humanity, and national honor. I would shirk this task if I could, but I dare not. I cannot satisfy my conscience except by speaking, and speaking now.

I went to Cuba firmly believing that the condition of affairs there had been greatly exaggerated. . . . I never saw, and please God I may never again see, so deplorable a sight. . . . I can never forget to my dying day the hopeless anguish in their despairing eyes. Huddled about their little bark huts, they raised no voice of appeal to us for alms as we went among them. Men, women, and children stand silent, famishing with hunger. They have no homes to return to; their fields have grown up to weeds; they have no oxen, no implements of husbandry. . . .

IV. THE EXTEMPORE METHOD

A. The method explained. Extemporaneous speaking, which is often confused with impromptu speaking, involves the more preparation. The advocate who speaks extempore knows in advance what his proposition and side are to be. He has time to think, read, discuss with others, prepare an outline, and in other ways prepare himself, short of writing a manuscript. In the best extempore speaking, only the final pattern of language is composed while the person speaks. This pattern of language can be improved through continued practice in writing and speaking. Extempore speaking which is prepared as indicated here is usually the best suited 'to the presentation of argument; in fact, it is a practical necessity in a give-and-take situation. It permits careful preparation and, in addition, it is flexible, direct, and spontaneous. When it is poorly done, extempore speaking has some weaknesses in common with the other methods.

B. Its superiority to other methods.

1. **Impromptu speaking.** Done without any *specific* preparation, this is not limited to public occasions; it occurs in informal, argumentative conversations. One speaks impromptu when he has not taken time to prepare his remarks, but this does not rule out his drawing upon his background or *general* preparation. Facility in this kind of presentation is an asset because of the frequency of its use. However, beginners will do well to practice with prepared arguments first. Impromptu efforts are expected to measure up to the standards of analysis, reasoning, evidence, presentation, and so forth, which are met by the best speakers who are present. An advocate who is inexperienced, poorly informed, and conceited may display glibness, but his logical weaknesses can easily be pointed out. The superiority of the extempore method to the impromptu is obvious.

2. **Reading from manuscript.** This is a familiar type of delivery.

There is some justification for it in situations which demand verbatim accuracy or exact timing. Persons whose every word may be scrutinized, or those who speak via radio, may deem it wise to read from carefully prepared manuscripts. Most speakers, however, can rarely use this excuse legitimately. They should realize that many factors of effectiveness may be sacrificed by reading. Directness, animation, and adaptability always suffer unless the oral reader is uncommonly expert.

3. Speaking from memory. As the name indicates, this activity means that the speaker commits to memory the kind of manuscript which we referred to in the preceding paragraph. This type of delivery is required in school oratorical contests, for example. The disadvantages are those of reading, except that directness may not be so easily impaired. There remain the difficulties of adjustment to the situation and the hazard of forgetting. In fact, the uncertainty of recall and the concentration upon the exact language frequently inhibit genuine responses to meaning and mood, and the delivery becomes artificial, monotonous, or otherwise indirect. Both reading and memorization are inadvisable in arguments in which both sides are represented. The demands of adaptation, attack, and defense can rarely if ever be met properly with a manuscript or a memorized speech.

V. SOME SUGGESTIONS ON DELIVERY

A. A point of view on delivery. Any advocate who presents his case orally must communicate his ideas and feelings through audible and visible symbols. In other words, the elements of basic importance in delivery are voice, bodily action, and platform decorum. Without laboring the obvious premise that skill in delivery is important, we shall offer some practical suggestions concerning the elements of effective delivery in public speaking. In so doing, we do not pretend to offer a condensed substitute for chapters on delivery in the elementary public-speaking textbooks. Neither do we mean our separate treatments of voice, action, and the like to be construed as a denial of the many and complex interrelationships which exist among the several elements of delivery, and between delivery and other constituents of the speaker's task.

B. Desirable characteristics of voice. One's voice is of considerable importance; it reveals much about him, and it has effects upon others. Attitudes, personality traits, moods, and physical conditions are often revealed in the voice. That is why actors adapt their voices to their roles. If the voice is to communicate, which means to have an effect upon others, it must be heard, it should be pleasant to hear, and it should not be so unusual as to divert attention from the message.

1. Pitch. One of the desirable characteristics of voice is an acceptable range and flexibility of pitch. A speaking voice which is deficient in this respect is called a monopitch, and it is incongruous with the sincere, animated, intense expression of a conviction. In other words, much of a speaker's meaning can be conveyed by his variety in pitch or melody. This is the principal reason for varying one's pitch, but it is not the only one. A speaker who does not use his optimum pitch with some variety is likely, if he must talk a great deal, to experience throat tension and hoarseness, huskiness, breathiness, or a general weakness in the voice.

2. Time or rate. A second desirable quality is appropriate time or rate. We customarily think of variety, pause, and rhythm in this connection. Vocal sounds have duration in time; some may be drawled, while others are clipped. Some voices have pauses, but others seem not to be interrupted by inhalation. There are singsong rhythms, staccato rhythms, and patterns that lack any meaningful rhythm. Variety in these elements of time prevents a mono-rate which is a form of indirectness. The direct communication of nuances of meaning demands vocal variety.

3. Force or adequate and varied loudness. This has to do with the carrying power and emphasis of a voice. An advocate should speak loudly enough to be heard, and he should vary his loudness or intensity to indicate the stress he wishes to place upon each word. While doing this he should keep a reserve of force which can be brought to bear on the few high points in his speech. In order to project vocal sounds with ample intensity but without harshness, a speaker must maintain adequate breath support up to each pause for breathing, produce tones of good quality, and avoid excessive tension in the vocal musculature.

4. Voice quality. Observable in the resonance, clarity, purity, and general timbre of the speech sounds, this is intimately associated with the sincerity and intensity of a speaker's emotional reactions. An advocate's voice should be a responsive instrument which registers emotional color that springs from genuine, appropriate feelings.

5. **Articulation.** If this is not clear and distinct, understanding, to say nothing of conviction, is difficult to secure. Articulation which will not distract attention from the speaker's message can be achieved through the proper use of the tongue, lips, palate, soft palate, and related structures in the shaping of consonants.

C. Action. Bodily action is the visible code of communication: posture, movement, and gesture. This part of delivery is important both to the speaker and the audience. It frees the speaker for more effective communication, conveys additional meaning to the listeners, and is, therefore, an important aspect of directness. Precise, mechanical instructions on how to stand and move must not be given, but a few basic principles are useful. First, effective movement is coordinated; all of the body must work as a unit. In other words, the entire person should convey the desired, single impression. Secondly, the entire body should be animated and responding actively to what the voice and language are saying. Third, all action is better when it is integrated with the ideas, inwardly motivated, and mostly uninhibited. Fourth, a speaker's action should indicate some reserve. That is, gestures should be spontaneous, but they should not give the impression of going the limit. Some control is preferable to complete abandon.

D. General appearance. Some of a speaker's effectiveness or lack of it can be attributed to his platform manner and personal appearance. Platform behavior includes taking the platform, sitting in the view of the audience, and indicating an attitude toward the situation. Before he rises to speak, the advocate ought to appear interested in the proceedings and courteous toward the persons present. When a speaker takes the platform, he should do so confidently and deliberately, acknowledge the introduction gracefully, face the audience pleasantly and quietly for a few seconds, and then begin speaking in a conversational manner. Such behavior indicates poise and good breeding.

Personal grooming likewise reveals the real person, or at least most listeners think it does. Neatness of clothing and the person, good taste in the manner of dress, discriminate use of cosmetics, and a fitting choice of coiffure are obvious principles of personal grooming. This aspect of general appearance affects attention and suggestion just as platform decorum does.

Exercises

1. Let each member of the class write a rank-order list of the five most persuasive speakers he has heard. One person or a committee might then prepare a list of the speakers who were ranked on several ballots. When the second list is issued to the class, each student will rank each speaker he has observed, using these criteria of ethical persuasion: assurance, evidence of preparation, intensity, flexibility, sincerity, and directness. Observe the relationships between the rankings on general persuasiveness and ethical persuasion.
2. Write a critique of a public speech of advocacy which you have heard recently. This speech may be a lecture outside the classroom situation, or it may be one speech in a school debate. Evaluate the delivery and the ethical persuasion.
3. Deliver a short extemporaneous speech based upon one point in partition from your case outline. Exemplify the principles of ethical persuasion and delivery.
4. In terms of the printed record which appears in Appendix A or B, set out what seem to be the instances of ethical persuasion in the remarks of one of the debaters.

Chapter XVI · FALLACIES AND STRATAGEMS

Fallacies are usually defined as defects in proof or as instances of erroneous reasoning which render arguments logically unsound. Stratagems are commonly thought of as deceptive artifices which divert, distort, or confuse arguments. Although these categories overlap, they cover the obstacles to straight thinking.

Speakers, listeners, writers, and readers urgently need to understand the more common obstacles to sound thinking and reasoning. Some experiments have shown that resistance to propaganda is a function of sound thinking, and that the teaching of such thinking is the most successful educational procedure in developing more resistance to propaganda. Speakers and writers who understand how thinking can go astray should be able to strengthen their own arguments against refutation and to detect their own opportunities for refutation in case they reply to another speaker or writer. Practically the entire content of this book is relevant to these purposes.

Our discussion of fallacies and stratagems is closely related to our treatment of the kinds of arguments, the structure of argument, the rules of evidence, analysis, refutation, and, to a greater or lesser degree, all the principles of argumentation. We shall refer back to these principles as we show how any violations of them result in obstacles to straight thinking. In addition to knowing these principles, one should realize that illogical thinking is more likely to occur in relation to subject matter about which one is poorly informed, and that fallacies are more difficult to detect in context than they are in their simplified, shortened, textbook form.

I. FAULTY USE OF EVIDENCE

Any treatment of evidence which violates the tests which were discussed in Chapter VII may be regarded as an obstacle to critical thinking. We shall state the tests in positive form here for the purpose of pointing out that the use of evidence should measure up to these standards:

A. The evidence itself:
   1. Evidence must be used unless an unsupported assertion is admitted.
   2. It should be consistent with human nature and experience.
   3. It must be consistent with established facts, otherwise pseudo-facts, half-facts, and speculative hypotheses contrary to fact might be accepted.
   4. It must be consistent with itself.
   5. It must satisfy any appropriate "hearsay" test.
   6. It must be of the best available type. This might be (a) a statement contrary to one's own interest, (b) casual evidence, (c) negative evidence that has not been "doctored," and (d) real evidence if it is available.

B. The sources of ordinary (fact) evidence:
   1. The witness must be physically qualified to perceive what he reports.
   2. The witness must be mentally qualified in terms of memory and accuracy of verbal expression.
   3. The witness must be morally qualified in terms of his character and his stake in the outcome.
   4. The witness must have had an opportunity to get the facts.

C. The sources of expert (opinion) evidence:
   1. This kind of evidence should not be used in lieu of available facts.
   2. The witness should have uncommon knowledge and experience pertaining to the point in question.
   3. The authority should be recognized as such by the audience or reader. However, an attempt to discredit a source in advance is in itself a fallacy of "poisoning the well."

II. FAULTY ARGUMENT FROM SIGN

Any argument from sign which fails to meet the requirements as set out in Chapter VIII is likely to be an obstacle to critical thinking. Sign arguments should meet these standards:

A. The sign relationship must be more than accidental or coincidental.

B. A sign must not be mistaken for a cause or a functional inter-dependency.
1. To argue that a high fever is a cause of sickness, or to contend that shorter summer nights cause longer summer days is to commit the fallacy of *non causa pro causa*.
C. The sign relationship must be reciprocal if either element is to be taken as a sign of the other.
D. The possible intervention of special factors which may alter normal sign relations must be considered.
E. The concurrence of several signs is usually stronger than a single sign.

III. FAULTY CAUSAL ARGUMENT

Causal arguments should be tested by means of the following standards which were set out in Chapter VIII:

A. The connection between cause and effect must be close and un-broken.
1. The fallacy of "after this, therefore because of this" (*post hoc ergo propter hoc*) should be avoided.
2. The fallacy of "non-cause for the cause" (*non causa pro causa*) may otherwise occur as in the statement: "Since thrifty people have money, the way to make people thrifty is to give them money."
3. The fallacy of "it does not follow" (*non sequitur*) applies here and in other situations in which the conclusions do not follow from the premises.
B. The possible operation of other causes to prevent or alter the alleged effect must be considered.
C. The alleged cause must be adequate to produce the known effect.
1. Otherwise a fallacy of part cause is committed.
D. The known cause must be understood in terms of the alleged effect and other possible effects.
E. Conditions or reciprocal relations must not be mistaken for causes, otherwise fallacies of false cause will result.
1. Poor housing may be a condition favorable to crime, but it is not in itself a cause.
2. Political conditions foster some type of political philosophy, and the prevailing philosophy fosters certain conditions, but one is not the cause of the other.

IV. FAULTY ARGUMENT BY EXAMPLE

A. Examples must be fair in respect to the point involved.
B. The size of the sample of a large group must take account of the range of variability among the members of that large group, unless the selected sample is the least favorable one.
　1. Otherwise the fallacy of converse accident or hasty generalization will be committed.
C. Negative instances must be accounted for.
　1. Otherwise the fallacy of accident will be committed.
D. The examples must clearly exhibit the relation which is being generalized.
E. A generalization cannot infallibly predict the nature of the next specific instance.
　1. The "gambler's fallacy" results from such an assumption as that, if a tossed coin has shown "heads" in seven of ten tosses, the chances of "heads" in the eleventh toss are seven to three.

V. FAULTY ARGUMENT BY ANALOGY

A. Figurative analogies have no probative force.
B. Compared cases must be alike in all essential respects.
C. Differences in the compared cases must be accounted for.
D. Cumulated analogies are stronger than a single analogy.

VI. FORMAL FALLACIES

A. A categorical syllogism must include three terms.
　1. The fallacy of four terms (*quaternio terminorum*) is to be avoided.
B. The middle term must be distributed at least once in the premises.
　1. The fallacy of undistributed middle is to be avoided.
C. From two negative premises no conclusion can be inferred.
D. If either premise is negative, the conclusion must be negative.
E. The conclusion cannot be negative unless one of the premises is negative.
F. No term may be distributed in the conclusion which was not distributed in its premise.
　1. Any violation of this rule is the "illicit process" of the major term or the minor term.
G. From two particular premises no conclusion can be inferred.

H. If either premise is particular, the conclusion must be particular.

I. The alternatives in a disjunctive syllogism must be mutually exclusive.

J. The alternatives in a disjunctive syllogism must express all possible choices.

K. A hypothetical syllogism must not deny the antecedent.

L. A hypothetical syllogism must not affirm the consequent.

VII. DIVERSIONS AND SUBSTITUTIONS

A. Diversions to other arguments. These familiar fallacies and stratagems occur when disputants "change the subject," "get off the point," or use "red-herring" tactics. Since these have not been discussed previously, we shall explain briefly the most common ones.

1. The fallacy of irrelevant conclusion occurs when (a) some point which is not contradictory is proved in an attempt to disprove the point in question, or (b) some conclusion other than the one demanded is proved. In order to disprove the argument that "labor unions coerce their members," one must prove that "at least some unions don't do it." If, instead of proving this, one were to prove that "coercion is reprehensible," he would commit a fallacy of the first kind. To illustrate the second kind, suppose that instead of proving that "the accused is guilty of forgery," one proves that "forgery must not be condoned."

2. Appeals to interests, motives, or prejudices (*argumentum ad hominem*) are diversions from an intellectual appeal.

3. Attacking the person instead of his ideas (*argumentum ad personam*) is a fallacious procedure. We are reminded of the lawyer who said to his assistant, "No case—abuse the other attorney." This and other irrelevancies belong in the general class of fallacies of *ignoratio elenchi* (ignorance of the point at issue).

B. Diversions to stop argument on a point. These occur when persons find themselves near defeat on the point at issue, and they introduce statements which lead the opponent to concede the real point or to defer to the influence of the diversionary statement.

1. The use of specialized language, technical jargon, or abstruse statements is a familiar example.

2. The reliance upon appeals to authority (*argumentum ad*

verecundiam) rather than to reason involves an invalid use of evidence from authority or expert opinion.

3. Appeals to tradition or custom are fallacious if one argues that something should not be done because it has not been done before.

4. Mob appeal or "playing the gallery" is known as the fallacy of *argumentum ad populum*. This is the stock-in-trade of demagogues.

5. Closely related to mob appeals are those of pity and sympathy (*argumentum ad misericordiam*). An attorney might use this appeal to "soften" a jury.

6. Arguments based upon ignorance (*argumentum ad ignorantiam*) attempt to shift the burden of proof or the burden of rebuttal, as the case may be. For instance, one might argue, "Communication with deceased persons must be possible, for no one can prove otherwise."

C. Substitutions of nonrational matter and manner. These occur when one attempts to substitute irrelevant material or a contentious manner for the materials and attitudes of critical thought.

1. Appeals to force (*argumentum ad baculum*) involve "using the big stick." Among nations, this means war or at least a threat of war. This appeal says, in effect, "Will you agree, or must I twist your arm?"

2. The more obvious substitutions include the use of humor, ridicule, irony, bombast, and anger.

VIII. MANIPULATION TO DISTORT AND CONFUSE

An arguer who uses this type of crooked thinking does not abandon the point at issue; he manipulates it so as to distort the idea and to confuse other persons.

A. Unreasonable extension of the argument. This may occur when one alters the adjective "some" to "all," or when one unfairly uses *reductio ad absurdum* in refutation. Such extensions may take the form of urging an opponent to an unreasonable position or of deliberately misrepresenting and broadening his statement.

B. Special pleading. This device is sometimes defined as the use in one situation of an argument which would not be accepted in another. A citizen of the United States might urge the United Nations to take some action with respect to the internal affairs of Russia, but he might not agree that, under similar circumstances, the United Nations should treat the United States in the same way. Another definition of special pleading refers to the omission of evidence which is relevant to the point but at variance with the intended conclusion. It is one-sided reasoning in support of a preconceived conclusion. Partisans often omit facts and reasons which are at variance with their own conclusions. For instance, a politician might boast of his party's economical administration of the state by citing the absence of bonded indebtedness, state sales taxes, corporation taxes, etc., but fail to mention the inequitable tax base, the low state of the public schools, and the neglect of social services.

C. Genetic fallacy. When the truth or falsity of an idea is made exclusively dependent upon its source, this fallacious manipulation is present. Thus an idea is said to be "good" if a "good" person or group originated it, but "bad" if the source is in poor repute. "The Fair Employment Practices Act is un-American, because it is favored by Communists."

D. Forcing ideas into arbitrary categories. Such torturing of ideas may take the form of making sharp distinctions between items on a continuum, or of calling an idea valid because it is the "mean between extremes." Thus a person need not be a "radical" or a "reactionary," but this does not mean that his ideas are "right" if they are at the half-way point between the extremes.

E. Pigheadedness. A participant in a controversy exemplifies this trait if he refuses to admit something from which the point under discussion immediately follows, or if he admits the premises but denies the conclusion. Thus he might admit a theory but deny its practical application.

F. Stressing weak arguments. This occurs when an advocate refutes the weakest proof and claims complete refutation, or when he meets a superficial argument with another one of his own for the purpose of ridiculing his opponent.

G. **"Trick" questions.** In a give-and-take situation in which opposing advocates exchange questions and answers, we often observe this kind of dialectical stratagem.

1. Instead of asking questions in a logical order such as cause and effect, for instance, a person asks one on a cause, two on an effect, one on a cause, etc., so as to confuse the respondent who does not see the relationships in perspective.

2. The questioner might also use the respondent's answers for a purpose or a conclusion which their content does not warrant.

3. In a similar vein, the trickster might ask questions with several meanings and quickly advance the argument on the basis of a partial answer to one of the elements of the compound question.

4. A fourth variation involves asking the converse of an intended question in order to mislead the respondent. Thus if the respondent consistently gives negative answers to questions which the interrogator wishes affirmed, the questioner may ask the converse as if it were that which he wished to have affirmed.

5. A fifth variant involves the use of a series of questions which will establish a sort of habitual "yes" response before the crucial question is put.

6. The device known as the "complex question" rests upon the fallacious assumption that when one says he has not stopped doing something, he must still be doing it; whereas, he may never have done it at all. For example, "Have you stopped cheating during examinations?"

IX. MISUSE OF LANGUAGE

A. **Ambiguity.** This much-abused pattern of language usage often impairs communication seriously, but it does serve a basic purpose in humor and poetry. We shall identify three common forms of ambiguity.

1. **Equivocation.** Otherwise known as ambiguity of a single term or as equivocation in quality, this is often a fallacy of four terms. The single term appearing in two or more premises is treated as if its meaning were constant when it is not. Note these examples:

"Some dogs have pointed ears, my dog has pointed ears; therefore, my dog is *some dog*." "A dandelion is better than heaven, because a dandelion is better than nothing, and nothing is better than heaven." The Bill of Rights did not require revision after the freeing of the slaves because of the ambiguity of the word "person" in the Constitution.

2. **Composition and division.** These two variants stem from the ambiguous use of "all." They are equivocations in quantity. When used collectively, "all" means the total group, as in "all the building" (the whole building). When used distributively, "all" means each and every one, as in "all the members." The fallacy of composition occurs when one takes collectively that which should be taken separately: "High prices of grain are beneficial to farmers; high prices of clothing help the textile industry; high prices of machines help the manufacturers. Thus a general price rise would be economically beneficial to the country." The fallacy of division occurs when one takes separately that which should be taken collectively. "The Student Governing Board is a very active group. Joe Zilch, who is a member, must therefore be very active."

3. **Amphiboly.** The fallacy or stratagem of amphiboly arises from an ambiguous construction of the sentence as a whole. The misconception is usually traceable to confused antecedents, word order, relative and demonstrative pronouns, dangling participles, etc. The consequences may be amusing or serious. These are examples of amphiboly: "Wanted: An apartment by a young couple with a southern exposure." "Homemakers: save soap and waste paper." "Respectable entertainment every night except Sunday." When King Croesus of Lydia planned a war against Persia, he asked the Delphic oracle how the venture would turn out. The oracle replied that a great kingdom would fall. Croesus assumed that he would win, but he lost. The oracle had not specified *which* great kingdom would fall.

B. **Vagueness.** This results from the use of a term which has no well-defined meaning. Thus it can be more confusing than an ambiguous term which has two possible meanings. Some common kinds and sources of vagueness include technical jargon, argot, cant, abstractions, and a general lack of correspondence between words and their referents. However, we do not condemn all abstractions used by competent theorists in the process of conceptualizing a maze of specifics into a systematic theory. Some instances of vagueness follow: The defeat of France in 1940 was attributed by some commentators to the "weakening of the moral fibre" of the French people. Some ordinances forbid the wearing of "a bathing suit which indecently exposes any part of the wearer's person." Our troubles beset us, according to some persons, because we "don't read the Bible enough."

C. Accent. The stratagem or fallacy of accent occurs as a result of improper word stress. The unfair separation of a word from its context or the use of vocal inflection may create a false impression. The meanings of most sentences can be altered by either of these devices. These are some examples: "He spake to his sons, saying 'Saddle me an ass,' and they saddled him." In W. L. White's *Report on the Russians* we can find many isolated sentences which, if removed from context, would suggest a pro-Russian author. However, most reviewers classified the book as anti-Russian in general tone. Note how the censorious words are deleted from a critic's review before it is quoted in advertisements for movies, plays, books, etc.

D. "Loaded" words. Language is used not only to inform but also to express subjective feeling or to arouse emotional behavior in others. The matters of probability about which we argue seem to be most seriously plagued by the mixing of the informative and the affective functions of language. At any rate, all speakers, writers, listeners, and readers should be constantly aware of the use to which the language is being put. A few samples will indicate the type of suggestive pressure-technique which abounds in propaganda: "un-American handout to incompetents," "court-packing scheme," "Constitution defender (or wrecker)," "yes-man," "the American way."

E. Figure of speech and hypostatization. 1. The first device is used in two ways; one may argue from a grammatical or linguistic form to the nature of a real thing, or he may use figurative language as if it were literally intended. We cite, as an instance of the first type, the argument that a representative should be a mere "rubber stamp" for his constituents, because etymologically the word "representative" means passivity. The misuse of figurative language might occur in an expression such as Ingersoll's "Life is a narrow vale between the cold and barren peaks of two eternities."

2. The second device, hypostatization, is employed when one uses abstract terms as if they represented specific and concrete entities which are capable of independent existence and of producing real effects. The process of reification in mental stereotyping is a distressing case in point. These are examples of hypostatization: "Nature designed us to act, not to be acted upon." "His conscience told him what was right." "History has a way of calling the period an age of defeat." "We live in a world, as the poet Jeffers has it, that turns back upon itself terribly in incestuous relationship." In a lighter vein we recall the grinning cat (in *Alice in Wonderland*) which walked away and left its grin behind.

X. TAUTOLOGY AND BEGGING THE QUESTION

A. Definition. Some textbooks in logic distinguish between tautology and begging the question. They state that the former is formally valid while the latter is not. In the literature of argumentation, however, the two phenomena are treated as one under the heading of begging the question (*petitio principii*), which consists in having assumed in the premises that which is "proved" in the conclusion. Instead of analyzing this vexed question in detail, we shall simply point out that both patterns as illustrated below should be considered as obstacles to straight thinking.

B. Four forms of tautology.

1. **Argument in a circle.** "Because the testator had sufficient ability to do business, therefore it is to be inferred that he read and understood the letters; and because he read and understood the letters, therefore he is to be inferred to have been of sufficient ability to do business." (Wright *v.* Doe EX. DEM. TATHAM.)

2. **Question-begging words.** "Abolish the bungling bureaucracy." "Newfangled school subjects should be dropped." "Vote to clean the rascals out."

3. **Question-begging definitions.** "The Office of War Information

is a New Deal propaganda mill." "College-bred means a four-year
loaf." "The A.A.U.P. is a professors' union."

4. **Nonevident premise.** "Everyone knows that military training
teaches discipline; it would therefore make the country more law-
abiding." "I did not want aerial warfare," said Hitler on January 1,
1941. "Since tariff protection has made America what it is, we
should retain it."

C. The fallacy of begging the question. John Locke's *Essay Concerning Human Understanding* argues that we derive the idea of
the succession of events in time from our senses and reflections:

> It is evident to anyone who will but observe what passes in his own
> mind, that there is a train of ideas which constantly succeed one another
> in his understanding as long as he is awake. Reflection on these ap-
> pearances of several ideas one after another in our minds, is that which
> furnishes us with the idea of succession. . .

Other examples: "The belief in luck is universal, for everyone
believes in it." "When war is no more, the nations will progress as
never before, for in all their endeavors they will move forward
more rapidly than before."

Exercises

1. Select from advertisements, editorials, or printed speeches one example of each of the ten classes of fallacies and stratagems. Record
   the results of your "fallacy hunt."
2. Identify the obstacle to critical thinking in each of these items:
   a. "I ought not do this, because it is wrong."
      "How do you know it is wrong?"
      "Because I know I ought not do it."
   b. An Italian mathematician once defined equality between two
      numbers thus: "Numbers whose units correspond to one another
      uniquely and in the same order and of which the one is neither
      a part of the other nor equal to a part of the other are equal."
   c. Wordsworth is reported to have said that, if he had a mind to,
      he could write like Shakespeare.
   d. An employer has the right to pay the lowest wages a worker will
      accept, for an employer has a right to do whatever is not legally

forbidden, and the law does not forbid paying the lowest wages a man will accept.

e. Opinion pollster: "Do you favor the closed shop?"
Interviewee: "Well, it's a matter of opinion. Myself, I like a little ventilation when I work."

f. A democracy is a society in which the voice of the people determines governmental policy. Thus what I wish should be done by Congress.

g. Seated in his limousine, the scenery flashed by.

h. "Twice isolationism has failed, and now we must ask ourselves whether it will save us a third time," said a university president in an address of welcome in 1943.

i. A debater passes lightly over a weak spot in his own case but stresses a similar weakness in the opponent's argument.

j. A magazine article in 1944, "Can Our Schools Teach the G.I. Way?" argued that the teaching procedures used in classes for Army and Navy personnel would prove equally effective in civilian schools and colleges.

k. A receding chin indicates a lack of strong will.

l. "Butch wants a bicycle," according to an advertisement for a group of "business-managed, tax-paying" electric-light-and-power companies. "Lots of lawn and lemonade and baby-sitting lie between Butch and that bike, but we're betting on the boy. He has energy, vision, and our national habit of working hard for what he wants. He's American business in miniature. (He sells "leminade" at three cents per large glass, although it costs more to produce.) There are many names for Butch's philosophy. You can call it Free Enterprise, Opportunity, Democracy, or Capitalism, if you want." (See the New Yorker, June 7, 1947, for a clever retort to this.)

m. "By the time World War III arrives, a battleship will be about as useful as a wooden leg in a forest fire." (From a letter to an editor.)

n. You can cause a person to turn around by staring at the back of his head.

o. The "common-sense" argument against the Copernican theory was that people could "see" the sun rise and set and the stars revolve in circles around the pole.

p. In a British political argument, one speaker said that it could be judged what the Conservative Party was like from the fact that one of its ministers had a son who had broadcasted for the enemy during the war.

q. "I speak from experience in this case (for re-enactment of Prohibition) because I witnessed the terrible effect that liquor had on my sister's marriage . . . "

r. "No man can read the history of the U.S. and be convinced that the Democratic Party ever did anything good for it." (Plymouth, Neb., *News*)

s. "All women's dresses, in every age and country, are merely variations on the eternal struggle between the admitted desire to dress and the unadmitted desire to undress." (Lin Yutang)

t. Silent men are generally thinkers.

u. In the article, "Unschooled Women Seen As Our Hope," it was said that the declining birth rate can be attributed to "too much education for women." (Chicago *Sun*, Nov. 26, 1945)

v. The Hawley-Smoot tariff (1930) is sometimes blamed for the depression of 1929.

w. Concerning a pay raise for members of the armed forces, a housewife argued, "We will be paying out a good deal of money in other ways, so why not give it to those boys who will be away from their families and friends?"

x. Said General De Witt's final recommendation to the Secretary of War on February 14, 1942 (concerning the large-scale removal of Japanese-Americans from the West Coast): "The very fact that no sabotage has taken place to date is a disturbing and confirming indication that such action will be taken."

Chapter **XVII** · REFUTATION AND REBUTTAL

I. THE NATURE OF REFUTATION

Refutation consists in the destruction of opposing proofs. As suggested in this definition, refutation is, in form, destructive rather than constructive; but in its purposes and results it is no less serviceable than positive proof. With respect to any given proposition, if we can induce a hearer to reject the position of our opponent, we are thereby preparing him to accept our own view. There are two basic methods by which we may weaken or destroy the hearers' belief in our opponent's case: (1) by attacking directly what our opponent has said in support of his case, and (2) by building up a *counter*-proposition, or argument, until its acceptance makes the acceptance of the opponent's position impossible. Under the first we attack the evidence or the argument, showing its weakness. Under the second we argue that the accused was insane, or too young, or not present, and therefore the case against him cannot possibly be true—regardless of the evidence.

Aristotle's names for these basic forms of refutation were "counter-syllogism" and "objection." A counter-syllogism consists in offering argument and evidence to support a proposition which is logically incompatible with the proposition it is presented to refute. If the counter-argument is more convincing (more probable) than the argument it is offered to refute, it is presumed that the audience will accept the more probable of the two. "Objection" consists in attacking the premises or the inferences of an argument in such a way as to weaken it or render it improbable. Actually, these two methods are often used in combination to good effect. Thus, a debater will object to his opponent's argument on one or more grounds and go on to offer a line of argument of his own which is more convincing than the opposing argument in its now weakened condition. Refutation pure and simple is rarely, if ever, sufficient, so that to destroy without building up will usually not serve our purpose. Refutation, therefore, is properly auxiliary and supplementary to positive proof.

In our attempt to convince or persuade any man, we must realize that he will, almost surely, have in his own mind many preconceived ideas about the matter under discussion, and that many of those ideas are likely to be antagonistic to what we are trying to get him to believe. In such circumstances, our success must often depend upon our ability to destroy these hostile conceptions, thus preparing the way for the acceptance of our own contentions. The necessity for such destructive effort is, of course, peculiarly pressing in any form of argument where the advocate is confronted by some definite opponents, as in debate, or perhaps in a newspaper controversy. Here, the audience or readers are balancing the two sides of the question, and the competent debater tries to make them see that his side overbalances the other. Direct answers to *what the opponent has said,* if well done, counts heavily in the final balancing. This is refutation.

II. WHAT TO REFUTE

The partial or complete destruction of such opposing opinions and arguments often calls for a keener insight and a more adroit attack than does any of the positive work of construction. It therefore becomes of the first importance to decide what, and how much, one ought to refute. Concerning this question John Quincy Adams, in his "Lectures on Rhetoric and Oratory" (Lecture XXII), a century and a half ago gave us what is still excellent advice:—

There are three very common errors in the management of controversy against which I think it proper here to guard you, and from which I hope you will hereafter very sedulously guard yourselves. The first may be termed answering too much; the second answering too little; and the third answering yourself, and not your opponent.

A. Answering too much. Speaking of the first of these mistakes, he says:—

You answer too much when you make it an invariable principle to reply to everything which has been or could be said by your antagonist on the other side. . . . If you contend against a diffuse speaker, who has wasted hour after hour in a lingering lapse of words, which had little or no bearing upon the proper question between you, it is incumbent upon you to discriminate between that part of his discourse which was pertinent, and that which was superfluous. Nor is it less necessary to detect the artifice of an adversary, who purposely mingles a flood of extraneous matter with the controversy, for the sake of disguising the weakness of his cause. In the former of these two cases, if you undertake to answer everything that has been said, you charge yourself with all the tediousness of your adversary, and double the measure by an equal burden of your own. In the latter you promote the cause of your antagonist by making yourself the dupe of his stratagem. If, then, you have an opponent whose redundancies arise only from his weakness, whose standard of oratory is time, and whose measure of eloquence is in arithmetical proportion to the multitude of his words, your general rule should be to pass over all his general, unappropriate declamation in silence; to take no more notice of it than if it had never been spoken. But if you see that the external matter is obtruded upon the subject with design to mislead your attention, and fix it upon objects different from that which is really at issue, you should so far take notice of it as to point out the artifice, and derive from it an argument of the most powerful efficacy to your own side.

1. **Three objections to answering too much.** Answering too many of the lesser arguments of an opponent should be avoided for the following three excellent and practical reasons: (a) *In the first place, it involves a loss of time and energy.* This is particularly true in the case of the arguments of an opponent who wastes himself in "a lingering lapse of words," which have little or no bearing upon the issues. But it is also true, even when the efforts of an opponent are well directed at the points in issue. The greater part of the materials in any proof are, as we have seen, only secondary in nature; they are of force merely because they tend to establish some larger, more vital fact. The important thing is to reach and overthrow these more significant and critical parts of the proof: if they can be destroyed, the secondary facts fall with them. To sink a battleship does not demand that every foot of its armor be twisted and torn, that every turret and smokestack be demolished; one or two well-placed shots are enough. It is only necessary that the vulnerable spot be well chosen, and that the aim be sure. Consequently it should be the purpose of the debater, in his refutation, to let the lesser points of his opponent pass unheeded, and to give his attention only to vital elements.

(b) *In the second place, answering too much results in confusion.* To attempt to refute too many petty arguments weakens the discrimination between the important and the unimportant, which is always necessary in argumentation if we are to make a distinct and lasting impression. Emphasis, as a means to clearness and force, is just as desirable in refutation as elsewhere, and emphasis cannot be attained if attention is given alike to the great and the small points.

(c) *In the third place, answering too much gives undue dignity and importance to many points of the other side.* Insignificant remarks are better left insignificant. To bring them anew to the attention of the audience, and give them the compliment of a serious reply, may help, rather than hinder, an opponent. One way to dispose of a foolish or trivial point is illustrated by Cicero in his defense of Q. Ligarius:—

When Tubero, in his accusation of Ligarius before Caesar, has made it part of his charge, that Ligarius was in Africa during some part of the civil war between Caesar and Pompey; Cicero in his answer, not thinking it deserved a serious reply, contents himself with barely mentioning it ironically. For thus he begins his defense of Ligarius, *Caesar, my kinsman Tubero has laid before you a new crime, and till this day unheard of, that Q. Ligarius was in Africa.*

B. Answering too little. Of the second fault, which consists in answering too little, Adams says:—

The second error in controversy, against which I am anxious of warning you, is that of answering too little. It is not unfrequently found united with that against which I have last admonished you. When too much of our strength is lavished upon the outworks, the citadel is left proportionately defenceless. If we say too much upon points extrinsic to the cause, we shall seldom say enough upon those on which it hinges. To avoid this fault, therefore, it is as essential to ascertain which are the strong parts of your adversary's argument as it is to escape the opposite error of excess. To this effect it is also a duty of the first impression to obtain a control over your own prejudices and feelings. Nothing is so sure to blind us to the real validity of the reasons alleged against us, as our passions. It is so much easier to despise, than to answer an opponent's argument, that wherever we can indulge our contempt, we are apt to forget that it is not refutation.

Sarcasm and scorn may be *aids* to refutation, but they are not *substitutes* for it. In refutation, then, the first essential is to understand what are the few vital points of the other side; to analyze your adversary's case, pick out his "strong parts," and answer them.

C. Answering yourself: "Straw men." Concerning the last and very common error, which consists in "answering yourself," the comment made by Adams cannot be overemphasized:—

But the most inexcusable of all the errors in confutation is that of answering yourself, instead of your adversary, which is done whenever you suppress, or mutilate, or obscure, or misstate, his reasoning, and then reply not to his positions, but to those which you have substituted in their stead. This practice is often the result of misapprehension, when a disputant mistakes the point of the argument urged by his adversary; but it often arises also from design, in which case it should be clearly detected and indignantly exposed. The duty of a disputant is fairly to take and fully to repel the idea of his opponent, and not his own. To misrepresent the meaning of your antagonist evinces a want of candor which the auditory seldom fail to perceive, and which engages their feelings in his favor. When involved in controversy, then, never start against yourself frivolous objections for the sake of showing how easily you can answer them. Quintilian relates an anecdote of the poet Accius, which every controversial writer or speaker will do well to remember. Accius was a writer of tragedies, and being once asked why he, whose dialogue was celebrated for its energy, did not engage in the practice of the bar, answered, because in his tragedies he could make his characters say what he pleased; but that at the bar he should have to contend with persons who would say anything but what he pleased. There can be no possible advantage in supposing our antagonist a fool. The most probable effect of such an imagination is to prove ourselves so.

The words of Accius should be observed by every student of argumentation. It is easy to set up "straw men" and knock them down, but it is dangerous and contemptible. To suggest possible arguments, unless you are sure either that they have already been advanced or that they must be advanced by the other side, is foolish. If the arguments are worth-while, do not help your adversary by suggesting them; if they are not worth-while, it is a waste of time to notice them. Furthermore, it gives an opponent the opportunity to ridicule the effort, by admitting or ignoring the points thus suggested.

III. THREE FUNDAMENTAL REQUIREMENTS

Refutation has the same three fundamental requirements as positive argument. It must not be presumed that refutation is a separate and distinct kind of argumentation. To refute demands skill in the *three R's* of argumentation: *research, reasoning,* and *rhetoric.*

A. Research. Know both sides of the case if you wish to give effective refutation to your opponent's arguments. One needs adequate information to refute an opponent. The man who is informed on a question in controversy can best correct the mistakes of an adversary. Thorough knowledge of all phases of the question is needed, and since, in Webster's phrase, "acquisition is never extemporaneous," a wise debater will not rely on readiness of tongue alone in this department of argumentation. Being "quick with a gun" is of little use when one has no gun at all—or an unloaded one.

B. Reasoning. Sound reasoning, straight thinking, is needed in refutation. Any slip here when one is "correcting" the reasoning of others is doubly disastrous. Clear thinking plus common honesty will keep you from "answering yourself," will enable you to show your readers or hearers just what you are refuting. Only straight thinking will keep your shots true. Often most careful analysis of an opposing argument is needed in order to pick out the exact point to be refuted, or to show the exact clash of discussion. Sometimes throwing the argument into the form of a syllogism will make strikingly clear the basic structure of a confused argument. Lincoln used this device against Douglas in the debate at Galesburg:

Now, remembering the provision of the Constitution which I have read, affirming that that instrument is the supreme law of the land; that the judges of every state shall be bound by it, any law or constitution of any state to the contrary notwithstanding; that the right of property in a slave is affirmed in that Constitution, is made, formed into, and cannot be separated from it without breaking it; durable as the instrument, part of the instrument,—what follows as a short and even syllogistic argument from it? I think it follows, and I submit to the consideration of men capable of argument, whether as I state it, in syllogistic form the argument has any fault in it?

Nothing in the constitution or laws of any state can destroy a right distinctly and expressly affirmed in the Constitution of the United States.

The right of property in a slave is distinctly and expressly affirmed in the Constitution of the United States.

Therefore, nothing in the constitution or laws of any state can destroy the right of property in a slave.

I believe that no fault can be pointed out in that argument; assuming the truth of the premises, the conclusion, so far as I have capacity at all to understand it, follows inevitably. There is a fault in it, as I think, but the fault is not in the reasoning; the falsehood, in fact, is a fault in the premises. I believe that the right of property in a slave is not distinctly and expressly affirmed in the Constitution, and Judge Douglas thinks it is.

C. Rhetoric. Lastly, all that goes to make effective expression, rhetoric—oral or written—is of unusual importance in refutation. Careless, inaccurate, disorganized style, or a weak and listless delivery, will counteract the good effects of both thorough knowledge and sound reasoning. Fact is the bullet, reasoning is the aim, and expression (we trust no untoward application of our figure will be made) is the force that drives the bullet to its mark.

IV. POSITION OF REFUTATION

With respect to the method of handling refutation, a common word of advice is to follow up refutation with positive proof. This suggestion, however, is of a general nature and is open to exceptions. But it must not be forgotten that refutation is destructive; it demolishes, but does not build up. To make men act or thoroughly believe, it is not enough to make them see there is no reason why they should not be convinced; they must be made to see that there is a positive reason why they should be convinced. Consequently, pure refutation is weak and lacks the strongest elements of conviction; it is a necessary help, but is not sufficient in itself. It is, therefore, generally an anticlimax to place refutation at the end of the discussion, or at the end of any important division of the argument. Positive proof rather than refutation should be given the most emphatic place.

This leads to the matter of the *arrangement* of refutation. With espect to the strength and the weakness of the points of refutation, the same rules apply as in positive proof; the emphatic places are the beginning and the end. If, then, the answer to be made is strong, it may well be put first or toward the last. Weaker answers are best hidden in the middle. However, it often happens that an opponent makes a *point* or presents some idea, *which must be overthrown before the speaker or writer can proceed* with his own proof. In such circumstances, clearly, the answer to the point must be made at the *very beginning* of the rejoinder. Doubt often arises as to whether it is best to make the answer a distinct point in the discussion, or to introduce it merely as an incident to some other point. This depends upon the importance of the argument to be answered, and so is a question of personal judgment in each particular case. In general, however, such answers are best given in connection with those parts of one's own proof with which they are naturally associated. In fact, they should always be considered wherever they happen to arise in the course of one's own argument, except where there is a particular definite reason (such as extreme importance of the point made or effective challenge of the previous speaker) for setting this rule aside. Then usually such refutation should be given before constructive argument. It is therefore true in general that, with the exception of the most vital of the proofs of the opposition, *refutation is best made as the occasion for the answer arises in the course of one's own demonstration.* These individual points that may be taken up as they arise are sometimes called *"special refutation."* But if the answer to an opponent's argument is, under the circumstances, of such importance as to make any large part of the question depend upon it, there should be no hesitation in making it one of the *main points of the proof,* and emphasizing it as such. Such a main point may be taken up wherever it most logically fits into the case. These large fundamental points that make an important part of the case are sometimes called *"general refutation."*

V. BASIC RULE FOR ALL REFUTATION

Before taking up any of the particular methods there is one principle of refutation that should be emphasized. *Always make perfectly clear to the audience or reader just what is the point that is to be attacked, and the nature of the attack to be made.* Show *what* you are going to refute, and *how* you are going to refute it. Repeat what your opponent has said and then say that you will show this to be *false, irrelevant, unimportant, untrustworthy,* etc., as the case may be. The statement to which objection is made should always be *distinctly* made at the start, and its place in the case—its relation to main points, issues, or proposition—should be clearly shown. This statement should be supplemented, while the reply is being presented, by whatever explanations are necessary, in order to make evident the purposes and results of the answer. It must be made clear that there are two opposing arguments which directly meet, and that one overthrows the other. The force of refutation is destructive, and it cannot achieve its full effect unless the audience understands *just what is to be destroyed,* and *just how the refutation accomplished the destruction.* In order to apply this basic rule it is of course necessary that the debater know the kinds of weakness in an argument that are expressed by calling it false, irrelevant, unimportant, inadmissible, etc. Above all things be sure to use one of these legitimate attacks on the *argument of the opponent* rather than an attack on your opponent by calling him a liar, a dunce, a blundering debater, or one who is ignorant of the law. Attack the argument, not the arguer.

A study of forensic and deliberative oratory shows the painstaking care to observe this rule used by the ablest speakers and writers. The following is an example of Webster's method in forensic refutation, a model of clearness in introducing refutation. The quotation is from his speech in the case of Ogden *vs.* Saunders:—

Here we meet the opposite arguments, stated on different occasions in different terms, but usually summed up in this, that the law itself is a part of the contract, and therefore cannot impair it. What does it mean? Let us seek for clear ideas. It does not mean that the law gives any particular construction to the terms of the contract, or that it makes the promise, or the consideration, or the time of performance, other than is expressed in the instrument itself. It can only mean that it is to be taken as a part of the contract or understanding of the parties, that the contract itself shall be enforced by such laws and regulations respecting remedy and for the enforcement of contracts as are in being in the State where it is made at the time of entering into it. This is meant, or nothing very clearly intelligible is meant, by saying the law is part of the contract. . . .

Against this we contend:—

1st. That, if the proposition were true, the consequence would not follow.

2nd. That the proposition itself cannot be maintained.

To take an illustration from a deliberative oration: Webster, in replying to Calhoun in the Senate, on the question of the protective tariff, divided his speech into five parts, corresponding to the five main points of his opponent. The following are the sentences introductory to these parts respectively:—

I. In treating of protection, or protective duties, the first proposition of the honorable member is, that all duties laid on imports really fall on exports; that they are a toll paid for going to market.

II. Another opinion of the honorable member is, that increased production brings about expansion of the currency, and that such increase makes a further increase necessary. His idea is, that, if some goods are imported, the amount of exports still keeping up, the whole export being thus paid for by the import, specie must be brought to settle the balance; that this increase of specie gives new powers to the banks to discount; that the banks thereupon make large issues, till the mass of currency becomes redundant and swollen; that this swollen currency augments the price of articles of our own manufacture, and makes it necessary to raise prices still higher, and this creates a demand for the imposition of new duties. This, as I understand it, is the honorable member's train of thought.

III. There is a third general idea of the honorable gentleman, upon which I would make a few observations. It is, that the South and West are the great consumers of the products of the North and East; that the capacity of the South to consume depends on her great staples; and that the sale of these depends mainly on a foreign market.

IV. A fourth sentiment of the honorable member is, that the removal of all duties increases the exportation of articles manufactured at home.

V. Finally, the honorable member is of the opinion that the whole system of protection was prostrated, and is prostrated, cut up, root and branch, and exterminated forever, by the State interposition of South Carolina.

VI. METHODS OF REFUTATION

Refutation is the destruction of opposing proofs. Any method by which the proof of an opponent may be weakened or destroyed is a "method of refutation." There are four different sets of such methods in argumentation. It must be borne in mind, however, that these are *not mutually exclusive* lists. In many points they practically coincide, being simply different names for the same things, because these things are looked at from different standpoints. We have considered three of these sets under evidence, forms of argument, and fallacies. The fourth is "special rhetorical devices." It is needless to do more than mention the first three here.

A. Tests of evidence. Showing that the evidence presented by an opponent is unsound—in some way fails to meet the proper tests of such evidence—is effective refutation. (See Chapter VII.)

B. Attack on the forms of arguments. Demonstrating the weakness of any argument by the use of the tests discussed in Chapter VIII is also an excellent method of refuting an adversary.

C. Fallacies. When we expose a fallacy in another's argument we are using a very common and very effective method of refuting him. (See Chapter XVI.)

D. Special rhetorical devices. The fourth list of special rhetorical devices, not found in any of these other lists, is usually given separately in a list of the methods of refutation. These devices are (1) *reductio ad absurdum,* (2) dilemma, (3) residues, and (4) turning the tables.

1. **Reductio ad absurdum.** One of the most commonly used methods of refutation is that of reducing an argument to an absurdity, or, as it is named, the *reductio ad absurdum.* The refuter adopts for the moment the line of argument of his opponent; then, by carrying it out to its logical conclusion, shows that it results in an absurdity. For example, when a lawyer asserted in court that a corporation can make no oral contract because it has no tongue, the judge exposed the fallacy by saying, simply, "Then, according to your own argument, a corporation could not make a written contract because it has no hand."

Cicero uses this method in the following:—

Nor, if Publius Crassus was both an orator and a lawyer, is the knowledge of the civil law for that reason included in the power of speaking. For if any man, who, while excelling in any art or science, has acquired another, shall hold that his additional knowledge is a part of that in which he previously excelled, we may, by such a mode of argument, pretend that to play well at tennis is a part of the knowledge of civil law, because Publius Mucius was skilled in both.

Macaulay makes striking use of this device:—

Many politicians of our time are in the habit of laying it down as a self-evident proposition, that no people ought to be free till they are fit to use their freedom. The maxim is worthy of the fool in the old story, who resolved not to go into the water until he had learned to swim. If men are to wait for liberty until they become wise and good in slavery, they may indeed wait forever.

This method is effective because of its simplicity and directness; it also has in it an element of ridicule that is persuasive against an opponent. William Ellery Channing, in a reply to Henry Clay on the slavery question, used this method as follows:—

But this property, we are told, is not to be questioned on account of its long duration. "Two hundred years of legislation have sanctioned and *sanctified* negro slaves as property." Nothing but respect for the speaker could repress criticism on this unhappy phraseology. We will trust it escaped him without thought. But to confine ourselves to the argument from duration; how obvious the reply! Is injustice changed into justice by the practice of ages? Is my victim made a righteous prey because I have bowed him to the earth till he cannot rise? For more than two hundred years heretics were burned, and not by mobs, not by lynch law, but by the decrees of councils, at the instigation of theologians, and with the sanction of the laws and religions of nations; and was this a reason for keeping up the fires, that they had burned two hundred years? In the Eastern world, successive despots, not for two hundred years, but for twice two thousand, have claimed the right of life and death over millions, and, with no law but their own will, have beheaded, bowstrung, starved, tortured unhappy men without number who have incurred their wrath; and does the lapse of so many centuries sanctify murder and ferocious power?

Again:—

But the great argument remains. It is said that this property must not be questioned, because it is established by law. "That *is* property which the law declares *to be* property." This human law is made supreme, decisive, in a question of morals. Thus the idea of an eternal, immutable justice is set at naught. Thus the great rule of human life is made to be the ordinance of interested men. But there *is* a higher tribunal, a throne of equal justice, immovable by the conspiracy of all human legislatures. "That is property which the law declares to be property." Then the laws have only to declare you, or me, or Mr. Clay, to be property, and we become chattels and are bound to bear the yoke! Does not even man's moral nature repel this doctrine too intuitively to leave time or need for argument?

2. The dilemma. This is one of the oldest of all known rhetorical forms. As a method of refutation, it consists in reducing an issue to an alternative, and then showing that both members of the alternative are untenable. These two members are called the "horns of the dilemma." The refuter says in substance: "Now, with respect to this point at issue, there are two and only two possibilities, *viz.*, A and B. But A is not true, and B is not true; consequently your contention fails." In order to make the dilemma conclusive, obviously two things are necessary: (1) The horns of the dilemma must include all the possibilities in the case, *i.e., the alternative must be exact;* (2) *Both members of the alternative must be destroyed.*

James Wilson, speaking in the convention for the province of Pennsylvania, in vindication of the colonies, January, 1775, used the dilemma as follows:

In the first place, then, I say that the persons who allege that those employed to alter the charter and constitution of Massachusetts Bay act by virtue of a commission from his majesty for that purpose, speak improperly, and contrary to the truth of the case. I say they do not act by virtue of such a commission. What is called a commission either contains particular directions for the purpose mentioned, or it contains no such particular directions. In either case can those, who act for that purpose, act by virtue of a commission? In one case, what is called a commission is void; it has no legal existence; it can communicate no authority. In the other case, it extends not to the purpose mentioned. The latter point is too plain to be insisted on; I (will) prove the former.

Jeremiah S. Black, in defense of the right of trial by jury, thus attacked the contention of his opponents, which was that the law of nations was binding in the trial of the cause in question:—

Our friends on the other side are quite conscious that when they deny the binding obligation of the Constitution they must put some other system of law in its place. Their brief gives us notice that, while the Constitution, and the acts of Congress, and *Magna Charta*, and the common law, and all the rules of natural justice shall remain under foot, they will try American citizens according to *the law of nations!* But the law of nations takes no notice of the subject. If that system did contain a special provision that a government might hang one of its own citizens without a judge or jury, it would still be competent for the American people to say, as they have said, that no such thing should ever be done here. That is my answer to the law of nations.

a. More than two horns. Sometimes the possibilities with respect to the point in issue cannot be reduced to two. There may be a choice offered of any one of three or more possible conditions, or courses of action. In such a case, to state the issue in the form of a dilemma, presenting a single alternative, would not be an exact disjunction, and so would be fallacious; to be truthful it is always necessary to state *all* the possibilities of choice, whatever their number. When more than two possibilities are to be considered, the method is, properly speaking, not a dilemma; but the *modus operandi* is similar. Webster, in his argument in the case of the Providence Railroad Co. *vs.* the City of Boston, made a division into three possibilities. Mr. Webster is here contending against the proposition that a certain street or piece of land is a public highway:—

If this street, or land, or whatever it may be, has become and now is a public highway, it must have become so in one of three ways, and to these points I particularly call your honor's attention.

1st. It must either have become a highway by having been regularly laid out according to usage and law; or

2nd. By *dedication* as such by those having the power to dedicate it, and acceptance and adoption so far as they are required; or

3rd. As a highway by long use without the existence of proof of any original laying out, or dedication.

It is not pretended by any one that the land in question is a highway, upon the last of these grounds. I shall therefore confine myself to the consideration of the other two questions; namely, "Was there ever a formal and regular laying out of a street here? or was there ever a regular and sufficient dedication and acceptance?"

b. Faulty disjunction of the dilemma. In this situation, an opening is left for an opponent which may result in great discomfiture to the author of the defective dilemma.

Thus Lincoln, in his speech on the Dred Scott Decision, refused to accept either of the horns of the dilemma presented by Douglas. Lincoln said of Douglas:—

He finds the Republicans insisting that the Declaration of Independence includes all men, black as well as white, and forthwith he boldly denies that it includes negroes at all, and proceeds to argue gravely that all who contend it does, do so only because they want to vote, to eat, and sleep, and marry with negroes. He will have it that they cannot be consistent else. Now I protest against the counterfeit logic which concludes that because I do not want a black woman for a slave, I must necessarily want her for a wife. I need not have her for either. I can just leave her alone.

3. The method of residues. Like that of the dilemma, this method is founded upon a division of the point in question into parts. The difference is that in the dilemma all the parts are destroyed, whereas, in the method of residues, one of the parts is left standing. By the method of residues, the matter in dispute is divided into two or more sections, which include all the possibilities in the case; then all but one of these are demolished, the one left standing being the aspect of the issue which the refuter wishes to establish. "There are," says the refuter, "three possibilities, A, B, and C. But A and B are false, consequently the presumption is that C is true." This method is not, strictly speaking, a method of refuting. It is rather a method of using refutation: the ultimate purpose of the speaker or writer is not destructive, but constructive; he destroys some of the parts into which he divides the question, in order that he may establish the remaining part. He uses refutation to accomplish his end; but the end itself is constructive proof.

a. Division must be exhaustive. *The first requisite in using the method of residues is that the division of the whole into parts shall be exhaustive.* The strength of the method depends entirely upon the assumption that all the possibilities in the case are destroyed save one. If, then, the disputant omits, in his division, to mention one of the possibilities, he has proved nothing, for it still remains uncertain which possibility is true—the one he seeks to establish or the one he failed to mention. Again, in order to make the work complete, it is usually necessary that the residual part be enforced by positive demonstration. The refutation of all but one of the possibilities leaves a presumption that the remaining possibility is true; but there may well be a suspicion that even this last part too is false, or that there is some fallacy in the division. Consequently, to be at all convincing the residual part must be enforced by positive proof.

Burke, in his speech on conciliation with America, used the method of residues. He began:—

> Sir, if I were capable of engaging you to an equal attention, I would state, that as far as I am capable of discerning, there are but three ways of proceeding relative to this stubborn spirit which prevails in your Colonies, and disturbs your government. These are:—to change that spirit, as inconvenient, by removing the causes; to prosecute it as criminal; or, to comply with it as necessary. I would not be guilty of an imperfect enumeration; I can think of but these three. Another has indeed been started, that of giving up the Colonies; but it met so slight a reception that I do not think myself obliged to dwell a great while upon it. It is nothing but a little sally of anger, like the frowardness of peevish children, who, when they cannot get all they would have, are resolved to take nothing.

He then considered the first two ways at length and proved them impracticable, and concluded:—

> If then the removal of the causes of this spirit of American liberty be, for the greater part, or rather entirely impracticable; if the ideas of criminal process be inapplicable, or if applicable are in the highest degree inexpedient, what way yet remains? No way is open, but the third and last, to comply with the American spirit as necessary; or, if you please, to submit to it as a necessary evil.

4. "Turning the tables." By this is meant showing that something presented by your opponent really supports your case and not his. It is "stealing his thunder." To turn the argument of an opponent against him is not often possible. But circumstances sometimes give the opportunity. A piece of testimony may be used by a writer, when he has not fully considered all the interpretations that may be put upon it. It not infrequently happens that evidence, or an argument, is introduced to give support to some particular point, and, in its bearing on that phase of the question, the evidence may be favorable to the speaker or writer who introduces it; but as the discussion proceeds, it may turn out that, with respect to some other phase of the question, the evidence or the

argument may be interpreted in another way, adversely to the one who introduced it. The effect of such an unexpected turn of affairs is obvious; the opponent is "hoist with his own petard."

Lincoln "turned the tables" admirably in his speech at Cooper Union in February, 1860.

Some of you delight to flaunt in our faces the warning against sectional parties given by Washington in his *Farewell Address*. Less than eight years before Washington gave that warning he had, as President of the United States, approved and signed an act of Congress enforcing the prohibition of slavery in the Northwestern Territory, which act embodied the policy of the government, upon that subject, up to and at the very moment he penned that warning; and about one year after he penned it, he wrote Lafayette that he considered that prohibition a wise measure, expressing in the same connection his hope that we should at some time have a confederacy of free states.

Bearing this in mind and seeing that sectionalism has since arisen upon this same subject, is that warning a weapon in your hand against us or in our hands against you? Could Washington himself speak, would he cast the blame of that sectionalism upon us who sustain his policy, or upon you who repudiate it? We respect that warning of Washington and we commend it to you, together with his example pointing to the right application of it.

VII. REBUTTAL

A. Rebuttal explained. General refutation has already been defined as the destruction of opposing proofs. It is either evidence or argument presented, not for the purpose of directly advancing your own case, but of blocking or destroying the case of your opponent. It is the almost universal practice in courts, in contest debating, and in actual debates in assemblies of various sorts, to provide for special periods after the main case has been presented in which evidence and argument can be advanced in refutation of the main case. Such periods are called rebuttal periods. Speeches made at such times are called rebuttal speeches. In law, rebuttal is "the giving of evidence on the part of a plaintiff (affirmative) to destroy the effect of evidence introduced by the defendant (negative) in the same suit." (Webster's Dictionary.) In some debates, both contest and real, this legal precedent is more closely followed, and the affirmative only has rebuttal speeches. Of course, all speakers on both sides may have more or less refutation in the main speeches. Since the order of speaking and the nature of negative cases give the negative speakers superior opportunities for refutation in the main speeches, it is well to give the affirmative some compensating advantages in rebuttal. So even where both sides have equal rebuttal speeches, the negative leads in rebuttal, giving the affirmative the last rebuttal speech. Refutation is the broader of the terms (as we use them) and rebuttal is the refutation that is given in a special speech which has properly no (or very little) constructive material in it.

B. No new constructive points of importance should be allowed in the rebuttal speeches. Only such material as can be used *against the opponents' case as presented* should be permitted. It has already been suggested that it is well in a debate where a man may speak more than once to hold material in reserve for rebuttal. It is, of course, possible to repeat or refer to arguments and evidence already given, but such repetition or reference must be subordinate to rebuttal and used destructively, not constructively. But the repetition of old materials is never quite so strong as the production of new. So that it is sometimes good strategy, even at the cost of taking something away from the strength of a first speech, to hold back some good evidence as a reserve. The judges of contest debates, however, should always penalize debaters who simply repeat or continue their main speeches during the time allowed for rebuttal. All that has been said above concerning refutation applies to rebuttal speeches in debate. Refutation is the very essence of debate, and the power to refute well is one to be sought by a debater as earnestly as he would seek any single power that a public speaker may hope to possess.

C. The preparation of rebuttal. While this should be very carefully done, it does not mean that rebuttal speeches should be memorized, or even written out.

1. The rebuttal must be prepared in advance. The material out of which to fashion rebuttal speeches should be carefully gathered and arranged for rapid use. Many contest debaters fail in this phase of their work. In debate, rebuttal is *no less important than positive proof;* in intercollegiate debates it is most often the rebuttal that is decisive; in any discussion it is the "last speech" that is coveted; Webster's famous "Reply to Hayne" was almost pure refutation. And it is very seldom that successful refutation is *impromptu*. *Good rebuttal speeches are practically always extempore,* not impromptu, nor memorized. An anecdote in point is told concerning one of the most brilliant advocates of the English bar. This lawyer was one day arguing an important case before one of the highest tribunals of the country. In the course of the trial he was made the object of an attack, personal and political in nature, from his opponent, the attorney for the prosecution. The attack was bitter, but forcible and persuasive. It seemed to be unexpected by everyone; the court was surprised, but manifestly affected. The advocate arose to make reply, and in his introduction, with perfect calmness and great eloquence, he answered every charge, retrieved the lost favor of the court, and overpowered his assailant with an irresistible invective. After this trial was finished, one of the judges—a personal friend—expressed his surprise and admiration at the extraordinary eloquence of the reply, declaring the retort to be one of the most brilliant passages ever heard in an English court of law, and adding that he had never believed such impromptu oratory to be within the limits of human powers. In answer to these congratulations, the advocate invited the justice to accompany him to his law chambers. Entering his library, he walked to a desk, opened a drawer, and took from it a manuscript; it was his speech of the morning written out in full, nearly word for word as he had delivered it. He had foreseen a contingency that nobody else had expected or deemed possible, and had made ready to meet the situation. He won because he had prepared in advance.

Memorized preparation, however, is always to be avoided (if possible) in debate, and should rarely be attempted by beginners, especially in contest debating. There is, in the first place, too great danger that the opposition will not say just what you are prepared to answer—and there is in debate no greater exhibition of incompetence, no greater indication of weakness, than is afforded by a memorized rebuttal that does not *fit*. Preparation of material to meet extemporaneously *any* stand taken by the opposition is good preparation. Anything else is weak and dangerous. Daniel Webster declared that all the material of his "Reply to Hayne" had been gathered and waiting in his desk for months before the debate.

Speaking of Senator Hayne, he said to a friend: "If he had tried to make a speech to fit my notes, he could not have hit it better. No man is ever inspired with the occasion; I never was." Mere words and gestures do not make refutation any more than they make positive proof. There must be just as much evidence in the one as in the other. Rebuttal demands as careful a choice of weapons and as accurate a method of handling them as any other kind of proof. Invention, selection, and arrangement demand as much preliminary planning here as elsewhere.

2. **Know the other side.** Clearly, the primary necessity in preparing refutation is to know just what points we may be called upon to answer; we must have a clear and accurate understanding of the points our opponents need to establish, and of the methods they may adopt in the attempt. Would any capable general ever lay the plans for a battle without first considering the position of his enemy, his location, his points of strength and weakness? As we discovered earlier, the selection of the main heads of the brief in debate depends very largely upon what the opposition may be able to "do about it." Those points must be chosen for emphasis, points that hit hardest and straightest at *the necessary* proofs of the other side (when we are able to tell in advance what such necessary proof will be); and at the same time we must remember that these main heads will surely be attacked, and we must take up a position that is defensible against assault. All this means a study and comparison of the two sides of the question, so as to find out what arguments need to be attacked, and, on the other hand, how one's own arguments may be best defended against the particular attack the other side will have to make.

3. **Be ready for surprises.** But it is rarely possible to foresee every argument that an opponent may advance. No two persons reason just alike: an opponent may well look at the question from some peculiar standpoint, or, as more often happens, he may plan a surprise. Then, too, there are many minor questions that are raised in such a discussion, which it is hardly worth-while trying to anticipate, or which escape notice in preparation. Commonly, these minor points are best left unanswered; but sometimes circumstances make them worth notice. Whatever the reason, it is certain that all the incidents of a debate cannot be foreseen; we

must always expect the unexpected. A successful debater must always be ready to meet strange situations, and to manufacture more or less of refutation and of proof on the scene of action. A debater who has read only on those phases of the question that are of interest to him, or who undertakes only those parts of the discussion that he treats in his own proof, is helpless in such circumstances. He has no resources to draw upon. If the discussion were in writing, he might think it over, consult new authorities, and plan his answer; but in debate there is no such opportunity. He must act at once. He is in the predicament of a military expedition that sets out on a long campaign, with a day's rations and no base of supplies. When a debater is thus surprised, his only hope must lie in having a thorough knowledge of the question *as a whole, and in all its details,* a knowledge so thorough as to be ready at the call of any exigency. Furthermore, a broad understanding of the foundations and general conditions of the question is necessary, in order to be able to estimate rightly the force and bearing of arguments that are made by opponents. A debater who does not understand the basic assumptions or premises on which his own and his opponent's cases rest is almost hopeless in rebuttal. A superficial preparation always distorts the mental vision of a speaker, and confuses in his mind the real issues in the discussion. But debate demands an especially clear perception and quick judgment of what is vital; the debater must think as quickly and act as decisively as the broker on the exchange; superficial information or a confused understanding mean as sure disaster in the one case as in the other. A debater in action must be able, when any argument or any evidence is brought against him, to estimate in a few seconds just what the matter amounts to, how it is related to his own case, how much to say about it, and where—in what part of his speech—to answer it. *Here a stock of ready-made arguments becomes useless. Only a deep understanding of the subject to the very bottom can give the clear, ready insight, and the steady judgment that alone avails.*

D. Effect of time limit. These foregoing suggestions are especially applicable in preparation for school or college debates. There the limitations of time are very stringent: not the smallest fraction of a minute can be lost in confusion or unnecessary deliberation; the answer must be in the debater's head as soon as the argument has left his opponent's lips. This necessity for such preparation, important everywhere, here intensified by the circumstances, constitutes one of the most valuable phases of contest debating.

E. Answer whole case. Too much emphasis cannot be given to the remarks made earlier concerning what to answer in refutation. It is probably worth-while here to discuss this question with particular reference to the rebuttal speeches in formal debate. The great fundamental principle which should guide the preparation of all rebuttal speeches is: *Answer the whole case of the other side.* One of the fatal weaknesses in the equipment of any debater, and a weakness that is almost invariably displayed by a beginner, is the weakness of attacking only a part of an opponent's proof. It is easiest in refutation to pick out the weak points of the opposition and attack them, leaving the more formidable points standing. It demands less careful preparation, and a less accurate analysis of the case of the other side, and it often seems to make the greatest impression on the audience. Consequently there is a temptation to pick up the more obvious errors of an opponent and dramatically expose them, or to seize upon some foolish word or phrase and ridicule it; it brings a laugh or a burst of applause, whereas, in an attempt to refute any of the stronger proofs, success is not so easy, for the audience, feeling that there are two sides to the issue, is not so readily convinced. But in the end, the audience will probably adhere to the man who has made it believe that his case, as a whole, is the stronger. Consequently, to achieve final success, the debater must endeavor to make it see, not that he has destroyed an argument here and there, but that he has overwhelmed the proof against him in its entirety.

1. Find the fundamental points. In order to make an attack upon the whole case of the other side, *two things are necessary.* In the *first* place, *the speaker must analyze the entire proof of his opponents and pick out the few basic points in it.* It is necessary to determine upon the few fundamental points of an opponent's proof, for the same reason that it is necessary to determine upon those of one's own. It is necessary for the sake of *clearness;* to give the same attention to the large and the small points of the other side perplexes a hearer in his understanding of the question as a whole. It is necessary for the sake of *emphasis;* it is only by neglecting or slighting trivial facts and dwelling upon the important ones, that the vital points of the question can be brought out into a clear light. It is necessary for the sake of *saving time;* rebuttal speeches are usually short, and definitely limited. To give attention to the facts of secondary importance is to waste part of these precious minutes. If the vital points of an opponent's contentions are destroyed, his subordinate points fall with them and so do not need special rebuttal. These main contentions must be answered if an opponent is to be defeated at all, and, if they are answered, *to do more is superfluous.*

2. **Show the audience that these points cover the case.** But it is not enough for a debater merely to select the important points of the other side, and proceed to refute them; he must, in the second place, *make it clear to the audience that in answering these points he is meeting the whole case* against him—that these *are* the foundations of the opposing case. To give the rebuttal its full effect requires that the audience be made to see that the speaker is attacking the entire proof in opposition, and that, if he succeeds, he has won his case. To do this requires that the arguments to be answered shall be stated clearly beforehand, and that they shall be explained in such a way as to make it evident that in them is contained the whole of the other side. It is very often desirable, as a means of making it evident that the whole case of the other side is being attacked, to *analyze openly* before the audience the proof of an opponent, and explain just what his argument as a whole amounts to. For instance, a speaker in rebuttal might well begin in some such manner as this: "Everything of any importance that my opponent has had to say on this question may be reduced to these three propositions, *viz.,* first, etc., second, etc., third, etc.," or "My opponent's case, as far as it has been presented to us, can be stated in his own words, as follows, etc." In some such way the audience may be made to have faith in the speaker's sincerity and in the importance of his efforts in rebuttal, and so be made ready to acknowledge the full force of his refutation.

For example, Webster, in his "Reply to Hayne" in the debate on the Foote Resolution, devoted a great deal of his speech to the refutation of Senator Hayne's theory of states' rights under the Constitution. Before entering on this task, he set forth in full the case presented by Senator Hayne, stating all the essential propositions of his doctrine, and making it evident that taken together they embraced everything that demanded refutation:—

There yet remains to be performed by far the most grave and important duty, which I feel to be devolved on me by this occasion. It is to state, and to defend, what I conceive to be the true principles of the Constitution under which we are here assembled. I might well have desired that so weighty a task should have fallen into other and abler hands. I could have wished that it should have been executed by those whose character and experience give weight and influence to their opinions, such as cannot possibly belong to mine. But, sir, I have met the occasion, not sought it; and I shall proceed to state my own sentiments, without challenging for them any particular regard, with studied plainness, and as much precision as possible.

I understand the honorable gentleman from South Carolina to maintain, that it is a right of State Legislatures to interfere, whenever, in their judgment, this Government transcends its constitutional limits, and to arrest the operation of its laws.

I understand him to maintain this right, as a right existing under the Constitution; not as a right to overthrow it, on the ground of extreme necessity, such as would justify violent revolution.

I understand him to maintain an authority, on the part of the states, thus to interfere, for the purpose of correcting the exercise of power by the General Government, of checking it, and of compelling it to conform to their opinion of the extent of its powers.

I understand him to maintain that the ultimate power of judging of the constitutional extent of its own authority is not lodged exclusively in the General Government, or any branch of it; but that, on the contrary, the States may lawfully decide for themselves, and each state for itself, whether in a given case, the act of the General Government transcends its power.

I understand him to insist that, if the exigency of the case, in the opinion of any State Government, require it, such State Government may, by its own sovereign authority, annul an act of the General Government, which it deems plainly and palpably unconstitutional.

F. Have a clear and careful method. The natural tendency of young debaters in rebuttal is toward carelessness of method. It is true, even of more experienced debaters, that speakers who are very careful in arranging and presenting their original proofs, when they come to the work of refutation, forget themselves and degenerate into a weak informality, wandering from the point and mixing up their materials without regard for clearness of statement, the proper arrangement of evidence, or the natural sequence of the proofs. Rebuttal is not necessarily more informal than any other part of a debate or discussion, and requires just as much care in presentation. The materials for it must be selected as judiciously, arranged as logically, and stated as clearly. A young debater does well to watch himself consciously till he has formed firm habits of the right kind.

G. Be fair to opponents. The final word in regard to rebuttal speeches is: *Be fair, courteous, good-humored, and honest in dealing with the opposing case.* State the opposing arguments fairly. Do not color them to suit yourself by rephrasing, or substituting, or inserting words not used by your antagonist. In the use of charts and maps, in asking to examine evidence, in giving opponents an opportunity to examine your evidence, be courteous. You will hurt your own case and make your audience uncomfortable by being churlish and ill-tempered. It is probably not necessary here to advocate and advise common honesty. An honest man will be an honest debater. Manufacturing evidence, garbling quotations, falsifying references, misstating facts—these things are not "strategy," and "part of the game." They are simply cheap dishonesty—plain lies. No self-respecting debater will indulge in such practices. In contest debating when the stupid or dishonest are detected in such practices, permanent disbarment from platform activities should be the minimum penalty.

Exercises

1. Identify and explain the methods of refutation used in one of the debate speeches in Appendix A or B.
2. Evaluate the refutation in one speech in Appendix A or B in these terms:
   a. Was too much answered?
   b. Was too little answered?
   c. Was a "straw man" attacked?
3. Compare the research, reasoning, and rhetoric which went into two opposing speeches as in Dewey *vs.* Stassen or Gould *vs.* Lucas.

4. Select two opposing rebuttal speeches in a printed debate (as in the *University Debater's Annual*) and evaluate them in terms of the advice given in Section VII ("Rebuttal") of this chapter.

5. Oral assignment: a direct-clash exercise. Divide the class into groups of four or five persons. Each group should be assigned a carefully phrased clash point which has been drawn from a familiar proposition. Let the first speaker lead off with a five-minute defense of the point as phrased. Thereafter, all other members of the group should alternate by sides in attacking and defending that point in four-minute speeches. The criticism and evaluation should incorporate the doctrine of this chapter.

Chapter **XVIII** · KINDS OF DEBATE

In Chapter 1 we defined argumentation and debate and indicated some of the more important areas in which these forms of discourse operate. Here we are concerned specifically with debate and its applications in a free society.

I. WHAT DEBATE IS

Debate consists of opposing arguments on a given proposition between a supporting affirmative and an opposing negative. As such, it provides some of the more important applications of the principles of argumentation with which this book is concerned. Debates may take place wherever opposing arguments meet, whether it be a street corner, a radio microphone, a court of law, a political campaign, or a legislative assembly. Formal rules or no rules at all may govern these arguments, and the purposes of the participants may vary tremendously.

The discourse among persons in which debate plays an important role is conducted primarily for purposes of learning and action. And of these two, debate is more concerned with action. It is first and foremost a policy-determining technique. It is in this capacity that debate serves a social purpose of great practical importance. Indeed, it is difficult to conceive of a democratic society of any kind in which the members of this society did not resort to debate as a means of resolving issues and determining policy. Problems, differences, conflicts are inevitable in any society. Where these problems are of a sort that they must be settled in one way or another, and differences persist after every reasonable effort to secure a consensus, the logical and sensible recourse for civilized human beings is debate. The most usual form of this debate is parliamentary debate or legislative debate under the regulations of parliamentary procedure. Motions are made, debated, and acted upon, and the motions so adopted (usually by majority vote) become the law of the land or the policy of whatever group has taken the action.

II. LEGISLATIVE DEBATE

Legislative debate is conducted for the purpose of reaching a group decision on matters of policy in organized legislative bodies. All that has been said in this book about propositions, issues, evidence, kinds of argument, cases, and other matters applies to such debate. We present here the rules of procedure under which such debate is usually conducted. Further advice may be obtained by consulting handbooks on parliamentary law.

Parliamentary law consists of a system of common rules and practices for the government of deliberative assemblies. To this same body of rules and practices the name *rules of order* is often applied. The rules included are the ones that are employed in assemblies generally. In individual assemblies there are often special rules which arise as motions and which are not embodied in the *constitution* or *by-laws* of an organization. These special rules are known as *standing rules*. The record of standing rules is found in the written minutes of the organization; the rules of order are usually those contained in some manual of parliamentary law; while the constitution and by-laws are usually the written instruments of an organization.

In so far as there is an ultimate authority for parliamentary law, it will be found in the practices common to deliberate assemblies generally. General usage is the ultimate authority, and this usage has been the slow evolution of centuries. It has been added to now and then by legal-minded philosophers, and "infiltrated with the common sense of the many," so that while even yet it is not a perfect system, it is well adapted to the needs of ordinary deliberative assemblies.

Parliamentary law may vary in the details of its rules, but underlying it all there are found four invariable foundation principles or corner stones, upon which every portion of the superstructure rests. They are (1) justice and courtesy to all, (2) one thing at a time, (3) the rule of the majority, (4) the rights of the minority.[1]

The following table of motions represents those used in most deliberative assemblies:

[1] F. M. Gregg, *Handbook of Parliamentary Law*, Chicago, Ginn and Company, copyright 1910, pp. 51–52.

TABLE OF PARLIAMENTARY MOTIONS

Motions	Need a Second?	Amend-able?	Debat-able?	Vote Re-quired	May Inter-rupt a Speaker
I. Principal Motion					
1. Any main question or any independent matter of business before the meeting	yes	yes	yes	maj.	no
II. Subsidiary Motions					
2. To amend	yes	yes	yes	maj.	no
3. To postpone indefinitely	yes	no	yes	maj.	no
4. To refer to a committee	yes	yes	yes	maj.	no
5. To postpone to a certain time	yes	yes	yes	maj.	no
6. Previous question	yes	no	no	$\frac{2}{3}$	no
7. To lay on (or take from) the table	yes	no	no	maj.	no
III. Incidental Motions					
8. To suspend a rule	yes	no	no	$\frac{2}{3}$	no
9. To withdraw a motion	yes	no	no	maj.	no
10. Question of consideration	no	no	no	$\frac{2}{3}$	yes
11. A point of order	no	no	no	Chair[a]	yes
12. Appeal from decision of chair	yes	no	no	maj.	yes
IV. Privileged Motions					
13. To make a matter of business a "special order" for a given time	no	no	no	$\frac{2}{3}$	yes
14. Questions of rights and privileges	no	no	no	Chair[a]	yes
15. To adjourn (unqualified)	yes	no	no	maj.	no
16. To fix time for next meeting.	yes	yes	no	maj.	no

[a] Require only decision of Chair; no vote unless appealed.

The sixteen motions listed in this table are divided into four groups and are arranged in the order of their precedence from the weakest to the strongest. Principal motions are characterized by the fact that they are never in order when there is any other question or business before the assembly. Subsidiary motions are applied to other motions for the purpose of modifying, or disposing of them, or of cutting off debate on them. It is important to note that these subsidiary motions are so arranged in the table that each one takes precedence over those preceding it in the list and yields to those following it. Incidental motions are motions that arise out of other motions and come up in an incidental way. The order in which these five appear is not significant, as these motions rarely come in contact with each other. Privileged motions arise independently of other motions and concern themselves with the needs and rights of the assembly, and therefore are of the very highest rank. They take precedence over all other motions, if made following them, though they yield to certain incidental motions arising out of them, and in some cases to subsidiary motions applied to them.[2]

Every motion we have listed has a definite purpose and is designed to meet a rather specific situation. To facilitate the use of the chart, therefore, we are listing these same motions below with their object or objects.[3]

OBJECTS OF MOTIONS

1. Main motion—to bring original business before the assembly.
2. To amend—to modify a question that is before the assembly.
3. To postpone indefinitely—(1) to dispose of a question for the session without voting on it directly; (2) used by the opponents of question to determine their strength.
4. To refer to a committee—to secure the advantage of action by a smaller group, or of greater freedom in debate in dealing with a question.
5. To postpone to a certain time—to defer action on a question to a certain time.

[2] Quoted with some changes from Gregg, *Handbook of Parliamentary Law*, pp. 71–72.
[3] Taken from Gregg.

6. Previous question—to suppress debate and bring the assembly to a vote.

7. To lay on the table—(1) to postpone a subject so that it may be taken up at another time during the same session; (2) to stop debate and suppress a question for the session, provided a majority cannot be secured to take the question again from the table.

8. To suspend a rule—to make temporarily possible an action contrary to the standing rules or rules of order of an organization.

9. To withdraw a motion—to expedite business in case of a changed opinion by the maker of the motion.

10. Question of consideration—an objection to the consideration of a question to enable the assembly to avoid irrelevant, unprofitable, or contentious questions.

11. A point of order—to correct a breach of order or an error in procedure.

12. Appeal from decision of chair—(1) to invoke a rule which the chairman has ignored or misinterpreted; (2) to appeal to the assembly to overrule the chairman on any rule where an opinion or a judgment may be exercised.

13. Special order—to set a specific time to consider a certain matter of business when all other things will be set aside.

14. Questions of rights and privileges—to secure to the assembly or any of its members some right with respect to safety, comfort, dignity, reputation, or freedom from disturbance.

15. To adjourn—to bring a meeting to a close.

16. To fix a time for the next meeting—to fix a time or place for reassembling.

III. JUDICIAL DEBATE

Judicial or forensic debate is conducted for the purpose of adjudicating questions of fact, usually in a court of law or in some other tribunal organized for this purpose. The affirmative is the plaintiff and the negative is the defendant in such actions. Decisions are usually rendered by judges, juries, or both.

As in legislative debate, a speaker in judicial debate makes use of most of what has been said in this book about propositions, issues, evidence, kinds of argument, briefing, and other matters. The debate, however, is conducted under the special rules and conventions which obtain in the jurisdiction under which the court operates.

IV. POLITICAL DEBATE

Political or campaign debate is conducted in democratic societies for the purpose of selecting candidates and electing persons to public office and for the purpose of reaching decisions on public issues which have been referred to the people for vote. No body of procedural regulations exists to govern political debate such as parliamentary law or the rules of legal pleading. The only limitations imposed are the regulations governing elections and the general laws governing libel and slander.

V. ACADEMIC DEBATE

Academic or "school" debate is conducted for the purpose of developing skill in the art of debate. *Debate as Training* is discussed in Chapter xix. Such school debates are frequently organized to simulate legislative debate, judicial debate, or political debate. It is hardly necessary to observe that only the most naïve student of the subject would seek to limit the applications of "argumentation and debate" to school debates, valuable and useful as they are for educational purposes.

Exercises

1. Select a problem for class debate. Each member of the class is asked to investigate the problem and phrase a proposition as a motion expressing the action he wishes to propose. Be prepared to present this motion and defend it in a three-minute speech. Use the table of parliamentary motions given in this chapter as a basis for guiding parliamentary debate on the motions. Appoint a chairman and make it a rule that each member of the class be prepared to support each main motion, amend it, or oppose it with the parliamentary motion best suited to accomplish his purpose. Use this exercise as a drill in parliamentary procedure. Experiment with different types of motions until you understand them and know how to use them.

2. Select a problem for class discussion and debate. Investigate this problem carefully and conduct a class discussion (See Chapter vi). Follow this discussion with a parliamentary debate on the same problem.

Chapter XIX · DEBATE AS TRAINING

I. DEBATE AS AN EDUCATIONAL METHOD

A. Its origin and development. Debate and its predecessor, disputation, were among the earliest known teaching devices. Protagoras, who taught in Athens approximately 2,400 years ago, is referred to as the "father of debate." He is said to have been the first to encourage regular discussions on set subjects and to organize argumentative contests among pupils. Aristotle, who taught a century later in Greece, commented on debate as a school exercise in his *Rhetoric*. Historically, the teaching and the practice of debate have flourished and declined concomitantly with democracy. Tyrants have had no use for debaters and their teachers.

Contest debating began in this country as an intramural activity of college literary societies. Some writers have stated that the first intercollegiate debate took place between Harvard and Yale in 1892. The first intercollegiate debate in which Northwestern University took part was held on October 10, 1873, when the Hinman Society team met a Tri Kappa Society team from the University of Chicago in a "friendly contest," as non-decision debates were called. Decision debates between Northwestern and Michigan took place in 1894 and 1895. A "Forensics" course was inaugurated at Northwestern in 1892. The movement spread to hundreds of colleges and thousands of high schools across the land. There are countless leagues and tournaments, and teams travel in all states and even to foreign countries. This tremendous growth has raised questions concerning the place of debate in the educational scheme. These will be considered in the following comments on objectives and criticisms.

B. Important objectives. An argument between advocates, such as one finds in a debate, affords excellent training in argument. The presence of opposition stimulates the participants to greater endeavor and compels them to consider both sides of the question.

The real issues are more likely to develop if both sides are represented by carefully prepared advocates. The presence of such opposition motivates greater consideration of the logical adequacy of evidence and reasoning. The rules of debate, furthermore, promote the observance of certain standards of decorum which keep the controversy within bounds and insure to both sides a fair hearing.

A second objective is improvement in extemporaneous speaking. Competent debating demands, and provides practice in, this kind of speaking. The debater learns to think on his feet, to adapt his arguments to those of his opponent, and to adjust himself in various ways to the situation at hand. Debating can develop a self-reliant, ready speaker who is able to meet situations as they arise.

Ability in the analysis and investigation of public questions is a third objective. Rarely in other situations do school and college students study these questions with the enthusiasm and thoroughness which debaters exhibit in preparation for debates. They know that they cannot do a good job unless they are well prepared. The importance of these skills and habits of mind should be obvious.

Skill in critical thinking is a fourth general objective which in part comprehends the others. It is useful in speaking, listening, writing, and reading. A critical thinker habitually applies the precepts of argumentation: he discerns propositions; he discovers issues; he knows how to study a subject; he is aware of the proof requirements of a proposition; he applies the tests of evidence; he distinguishes between valid and fallacious reasoning; he identifies implicit assumptions; he recognizes the non-logical means of persuasion. This skill in critical thinking is no mere by-product if the debating is based upon the sound principles of argumentation.

We look upon school debate as a preparation for policy-determining debate such as we observe in the courtroom, the legislative assembly, and in countless less formal situations of life. As such a preparation it is one of the most valuable educational experiences in which competent students can take part. Some of the many types of debate have been used successfully as teaching devices in classes in public speaking, argumentation, and social studies. An exposition of each of these types of school debate appears later in this chapter.

C. Criticisms of the activity. For the purposes of this discussion we shall ignore the superficial objections which have to do with the number of students who receive the benefits of debate, the classes missed because of trips, and other allegations of overemphasis. These are superficial because they do not allege inherent faults in debate as an educational activity. We shall direct our attention to the more significant attacks. In this connection we refer our readers to the defense of real-life debate in Chapter I.

Several criticisms can be grouped under the general charge of intellectual perversion. This charge is stated in the following ways: debate fosters insincerity for the sake of victory; a debater's mental activity is characterized by wish-thinking and opportunism; young people are harmed by being forced to argue against their convictions; debaters do not search for truth, because their thoughts and feelings are predetermined.

It is easier to make the charge of dishonesty and sharp practice than to prove it. Persons with little knowledge and strong prejudice, which they dignify as "conviction," find it hard to believe that those who espouse the opposite side are anything but knaves or fools. From the point of view of the audience, the issue is not how strongly the debater believes his argument but whether it is significant and valid. If it is not, the opposition should point out this fact. The presence of a competent opponent is a deterrent to dishonesty. The assumption of democracy is that when both sides have been advocated, the listeners can be trusted to make a wise decision.

The charge that school debaters are harmed because of their being forced to argue against their convictions has not been proved. Neither the extent of the practice nor its harmfulness has been substantiated. We state that the only responsibility of a debater is to set up the best possible case for his side in terms of the available proof. His convictions are in no way at stake. The rhetorical competence which is sought in school debates must not be confused with the ethical question of how one may use that competence in the policy-determining debates of later life. Our observations of thousands of debaters lead us to conclude that one is a better advocate for having prepared, not only his side, but the other as well. Then, too, a vast number of school debaters have no preference for one side until they have debated both. Frequently those who have an initial preference change their minds after they work on the other side. Why take so seriously a "conviction" which often is merely a snap judgment based upon little or no study?

Let us consider another aspect of the first general charge of intellectual perversion; namely, that debaters cannot seek the truth because their thoughts and feelings are predetermined. Debate does not require one to investigate a problem by first deciding what he will think about it. There is a place for open-minded investigation, and that place is in the investigation and analysis which precede debate. Even so, there are times when we must work from axioms and beliefs. From the audience's point of view, this is better than listening to speakers explore their minds in public while the listeners wait for an intelligible statement. Debate need not be characterized by sketchy and opportunisitic investigation. Nor does the so-called "deductive" method of presentation inevitably mean that no "inductive" inquiry preceded it. We see no reason to discard the eagerness to declare a conviction, the practice of stating proof concisely, and the willingness to change one's belief as investigation and argument may direct.

A second criticism of debate is that competition encourages contentiousness or fosters attitudes of conflict. A debater, according to this view, represents militarism in intellectual life. We recall that Aristotle cautioned against drawing a point of issue when it could be avoided, but he also provided most systematically for vigorous attack and defense if conciliation failed. As we stated before, there is no wisdom in glossing over real clashes of interest as if they did not exist. If feelings run high in debate, the form of the activity is not the cause; the fact that personal interests are at stake brings out conflict. If labor and management spokesmen debate, is it because these men were school debaters, or is it because their drives for wages and profits clash? As we have said, if exploitation and force are to be avoided in such cases, we must have available an orderly method of handling these differences. Debate is such a method. Since this is the case, training in the method merits a place in the educational scheme.

A third criticism is that school debate seeks only a temporary decision rather than a solution to the problem about which the controversy centers. "Solution" has a noble sound, but discussions of current problems do not reach ultimate or final answers. The "solutions" reached in discussions, either in real-life situations or in school exercises, are a series of temporary decisions en route to the ultimate, just as are those of debate. What, for instance, is the "solution" to a labor-management disagreement over wages, and would it be permanent? We see that in many practical matters there is not time for endless quest of certainty. There are important differences between the laboratory ideal and the expedient handling of pressing current problems. Realities of life demand decisions. If we delay, we may lose all power to act.

Fourthly, school debate is accused of harmful emphasis upon "two-sidedness" or "two-valued orientation." The same has been said of real-life debates, and that charge has been answered in Chapter ix. The same reply fits this situation, because we view school debate as preparation for the debates of life.

Finally, let us consider the fifth general objection: debate is futile because an advocate can seldom, if ever, convince his opponent.

> A man convinced against his will
> Is of the same opinion still.
> A woman convinced against her will
> Is of the same opinion, but is never still.

It is said that one may vanquish an opponent but still not persuade him. This is obviously sometimes true and sometimes not. Even if it were always true it would not be a very discerning criticism. Under normal circumstances a debater is attempting to convince some third party rather than his opponent. This third party may be an audience, or it may be a judge; but it is some man or group of men whose judgment on the matter is significant to him. The very fact that the debaters have found themselves unable to agree is usually the precise reason why the debate takes place. Ideally, at least, people will first make every effort to come to some kind of agreement on a problem through reflective deliberation or discussion. Failing in this, they will then resort to debate, wherein the decision is submitted to a popular vote or to some supposedly neutral third party. In a debate, both parties frankly and openly *desire* to maintain their proposition, and the debate is over as soon as one party concedes the position of his opponent. Convincing one's opponent may be one purpose of a debater, but in the great majority of cases, this is only incidental to winning the support of others.

II. APPROACHES AND ATTITUDES IN DEBATE

A. The strategic approach. Some ingenious persons have written chapters and even books on the ways to gain unexpected advantage over an opponent in an argument. A few of them have gone so far as to express these tricks in sophistic terms, such as "not showing one's hand," "bottling-up the enemy," and "splitting hairs." We do not subscribe to this doctrine which attempts to exploit the audience at the expense of one's opponent and at the expense of a reasonable decision on the proposition. A less philosophical objection is that trickery can usually be exposed by a seasoned debater. Furthermore, the tricksters do much harm to the repute in which debate is held by thoughtful persons. About the only strategy that cannot be exposed to the discomfiture of the person who is trying to use it is that of sound, vigorous argument; and, of course, this is not strategy in the sense in which we have used the term.

B. The straightforward approach. The best approach in almost any argument, both from the logical and the psychological points of view, is that of a sound analysis supported by as few carefully chosen lines of argument as will constitute prima facie or logically adequate support for this analysis, with each of these lines of argument thoroughly bolstered with the best available evidence. A case built along these lines has the merit of being simple, clear, and, at the same time, completely fortified from every point of view. Scattered and complex cases are seldom so effective as those which are organized around a few simply stated and well-supported arguments. If this be strategy, then it is the kind which will not thwart intelligent deliberation.

C. Desirable personal attitudes. "Magnanimity" or "fair play" is the best term to characterize the desired personal behavior of a debater. He should not be a little pettifogger "skilled in delays, sophisms, and misapprehensions." Rather, he is a person whose interest in the issue is unmistakable and who is capable of rising above personal embroilments, petty trickery, meanness, and vindictiveness. The attitude that we are describing here is not stuffy self-righteousness, but the kind of earnestness, tempered with generosity and frankness, which makes pettiness suffer by comparison. Edmund Burke once said that magnanimity in politics is "not seldom the truest wisdom." Assuming this to be true, we say that the attitude which we recommend not only makes for more intelligent deliberation, but is good persuasion as well.

III. BUILDING THE CASES

A. Suggestions for affirmative debaters. If the issues as set out by the first affirmative speaker are accepted as the basis of the argument, the affirmative case becomes the ground on which the contest will presumably be conducted. Affirmative speakers will do well to make their case stand out clearly throughout the debate and to press the negative to meet it. We stress this because negatives often seek to draw the argument toward their stand. Negative objections should be answered in terms of the affirmative case, either by meeting them with a reinforced case point or by showing the objection to be irrelevant or inconsequential in terms of the affirmative case point as stated.

The burden of proof should be accepted and met specifically. However, the negative must be prevented from avoiding its logical responsibilities and foisting undue burdens upon the affirmative. To meet a reasonable burden of proof on a proposition of policy, the affirmative must establish the extent and seriousness of the problem, the inherency of causal factors in the present situation, the workability of the proposal in terms of meeting the cause for action, and the probability that the solution will not entail new and greater problems. It seems that most of the weak affirmative cases are so because of a failure to clinch the second point: the inherency of causal factors in the status quo.

Affirmative cases on propositions of value and fact must also meet the burden of proof, but the issues and the points in partition are unlike those of propositions of policy. These matters are treated basically in Chapter IV. Since propositions of value are used infrequently in school debates, we shall refer here to only one example in order to make our point about the building of a debate case. In debates on the proposition of value which declared chain stores to be detrimental to the public welfare, the most successful affirmative teams first set out and defended their criteria for judging a system of retail distribution in terms of public welfare. Then they went on to show that chain stores as defined did not measure up to those criteria.

We have urged affirmatives to prevent their opponents from foisting undue burdens upon them. There are situations in which the affirmatives take undue burdens upon themselves without any urging from the negative side. This happens when the affirmative case goes beyond the requirements of the proposition. For instance, if the proposition demands the nationalization of basic, nonagricultural industries, any affirmative case which stands for total nationalization is really affirming a new proposition or motion, or at least a motion as amended. In terms of basic industries, this stand is more nearly a negative case, but not necessarily a safe one.

B. Suggestions for negative debaters. The negative case must constitute a vital objection to the proposition. As in the case of the affirmative, it is generally advisable to take a conservative position and to concentrate on a few decisive points. Some negative cases on propositions of policy have stood on one point: "It won't work."

The suggestions concerning affirmative cases indicate some potential weaknesses which the negative should be prepared to attack. To this end the negative debaters should prepare, not only a case of one of the four types discussed in Chapter xii, but also several optional blocks of material which can be adapted to the peculiar weaknesses of various affirmative cases. This flexibility of attack distinguishes the best negative teams.

A reminder of the special risks involved in a counter-proposition attack is in order at this point. The negative counter-proposition must be clearly stated and must be truly counter. If the affirmative can adopt it as a means to their end, the negative case fails. However, as we also said previously, the negative plan need not be adopted if it defeats the affirmative. That adoption may grow out of another debate. Thus the proposal of a new rural school building might be defeated by a counter-proposal of a fleet of school busses, but the latter should be debated as a new proposition before it is adopted.

IV. REBUTTAL PRACTICE

A. How to prepare for it. Effective rebuttal requires careful preparation. In fact, it is more difficult and may be more important to the outcome than the constructive effort is. Debaters who view rebuttal as an impromptu exercise are deluding themselves. Both the constructive and the rebuttal speaking should be extemporaneous. Both should be prepared equally well. A sound case is harder to attack, and prepared rebuttal enables a debater to defend his case and attack that of the opposition more efficiently.

Rebuttal preparation differs somewhat from constructive preparation. A team or a squad ought to consider all the individual arguments and all the case plans which they may face. Each argument should be written on a separate card or added to a large rebuttal chart. Below this statement on the card, or in columns to the right in the instance of a chart, the argument should be followed through three or four possible exchanges between the two teams. This should prevent mere repetition of old evidence and reasoning which do not suffice to meet a new attack. It might be called defense-in-depth. The debaters who will use this material should do the major portion of the work on it. The faculty director should only direct, guide, or advise.

Such preparation is not "canning" rebuttal. The objectionable "canned rebuttal" is that which is written and memorized in advance and used regardless of the trend of the debate. Rebuttals which are read from cards or papers are likewise objectionable; neither type of presentation develops the debater.

One convenient type of oral practice effectively discourages the "canning" of rebuttal material. It is a practice rebuttal session conducted according to a modified direct-clash sequence. The director designates an affirmative speaker to present one small point in three minutes, calls on a negative speaker to reply for two minutes, calls on an affirmative to reply for two minutes, and calls on a negative to close for his side. The second clash may be started with a negative point, and so on. Other devices, such as cross-examination, also discourage improper preparation.

B. How to conduct it. As we have said in a previous connection, every speech in a debate after the first affirmative should include some rebuttal. We refer the student to Chapter xvii for the methods of refutation. The use of some rebuttal in most constructive speeches follows logically from the fact that proof in a debate is cumulative; *i.e.*, the second speaker of a team builds upon a foundation laid down by the first speaker. Thus a second affirmative should re-establish his colleague's cause for action before going on to set out the plan and its advantages. Each speaker after the first one in a debate should open his speech by "taking one hot off the bat." This is done by isolating and refuting tersely and effectively the last telling point made by the preceding opponent.

Although adaptation and refutation are needed in constructive speeches, these processes must not cause one to neglect his constructive responsibilities. Affirmatives are more likely to spend so much time refuting that they fail to present a prima facie case. A similar danger confronts a negative whose attack includes a preconceived case.

Furthermore, the use of refutation in constructive speeches should not result in a loss of organization and coherent development. Both sides have this risk. Otherwise well organized cases become muddled if refutation is poorly handled. If the attack or defense is germane to a constructive point that is to be taken up in the speech, all can be woven into one argument. If the refutation material does not apply to the constructive point under discussion, it is better to take up the refutation first and then turn to construction. Even in negative speeches based entirely on refutation there should be evidence of planned progression. Both sides are expected to present sequences of arguments which can be followed.

There should always be some guiding plan in rebuttal. This includes the division of labor between team mates and the organization of each rebuttal speech. We shall consider first the distribution of duties between teammates. Whatever plan is devised must not be thought inflexible; provisions need to be made for freedom to meet important arguments as they arise and to handle unforeseen situations promptly. One scheme of rebuttal is called "man-to-man" defense. The first speaker on one team handles what is said by the first speaker on the other side, the second speaker meets the arguments of his opposite speaker, and so on. A more effective plan is called the "zone" defense in which each debater is assigned specific ideas or portions of a case to attack or defend. A rough division may be made according to the cause for action, the plan, counter-propositions, etc. In general, we prefer that division of labor which assigns to each speaker the handling of whatever points seem to need prompt attention when he gets up to speak. No one can reliably predict what those will be. This scheme stresses the timeliness of rebuttal and demands versatility in a debater.

Another aspect of this division of labor concerns the proper function of the last rebuttal speaker for each side. In general, it is the presentation of a contrasting summary rather than a sketchy treatment of many scattered points. Roughly two-thirds of the allotted time is sufficient for this purpose. One method is to summarize only what has been said against each main opposing argument, and then climax the statement with a terse review of one's own case. Another method is the contrasting summary of the main points of conflict under the headings of ultimate issues. Herein one not only "boils down" the arguments but also attempts to point out his team's advantage. For the latter purpose it is often better to organize the rebuttal around one's own case.

The second aspect of the guiding plan is the organization of each rebuttal speech. Definite points should stand out in a clear relationship to the case as a whole. Hit-or-miss rebuttal consisting of a disconnected series of remarks is not effective. It is better to use topic sentences, carefully selected forms of support, transitions between points, and a conclusion which clinches the main ideas.

The following miscellaneous items of advice on the use of rebuttal in debate have been given by many coaches and judges:

1. Don't try to hit everything. Use few points, and group related questions and arguments under each.
2. If necessary, use anticipatory refutation to dispel common misconceptions before they are stated, but do not set up "straw men."
3. Show the relationship to the whole case when defending or attacking a point.
4. When refuting a point, state it tersely but fairly, indicate its importance to an issue or the case, attack it, and assess the damage.
5. Keep running notes, possibly in parallel columns, for convenience in checking what remains to be done.
6. When on the affirmative, press the negative to show how the

repairs or the counter-proposition will meet the need better than your plan will. If the counter-proposition is not truly counter, adopt it as a part of your plan.

7. It is not enough merely to repel an attack; the strong points of one's own side and the admissions and the omissions of the other side should be stressed.

8. In making a second reply, do not repeat the proof; use new evidence and reasoning. New constructive argument, however, is not admissible.

9. In the interest of appropriate style, avoid the specialized vocabulary of argumentation and the use of stereotyped expressions such as: "we have proved," "my constructive speech," "Mr. Chairman, honorable judges, worthy opponents, ladies and gentlemen," etc.

10. Observe the standards of delivery that characterize the best public speaking.

11. Finally, avoid overstatement, mere assertion, misquotation, personal attack, and, in general, the "hammer-and-tongs" approach.

V. CONDUCTING THE DEBATE

A. Presiding officer. Anyone who participates in a debate, either educational or policy-determining, should know and observe the customs of the activity. A debate is usually presided over by a chairman who opens the meeting, introduces the speakers, and perhaps sets the tone of the program. He announces the decision of a panel of judges, or introduces a single critic judge who gives a critique. The chairman announces the proposition but does not discuss it. This is good advice for all introducers of public speakers. The chairman should announce a speaker and remain standing until the speaker approaches the lectern and recognizes him.

B. Salutation. When the speaker reaches the front of the platform, he should pause momentarily and then address the audience. "Ladies and Gentlemen," "Ladies," "Gentlemen," or "Members of the Tuesday Study Club" suggest the apppropriate kind of salutation. It is both superfluous and in poor taste to call the roll as in "Mr. Chairman, Honorable Judges, Worthy Opponents, Ladies and Gentlemen." The timekeepers may feel slighted. Instead of addressing the opponents or the judges during the debate, it is better to speak to the audience. It is assumed that the judges and the opponents will hear what is said.

In case a visiting team is being entertained, the first speaker for the home team may give a brief and genuine expression of welcome. The following speaker for the visiting team may respond appropriately.

C. Judges or critic. The panel of judges or the critic judge should be seated in the audience and be provided with satisfactory facilities for writing notes. If the decision and critique are to be given orally by the critic judge in the presence of the audience, he should be apprised of the arrangement when he is engaged. At the close of the debate the chairman should introduce the judge. If, as in the case of a three-judge panel, no oral critique is presented, the ballots should be collected by ushers or timekeepers and brought to the chairman for announcement.

D. Audience. When the debaters have achieved sufficient competence to be worthy of an audience, a public situation adds much to a debate. Although one campus affords only a few opportunities per season, the program can be expanded by taking debates to civic clubs, school assemblies, and other such groups. This is not to say that tournament debating needs to be dropped from the schedule. Audience interest can be built up by using propositions that concern them and by modifying the traditional pattern through the use of direct-clash contests, a cross-examination period, an open forum, and shift-of-opinion ballots. The audience situation can be educationally more useful if the debaters are taught to address the listeners as persons who are to settle the question at the close of the debate.

E. Attitude toward opponents. The behavior of debaters toward each other should be fair, courteous, considerate, and honest. Any evidence of poor sportsmanship turns an audience against a speaker. This includes the conduct of debaters at their tables while another person is speaking. Loud whispering, talking aloud, grimacing, noisy handling of papers, yawning, and other evidences of bad manners should be avoided.

F. Timekeepers. Most formal debates in this country are conducted according to customs or rules, one of which concerns the time limit of each speaker. Ten-minute constructive speeches and five-minute rebuttals are the most common. Rarely there is a three-minute intermission between the constructive series and the rebuttal series.

Two timekeepers, usually one from each of the competing schools, sit near the front and signal each speaker. During a ten-minute speech, the timekeepers display ten cards, changing them at one-minute intervals to show the remaining time. As the speaker begins, the card marked "10" is shown, and after one minute has elapsed, card "9" is shown, and so on. The expiration of the allotted time is indicated by the timekeepers' rising or by the use of an audible signal. The speakers and the timekeepers should "check signals" before the debate begins.

G. Properties. The stage setting for a debate customarily includes a table and the required number of chairs for each team, a chair for the presiding officer, and a speaker's stand. Occasionally, water pitchers and glasses are provided. It is customary to place the affirmative team on the right side of the platform. It is the left side as seen by the audience. Charts are sometimes added to the list of properties. The little they add to the effectiveness of a team can readily be offset by their susceptibility to damaging refutation. If a chart is used, it should be large enough for all to see, and it should be left in view until the debate is concluded.

VI. EVALUATING A DEBATE

A. Criticism and judging. The criticism of a debate and the decision in a debate should not be confused. It is possible to have a criticism without a decision, and vice versa. In interscholastic debating, criticisms are rarely given without a decision. The decision is seldom accompanied by a critique when three judges are used, but a single critic judge customarily offers suggestions. This critique may be given in the presence of the audience or presented to the interested persons after the presiding officer has read the decision to the audience.

A competent, thorough criticism contributes greatly to the educational opportunities presented by a debate. After a debate in the classroom or on the public platform, such criticism should be given by someone whose understanding of argumentation and debate qualifies him to evaluate the work of the debaters. His function is that of a teacher.

B. Types of votes. There are three different kinds of decisions which can be given in debates. Each has its unique purpose, method, and meaning. The first of these is the legislative vote. The judge bases his decision upon the merits of the proposition. That is to say, he votes for the side in which he believes. This type of decision should not be given by a judge or a board of judges in school debates. The legislative vote belongs in legislative assemblies where policy-determining debate takes place.

However, in audience-decision debates, a legislative vote is used. This situation is different in that the average listener does not assume competence to give a critic's vote. The outcome should not be construed as a critical decision. If there is to be an expression of opinion from the audience, a legislative vote in the form of a shift-of-opinion ballot should be used. The Woodward ballot shown below is issued to each listener before the contest, and he records his general opinion before and after the debate.

Before the Speech	*After the Speech*
	Mark only one Place
—YES (This expresses my belief on this question).	I have heard the entire discussion, and now: —The only change in my original opinion is that I am LESS SURE my opinion is right.
—I am UNDECIDED.	—The only change in my original opinion is that I am MORE SURE my opinion is right.
—NO (This expresses my belief on the question)	—My original opinion has been changed to YES.
	—My original opinion has been changed to NO.
	—My original opinion has been changed to UNDECIDED.
	—NO CHANGE. I vote the same as before the speech.

A brief explanation of the scoring procedures is pertinent here. The point values of the several degrees of shift following a *single speech* in favor of a given policy are these:

from no to yes = 4
from no to undecided = 3
from undecided to yes = 1.5
from yes to more sure = 1
from no to less sure = 1
no change = 0
from yes to less sure = −1
from no to more sure = −1
from undecided to no = −1.5
from yes to undecided = −3
from yes to no = −4

For a *debate,* use the following formula instead of the foregoing. Whichever team has the larger numerical shift is the winner of the legislative decision.

Affirmative shift $= \dfrac{\text{number original no}}{\text{number original yes}} \times$ (number shifted from yes to more sure) + (number shifted from no to less sure) + ⅗ (number shifted from undecided to yes) + 3 (number shifted from no to undecided) + 4 (number shifted from no to yes).

Negative shift = (number shifted from no to more sure) + ⅗ (number shifted from undecided to no) + $\dfrac{\text{number original no}}{\text{number original yes}} \times$ [(number shifted from yes to less sure) + 3 (number shifted from yes to undecided) + 4 (number shifted from yes to no)].

The juryman's vote, which is the second type, is one in which the decision is based solely upon the evidence submitted. In the opinion of the judge, the weight of evidence lies with the side to whom he awards his decision. Since the matters of evidence constitute only one of several criteria in school debates, a decision based solely upon the weight of evidence is obviously inadequate. Furthermore, the juryman's vote is suited to propositions of fact, not policy. Finally, in the juryman's vote the jury is under oath to vote for the negative unless the affirmative proves its case beyond a reasonable doubt. In a school debate the time limit might prevent the affirmative's proving its case so conclusively, and thus the negative would have an advantage.

The critic's vote, which is the third type, is based upon the quality of the debating. The judge indicates which team, in his opinion, did the more effective debating. This does not mean that he agrees with the arguments or the side of the winning team, or that one side had merely the greater weight of evidence. It is his educational job to point out the strong and the weak points of the debaters in terms of acceptable criteria such as those which appear in the ballot below. The debaters should be able to learn something about their activity as a result of this kind of decision. For this reason it is the best one to use in school debates.

C. **Criticism blanks and rating scales.** The critic's vote may be registered by the writing of one word ("Affirmative" or "Negative"), by giving credits for items on a score card, or by assigning quality ratings. The list of criteria may vary in length from four to ten items, but it should cover analysis and case, evidence, attack and defense, and delivery. Below is one type of ballot used in tournaments.

Some leagues and conferences use official ballots for the guidance of judges and for convenience in keeping records. The arbitrary designation of percentages for each criterion is questionable, but the practice prevails in some places. Items such as the following appear on some official ballots:

> Analysis and Case
> > clear
> > logical
> Evidence
> > pertinent
> > dependable
> > sufficient
> Argument
> > sound
> > comprehensible
> Rebuttal
> > adaptation and attack
> > defense of own case
> Delivery
> > easily heard
> > extemporaneous
> > direct
> > courteous

JUDGING SCALE

Affirmative Team

Round_____ Room_____

Rating Scale: 1–Poor, 2–Fair, 3–Good, 4–Excellent, 5–Superior.

First Affirmative Speaker

	1	2	3	4	5
Analysis and Case	—	—	—	—	—
Attack and Defense	—	—	—	—	—
Evidence		—	—	—	—
Delivery		—	—	—	—
Total Score____					

Second Affirmative Speaker

	1	2	3	4	5
Analysis and Case	—	—	—	—	—
Attack and Defense	—	—	—	—	—
Evidence		—	—	—	—
Delivery		—	—	—	—
Total Score____					

Affirmative's Total Score_____

Negative's Total Score_____

Team's norms: 8 to 17, Poor; 18 to 24, Fair; 25 to 30, Good; 31 to 35, Excellent; 36 and above, Superior
(Norms of 576 ratings in 72-unit tournament at N.U. in 1950)

In my opinion, the better job of debating was done by:

_____, _____
    school and number   side

Signed_____
             judge

Put comments for *Affirmative* team on reverse side of this half of the ballot.

JUDGING SCALE

Negative Team

Round_____ Room_____

Rating Scale: 1–Poor, 2–Fair, 3–Good, 4–Excellent, 5–Superior.

First Negative Speaker

	1	2	3	4	5
Analysis and Case	—	—	—	—	—
Attack and Defense	—	—	—	—	—
Evidence		—	—	—	—
Delivery		—	—	—	—
Total Score____					

Second Negative Speaker

	1	2	3	4	5
Analysis and Case	—	—	—	—	—
Attack and Defense	—	—	—	—	—
Evidence		—	—	—	—
Delivery		—	—	—	—
Total Score____					

Affirmative's Total Score_____

Negative's Total Score_____

Team's norms: 8 to 17, Poor; 18 to 24, Fair; 25 to 30, Good; 31 to 35, Excellent; 36 and above, Superior
(Norms of 576 ratings in 72-unit tournament at N.U. in 1950)

In my opinion, the better job of debating was done by:

_____, _____
    school and number   side

Signed_____
             judge

Put comments for *Negative* team on reverse side of this half of the ballot.

VII. TYPES OF SCHOOL DEBATE

A. Definition of school debate. We use the term "school debate" to designate the various types of this activity which may be undertaken for the purposes of informing an audience on public questions and training students in certain speech skills. It should be understood that debate and some types of discussion are more often used as policy-determining techniques in legislative, forensic, and political deliberation. The chief purpose of educational speech activities is to develop attitudes and skills which will enable individuals to participate more competently in the important discussions and debates of life.

B. Discussion-debate modifications.

1. Three-team debate. A slight modification of debate in the direction of discussion is seen in a debate among three sides or teams, each of which supports a solution or plan. The three positions may be a defense of the plan embodied in the proposition, a defense of the status quo, and a defense of a counter-proposition or alternative plan. The element of intentional reasoning, which is inherent in advocacy, is present in this modified form of debate. Assuming that team "A" represents the status quo, team "B" defends the proposed plan, and team "C" advocates an alternative plan, the following sequence of speeches might be used:

> First speaker of "B" team attacks the status quo for 8 minutes.
> First speaker of "A" team defends the status quo for 8 minutes.
> First speaker of "C" team attacks the status quo for 8 minutes.
> Second speaker of "B" team advocates the proposed plan for 12 minutes.
> Second speaker of "A" team defends status quo against the "B" plan for 12 minutes.
> Second speaker of "C" team advocates the alternative plan for 12 minutes.
> First speaker of "C" team attacks the "B" plan for 8 minutes.
> First speaker of "A" team attacks the "C" plan for 8 minutes.
> First speaker of "B" team attacks the "C" plan for 8 minutes.

2. Debate-forum. The open-forum debate commonly consists of any of the other types followed by a discussion in which the audience participates. Questions are directed to specific speakers through the presiding officer of the debate. The chairman has discretionary authority to rule out questions, to restate questions, to assign questions to speakers, and to call for certain types of questions. The open-forum debate is usually a no-decision contest. It is a modification toward discussion in the degree that audience participation takes place in the final stage.

3. **Parliamentary session debate.**[1] Several educational debate procedures have been patterned after the parliamentary methods of policy-determining groups. This one as developed at Pennsylvania State College requires a chairman, a secretary, four discussion leaders, and an audience. After the chairman opens the meeting and states the question, the first visiting speaker gives an eight-minute committee report on the matter of "evils" and their sources. If no "evils" are reported, the discussion is on the validity of the report. If "evils" are reported, the speaker moves the adoption of a solution. A second visiting speaker then talks for eight minutes on the plausibility of the solution. Next, each of the two home-team speakers has eight minutes in which to support, amend, or offer a substitute motion. Since no debate can take place if four speakers support the one motion, the home team might plan to offer an amendment and a substitute motion, or a substitute motion and its defense. After thirty-two minutes of platform speaking, the discussion is opened to the assembly.

4. **English debate.**[2] Visiting debaters from Oxford and Cambridge have attracted considerable attention in American forensics circles because of their unusual practices. The most noticeable of these are their use of entertaining wit and philosophic-literary style, their easy platform manner, their lack of teamwork, and, more fundamentally, their attitude toward the contest situation. This attitude which is foreign to American debaters is observable in the Oxonians' behavior. They are unusually open-minded in their concessions of points, their readiness to praise an opponent's ideas, and their general indifference to pugnacity. Their preparation is brief

[1] See J. F. O'Brien, "The Place of Extra-Curricular Speech in the College or University of Today," *Quarterly Journal of Speech,* November, 1935, pp. 583–584.

[2] See *Quarterly Journal of Speech Education,* June, 1923, pp. 215–222; *ibid.,* February, 1925, pp. 45–48; *Quarterly Journal of Speech,* February, 1948, pp. 46–53.

and casual; they do not use "set" case outlines and card-index boxes, and they are not directed by a faculty sponsor.

These differences, which are dramatized whenever English and American debaters meet, stem from the practices of the Oxford Union Society. Hundreds of students from twenty-odd colleges of Oxford meet to discuss major public questions in this old literary-social club. It duplicates the House of Commons in that it has a chairman's dais, benches for the government and the opposition, party leaders and "aye" and "no" exits. Each of the four main speakers for the evening is assigned to the side in which he believes. Evening dress is customary. Without much reference to his colleague he speaks fifteen or more minutes without a prepared brief or manuscript. A note from the secretary is the only notification of the elapsed time. The occurrence of heckling and the fact that the audience will vote serve to make the speaker use wit, informality, and general persuasion instead of debate evidence in the American sense. After an open-forum period the audience divides and votes by exits, not on debating excellence, but on the merits of the question. The motivation for this activity is the possibility of a career in public life.

Some persons have become enamored of the Oxford Union style and have advocated its adoption in place of our present programs. But there is a possibility that the foreign procedure is overrated. An American Rhodes Scholar and a don of Balliol College have agreed that most of the speaking in the Oxford Union Debating Society is very dull.[3]

British and American debaters who have recently exchanged visits have pointed out additional differences between the practices in the two countries. In the Cambridge and Oxford Unions as well as in Parliament, all remarks are addressed to the President or the Speaker. The members of student societies occasionally invite outside speakers of distinction to participate in debates. There is always an audience of at least fifty or sixty persons for the weekly debates, each one of which lasts longer than an American intercollegiate contest. In this connection, it is interesting to note that the Unions do not engage in interuniversity forensics or have more

[3] "Oxford: Two Views in Vivid Contrast," *New York Times Magazine,* April 30, 1950.

than one debate on a proposition, except when two of their members tour this country for fees.

An American version of the English-style debate involves changes which impose time limits, maintain orderly procedure, and equalize participation. From four to eight persons are required to assume responsibility for the delivery of speeches. The following are eleven rules of procedure:

(1) The President calls the House to order and announces the motion for debate.

(2) Ten-minute speech by a previously designated speaker moving the adoption of the motion.

(3) Ten-minute speech by a previously designated speaker opposing the motion.

(4) Seven-minute speech by a previously designated speaker seconding the adoption of the motion.

(5) Seven-minute speech by a previously designated speaker opposing the motion.

(6) At this point the floor is open to any member of the House who desires to speak. The time limit on these speeches is five minutes. No member may speak more than once, points of order or information excepted. Members favoring the motion and those opposing it speak alternately. The President indicates the side entitled to the floor by announcing, "I will now recognize a speaker for the motion," or "I will now recognize a speaker opposed to the motion." (Insofar as practicable, each school represented splits its delegation so that it has an equal number of speakers favoring and opposing the motion.)

(7) Any speaker except the one who opens the debate may be interrupted by any member of the House at any time. Such interruptions take one of two forms. (1) If the rules have been infringed, a member is entitled to rise and point this out to the President, at the same time describing the infringement which he believes to have taken place. (2) The second type of interruption permitted is a direct request for information addressed to the speaker who has the floor. To make this sort of interruption a member must first rise to his feet in such a manner as to attract discreetly the attention of the President. The speaker, if he wishes to be interrupted, will sit down. If he does not sit down, and ignores the member who desired to interrupt, the latter must resume his seat. An interruption on a point of information must be made in the form of a question, and is addressed to the speaker through the President. The interrupter may not himself impart information to the House; he may only seek to elicit information from the speaker. The

President will rule the speaker out of order if his interruption does not constitute a genuine request for information.

(8) The debate on the motion proceeds in the fashion outlined for one hour and thirty minutes, at which time the speaker who originally moved the adoption of the resolution presents a five-minute speech answering the arguments which have been presented against it and summarizing the discussion. Immediately following this speech there is a division of the House. Abstentions are intimated by informing the tellers. The numbers having then added up, the President announces the results from the Chair.

(9) Members favoring the motion sit facing those who oppose it, the former ranging themselves on the President's right, the latter on his left . . .

(10) The speeches are clocked by a timekeeper. Members must bring their remarks to a close upon receiving his signal.

(11) A member may speak on any phase of the subject he desires. The President will, however, rule out of order any member who attempts to introduce material which is obviously not germane to the discussion.[4]

5. **Problem-solving debate.**[5] The schemes of problem-solving debate provide for three sets of speeches (analysis, solution, and evaluation) by two teams of two or three speakers each. The problem is phrased as a question rather than a proposition. All of the speakers attempt to solve the problem, and in doing so they may agree or disagree with any other speaker, including their own colleagues. Those who favor this mixed type of procedure say that it provides greater freedom to argue one's convictions, it encourages reflective and cooperative thinking, it prevents the choosing of sides too soon, it informs audiences more effectively, and it provides excellent early-season practice for school debaters. However, unless some precaution is taken to organize teams whose convictions on the problem are identified with different proposals, there may be no semblance of a debate.

The sequence and functions of speakers require special attention. "Analysis" speakers attempt to interpret the question, to set out what they conceive to be the disturbing factors and their causes, and to develop criteria by which solutions may be judged. Each

[4] D. Ehninger, "Outline of Procedure for the English-Style of Debate," *The Gavel*, copyright March, 1948. Used by permission of Delta Sigma Rho.

[5] See F. W. Orr and A. L. Franzke, "The University of Washington Plan of Problem-Solving Debate," *Bulletin of the University of Washington* (Extension Series), No. 8, January, 1938.

"solution" speaker explains and defends a solution which his team believes to be the most satisfactory in terms of the analysis of the problem. The function of an "evaluation" speaker is to compare and evaluate the proposals. His responsibility is not to attack or defend any proposal, but rather to interpret, compare, and evaluate in terms of available evidence and argument. According to one version of the problem-solving debate, two "analysis" speakers have ten minutes each, two "solution" speakers have twelve minutes each, and two "evaluation" speakers have eight minutes each. This scheme is often modified to include only one "analysis" speech, from two to four "solution" speeches, and only one "evaluation" speech. The latter sequence eliminates any possibility of repetitious speeches in the first and third stages, and it provides for the introduction of more than two solutions. If periods of questioning are desired, the following order would be followed by two-man teams: (1) an eight-minute analysis by the first speaker of team "A," (2) an eight-minute solution by the first speaker of team "B," (3) a five-minute questioning of the first speaker of team "B" by the second speaker of team "A," (4) an eight-minute solution by the second speaker of team "A," (5) a five-minute questioning of the second speaker of team "A" by the first speaker of team "B," (6) an eight-minute evaluation by the second speaker of team "B."

6. **Student congress or legislature.**[6] Like the problem-solving debate, the student congress or legislative assembly works on one or more problems rather than a proposition. The students' investigation consists in a thorough study of the subjects which are announced two months prior to the opening of the session. The purpose of this investigation is to analyze the problems and to consider solutions, to the end of drawing a bill or resolution which will be introduced in the meetings. On an intercollegiate basis, individual school delegations come prepared to introduce and defend their respective bills. The delegates need to understand committee work, parliamentary procedure, and other details of routine in addition to the subject-matter aspects of the assembly.

The National Student Congress of Delta Sigma Rho usually involves a three-day series of meetings, including the opening assembly, preliminary committee meetings, main committee meet-

[6] See L. S. Judson, ed., *The Student Congress Movement*, New York, the H. W. Wilson Company, 1940; also *The Gavel* of Delta Sigma Rho.

ings, joint conference committee meetings, and general assemblies. The opening assembly provides for the election of a speaker of the house, the appointment of a parliamentarian, and the announcement of committee assignments. In subsequent committee meetings the bills which have been brought in by the several delegations are analyzed, discussed, and reported out as one bill per committee. Minority reports may be made also. The following general assemblies take action on the committee proposals under the usual rules of parliamentary procedure. This pattern may be varied in terms of the number of problems discussed, the length of the session, the number of houses (unicameral or bicameral), and the rules of procedure.

This type of educational speech activity provides a variety of experiences in conversation, discussion, debate, and in giving nominating speeches. The benefits of research and democratic participation are equally obvious. However, serious limitations become apparent if committee chairmen are unskilled, if a few dominant students hold the floor, or if parliamentary wrangling supplants sincere deliberation.

7. **Forensic experience progressions.** Several combinations of discussion, extemporaneous speaking, and debate have been used in lieu of intercollegiate tournaments. An intercollegiate conference held at Northwestern University in 1945 included a lecture-forum, a series of round tables corresponding to the steps in reflective thinking, a parliamentary meeting to frame resolutions, an extemporaneous speaking contest, and three rounds of debating. The number of round tables may vary from three to six or more.

The forensic experience progression as developed by Elwood Murray includes three forum-panel discussions, one extemporaneous talk, and six one-man-team debates, organized around five subtopics as indicated in the following stages. Each student's work in each stage is rated by a critic. The first is the problem phase in which a forum-panel discussion takes place on the question, "What is the problem, and to what extent is it significant?" Each participant presents a five-to-seven-minute speech of definition, analysis, and interpretation. This includes (1) the nature and extent of the problem, (2) analysis of divergent points of view, (3) possible future effects, and (4) the speaker's personal "stake" in the matter. Following the talks, each participant is allowed five minutes in which to comment on other talks and to defend or modify his own position. The chairman conducts a forum at the end of each phase.

As a continuation of the problem phase, the second stage is conducted as a formal panel discussion on the question, "What are the major causes of the problem?" The speaking procedure of the first stage is continued, but the analysis is deeper. Each talk is concerned with these points: (1) origin and causes of the problem, (2) the accepted criteria for the evaluation of any solution, and (3) the differences in criteria which must be resolved.

The third stage, called the solution phase, consists in a series of extemporaneous talks on the question, "What are the solutions to the problem?" Each person has five to seven minutes in which to outline solutions but not to argue them. All speakers after the first may need to adapt their remarks to prevent repetition.

Continuing the solution phase, the fourth stage involves debates on the question, "What is the best solution?" A proposition is formulated by the speakers and the critic at the end of the third stage. Each speaker chooses a solution which he will advocate in the fourth stage. He will engage in six debates, in three of which he defends his plan and in three of which he opposes other plans. An affirmative speaker is allowed periods of six, six, and three minutes. A negative speaker is allowed periods of eight and seven minutes.

Stage five, the action phase, is conducted as a forum-panel discussion on "What, as citizens, will be our program to put into effect the necessary remedies?" The speaking procedure is the same as that in stages one and two. Each talk includes (1) a statement of the effects of participation upon the speaker's thinking, (2) a summary of his favorite solution, (3) an indication of the obstacles to be confronted by this solution, (4) proposed procedure to deal with obstacles, and (5) an outline of the speaker's program for preparing himself for action on the problem.

8. **Debate symposium.**[7] The debate symposium provides for four two-man teams. The first speaker for each team states his team's position, and the subsequent speakers may amplify their colleagues' remarks, cross-examine any of the speakers of the other teams, refute any of the preceding arguments, or restate and summarize

[7] See H. F. Harding, "A Debate Symposium," *The Speaker*, Vol. XX, May, 1938, p. 6.

their own positions. A forum for audience participation usually follows the series of debate speeches.

9. Cooperative investigation.[8] In the cooperative investigation, a problem is analyzed in a manner similar to that of Dewey's steps in problem-solving. Each of the six speakers is given a topic. The first three topics relate to "understanding the problem," and the last three pertain to "suggested solutions." The first three speeches are explanatory and investigative, whereas the last three are advocatory.

10. Intercollegiate forum.[9] The intercollegiate forum provides for a group of four speakers, the first of whom explains the background and present status of the problem. Each successive speaker then presents a proposed solution and restates or refutes other plans. One need not maintain his original point of view as in a traditional debate; in fact, he may withdraw his proposal and defend that of another speaker. This is a mixture of debate and discussion for these reasons: (1) it includes advocacy, (2) it provides for definition and analysis of a problem, (3) it presupposes the introduction of several proposals, and (4) it permits the modification of one's original position.

C. Variations in traditional debate.

1. Two-man debate. A convenient, short form of the traditional debate for classroom use is that in which only two persons participate. This permits debating when team work is difficult to arrange. The affirmative opens the debate with a ten-minute constructive speech; the negative replies with a fourteen-minute rejoinder; and the affirmative closes the debate with a four-minute rebuttal. These time limits may be changed to suit the occasion, but each side must have the same amount of time. The chief variation in method lies in the negative rejoinder which includes attack and defense in one speech.

2. Two-man teams. Traditional debates ordinarily take place between affirmative and negative teams of two or three speakers each. The trend in school and college debating is toward the exclusive

---

[8] See H. L. Ewbank, "The Wisconsin Public Discussion Contest," *The Gavel*, Vol. XX, May, 1938, p. 54.
[9] See A. B. Williamson, "A Proposed Change in Intercollegiate Debating," *The Quarterly Journal of Speech*, Vol. XIX, February, 1933, pp. 192, 200–202

use of two-man teams in contest situations. A typical arrangement of speeches is as follows:

Constructive Speeches

First affirmative .... 10 minutes
First negative .... 10 minutes
Second affirmative .... 10 minutes
Second negative .... 10 minutes

Rebuttal Speeches

First negative .... 5 minutes
First affirmative .... 5 minutes
Second negative .... 5 minutes
Second affirmative .... 5 minutes

The affirmative opens the constructive speeches, and the negative opens the rebuttal speeches. In other words, the affirmative opens and closes the debate, and the negative has two consecutive speeches in the midst of the debate. The first affirmative states the proposition, gives the affirmative interpretation of it, and develops the affirmative answer to at least one issue. The following negative speaker must react to the preceding speaker's interpretation and reply to the opponent's argument. The affirmative's interpretation must be scrutinized to make sure that it places a legitimate construction upon the language of the proposition. The second speakers on both sides will offer necessary refutation, complete their constructive arguments, and summarize briefly. Rebuttal speakers will attempt to attack opposing arguments, to defend their constructive arguments, and to focus the debate upon the contested issues.

3. **Three-man teams.** Three-man teams were almost exclusively used for many years in school and college debating. The arrangement was obviously intended to divide the three stock issues among as many team members. The fact that it provided experience for more students was said to be an advantage. The procedure is the same as that in the two-man team except that there are more speeches, and the time limits are sometimes different. Each of the six constructive speeches is ten or twelve minutes in length, and each of the rebuttals is five minutes in length. In some cases the final rebuttal speakers are allowed seven minutes.

4. One-rebuttal debate. This simple variation of the traditional debate reduces the length to forty minutes and still utilizes four debaters. It encourages adaptation and rebuttal throughout the debate, since three of the speakers have no other opportunity to present refutation. The schedule of speeches may be arranged as follows:

Constructive Speeches

First affirmative	5 minutes
First negative	10 minutes
Second affirmative	10 minutes
Second negative	10 minutes

Rebuttal Speech

First affirmative	5 minutes

5. Split-team debate. In an effort to remove the element of institutional rivalry between debate teams, this deviation from the traditional debate was developed. One serious defect, however, is the difficulty or impossibility of teamwork and serious effort. If one considers team activity an important aspect of debating, he will not care to have competing schools or societies exchange one speaker unless there has been ample time for thorough collaboration before the contest.

6. Cross question debate.[10] This is a more radical departure from the traditional type of educational debate in that it includes constructive speeches, periods of cross-questioning by opponents, and rebuttal summaries. The following schedule of speeches involves four debaters and requires eighty minutes:

First affirmative presents an entire case...............	20 minutes
First negative questions the first affirmative..........	10 minutes
Second negative presents an entire case...............	20 minutes
Second affirmative questions the second negative	10 minutes
First negative presents rebuttal............................	10 minutes
Second affirmative presents rebuttal.....................	10 minutes

The schedule above may be modified for classroom use by reducing the case speeches to twelve minutes each, the questioning periods to four minutes each, and the rebuttals to five minutes

[10] See J. S. Gray, "The Oregon Plan of Debating," *Quarterly Journal of Speech Education,* April, 1926, pp. 175–179.

each. Three-man teams may be used if the third speaker on each team gives the rebuttal summary. Still another schedule enables each speaker to join in the cross-examination:

First affirmative speech.. 10 minutes
Cross-examination by second negative................ 3–5 minutes
First negative speech.. 10 minutes
Cross-examination by first affirmative.................... 3–5 minutes
Second affirmative speech .... 10 minutes
Cross-examination by first negative........................ 3–5 minutes
Second negative speech.. 10 minutes
Cross-examination by second affirmative.............. 3–5 minutes
Negative rebuttal summary .... 5 minutes
Affirmative rebuttal summary................................ 5 minutes

Since the most unusual aspect of this type of debate is the question-and-answer period, we shall offer some suggestions for conducting it. The time belongs to the questioner for use in drawing out the respondent, but not for the delivery of a speech. Questions and answers must be brief and clear. The respondent may request a restatement of an unclear question, and the questioner may insist upon brief answers. The questioner should lead up to the admission of a premise or an analogy, but he should not press for a final admission; it can be deduced in rebuttal. This type of debate, perhaps more than any other, demands for its success an attitude of fair play and an honest attempt to get at the real issues. The participants must be courteous and abide by rulings from the chair rather than indulging in quibbling about procedure. It is better to reserve direct rebuttal for the final period in which one deals with the final bearing of the cases, the answers, and ignored questions. Since the purpose of questions is to get at analysis, evidence, and inference, it it advisable to group one's questions under the case headings. Obviously, a questioner must be ready to adapt to any of the possible answers which may be given. Finally, both speakers should stand near the lectern and speak loudly enough for all to hear.

It is apparent that this type has certain advantages and limitations. One advantage is the considerable audience interest which is stimulated by the similarity to hearings and trials, the spontaneous adaptations which are made, and the sharp focus upon contested points. Another advantage, in terms of the training of speakers, is the necessity of careful preparation. As we pointed out earlier, the question-and-answer period will degenerate into mere bickering unless there is fair play and an honest effort to deal with issues. Then, too, the debaters should adjust their questions to the opposing case and make some use of the answers. In short, the technique of questioning is vital.

7. **Direct-clash debate.**[11] This departure from the traditional debate form was first tried in the season of 1931–1932. In addition to providing variety in the forensic program, it disciplines debaters in extemporaneous speaking and in clashing directly on the point at issue.

Although the same propositions that are used in other debates may be used in the direct clash, there are differences in the size of teams and in the method of judging. A team may consist of no more than five and no fewer than two debaters, and opposing teams need not be of equal size. The speaking order need not be fixed, but no one may speak twice in succession during a clash, and no one may begin successive clashes. If the unique scoring procedure which is described later is not used, the debate may be a non-decision or an audience-vote affair.

The opening phase of the debate consists in definition and analysis by both sides. An affirmative speaker has eight minutes in which to define terms, explain the proposed plan, and set forth what his team believes to be the issues. Proofs are not advanced in this phase. A negative speaker then has eight minutes in which to indicate the issues which his side accepts for clash and to outline a counter-proposition if one is to be used. Thus the debate is limited to those issues upon which disagreement exists. If the clash is on only one issue, it must be subdivided for use in subsequent phases.

Following the two eight-minute speeches, each side may speak for another three minutes to clarify some points or, in the case of the affirmative, to indicate its attitude toward the counter-proposition. In some tournaments these two stages are replaced by a general meeting in which clash points are selected.

The first clash is opened by an affirmative speaker in a three- or

[11] See Edwin H. Paget, "Rules for the Direct Clash Debate Plan," *Quarterly Journal of Speech*, October, 1937, p. 431.

four-minute speech which presents a point in partition or one of its main subpoints within an issue upon which the teams have agreed to clash. The judge is instructed to penalize a team for presenting irrelevant or inconsequential points. The first negative speaker has two minutes for a pointed reply to the specific argument of the preceding speaker. The second affirmative must then, in two minutes, answer directly the first negative. This exchange continues until each side has given three two-minute speeches. The closing speech is a two-minute, affirmative summary. Hence, the total elapsed time is fifteen or sixteen minutes per clash.

At the end of each speech after the first five minutes, the chairman shall await a signal from the critic judge before allowing the debate to proceed. This permits the judge to terminate the clash and award a point to the team whose opponent replied weakly, dodged the point, or shifted ground. An even clash is allowed to continue for seven speeches before a decision is given on the merits of the debating.

The second clash is opened by the negative, and the routine continues as in the first clash. No point may be initiated twice in a series of clashes, except that the side losing a clash may initiate the same one again.

The affirmative and the negative alternate in initiating clashes until one side has won three. The judge may waive the score-by-points rule if he believes that one team has conceded or has won the all-important point in the debate. If no critic judge is used, each side shall present two or three points, and each clash shall continue for seven speeches. A shift-of-opinion ballot may be used to obtain an audience decision.

8. **Mock trial.**[12] This plan grew out of a search for new and interesting varieties of public-speaking events for off-campus audiences. In essence it is a modified jury trial based upon a debate proposition. Its appeal may be traced to the dramatization of conflicting ideas. In one of the experimental debates an injunction was sought restraining the United States from protecting, by armed force, the lives and properties of her nationals abroad in the event of foreign war. Three students who carried major roles represented

[12] See Warren Guthrie, "The Reserve Plan for Intercollegiate Discussion," *Quarterly Journal of Speech*, October, 1939, pp. 392–396; also *University Debaters' Annual* (1937–1938), H. W. Wilson Company, New York, pp. 327–388.

the judge of the court, the Attorney General of the United States, and the attorney seeking the injunction for the plaintiff. Seven minor roles were those of three witnesses for the plaintiff, three for the defense, and a bailiff. Each witness represented a prominent authority and confined his testimony to statements of historical fact or to the printed statements of the person he represented. Some witnesses impersonated the originals. The bailiff opened court and swore in the witnesses. Twelve members of the audience served as jurors.

The following is a sketch of the procedure:

1. The bailiff calls the court to order.
2. The judge gives a three-minute speech on the background of the question (as in a first affirmative speech).
3. The attorney for the plaintiff has three minutes in which to outline the case he hopes to establish through the examination of his witnesses.
4. The attorney for the defense has three minutes for a similar presentation.
5. The attorney for the plaintiff calls his three witnesses singly. He may have four minutes for the direct examination of each. The attorney for the defense may ask three questions of each witness in cross-examination.
6. The same plan is followed for the defense.
7. The attorney for the defense has three minutes in which to summarize his case and make a final plea to the jury for the rejection of the injunction.
8. The attorney for the plaintiff makes a similar summary and plea for the granting of the injunction.
9. The judge instructs the jury to decide the case solely on the evidence and to return a verdict.

If the proposition calls for the adoption of a new policy instead of the abandonment of an old one, a decree of specific performance or a writ of mandamus may be sought by the plaintiff.

9. Heckling debate.[13] The practice of heckling opponents is not new, but the procedure described here was introduced into intercollegiate debating in 1926. The originator sought to stimulate interest among debaters and audiences by introducing a life-situation element which intensifies conflict. Perhaps there is "never a

[13] See Charles H. McReynolds, "A New System of Debate," *Quarterly Journal of Speech*, February, 1940, pp. 6–11.

dull moment" in such contests, but there is some danger that the exchanges will degenerate into a chaotic wrangle in which the speakers as well as the audience will become lost. At least this is not the type for novices.

The following principles or rules have been offered for the conduct of heckling debates:

1. The speaking order is first affirmative, first negative, second negative, and second affirmative. Each one has ten minutes (or fifteen to eighteen if agreed upon in advance) to present a speech and answer a heckler. There are no rebuttals.
2. Only the heckled speaker may reply. Each debater is assigned to heckle one opponent. Team members may confer quietly.
3. Before asking his first question, a heckler rises, asks the chair for permission to speak, and turns to face the speaker. He reseats himself during the reply. Thereafter the heckler does not address the chair.
4. The speaker should resume the speech as soon as he has answered a question briefly, pertinently, and politely.
5. The chairman should insist upon brief and pointed questions, he should curtail heckling if audience interest is jeopardized, and he should enforce the rules of courtesy.
6. Heckling should be aimed at developed points, not isolated sentences. Its purpose is to get at vital matters and not merely to harass a speaker. Interruptions are sometimes restricted to a five-minute period in the middle of each speech. In this case the last affirmative must not use a new argument in the non-heckling period.

10. **Direct-question or dialectic debate.**[14] The essence of this procedure is that the constructive speeches are replaced by dialogues between colleagues. It may be used with the cross-question or other types of debate. Although it has possibilities in variety and audience interest, there is a problem of maintaining unity and continuity.

In an experimental debate in 1935, the affirmative used fifteen minutes to present their case through a dialogue between the two colleagues. This team was then cross-examined by the negative for ten minutes. Following this, the negative developed their case in a fifteen-minute dialogue and were cross-examined by the affirma-

[14] See C. P. Lahman, *Debate Coaching*, New York, The H. W. Wilson Company, 1936, pp. 34–35.

tive for ten minutes. One negative speaker and one affirmative speaker concluded the debate with five-minute summaries.

11. Congressional style debate.[15] A combination of the usual procedure, cross-questioning, and heckling was developed at Purdue University about 1931. The number of speakers is variable, but two-speaker teams are recommended. The time limit of constructive speeches is twelve minutes, one-third of which may be used for heckling by the opposition. At any time after the third minute of the speech of either team's first speaker, heckling may commence. The limit is three interruptions per speech, but more than one question may be asked during one interruption. If interrupted in his last minute, a speaker shall have an extra minute for a conclusion. Each rebuttal speaker is allotted six minutes, one minute of which may be used for an interruption by an opponent, and the remaining five minutes are available for rebuttal or cross-examination of the opposition. The last rebuttal speaker on each side shall not be interrupted during his last two minutes. Two timers are needed: one for speakers and one for interrupters. The order of speakers is the same as that in a traditional debate.

D. Tournaments. Tournament debate is not essentially another type. It is rather a scheme which enables several schools to secure numerous debates for their teams in a short time and at less cost per debate. In every season there are countless one-day and two-day tournaments, usually during Fridays and Saturdays. The host school invites each visiting school to furnish one or more units, each one consisting of a judge and two or four debaters. In some cases each team remains on one side, while in others the teams alternate sides.

The schedule is usually divided into three or more rounds. Under the heading of each round are posted the affirmative teams, the negative teams, the judges, the rooms, the chairman-timekeepers, etc. The most difficult part of this scheduling is the pairing of teams and the assigning of judges so that no teams meet each other more than once, and so that a judge does not hear one team twice or judge a team before his own team meets it. The following schemes of pairing teams allow the preparation of brackets in advance, even if the number of schools exceeds or falls short of the expected

[15] *Ibid.*, pp. 35–36.

number. The important point is that each school delegation is given a number upon arrival.

For small tournaments which have fewer than nine numbered units, the Lambertson system is the most satisfactory. However, in some cases a judge will hear a team which subsequently meets his team.

Round I			Round II			Round III		
Aff – Neg		J	Aff – Neg		J	Aff – Neg		J
1 –	2	3	1 –	3	6	1 –	4	2
2 –	3	4	2 –	4	1	2 –	5	3
3 –	4	5	3 –	5	2	3 –	6	4
4 –	5	6	4 –	6	3	4 –	1	5
5 –	6	1	5 –	1	4	5 –	2	6
6 –	1	2	6 –	2	5	6 –	3	1

Round IV			Round V		
Aff – Neg		J	Aff – Neg		J
1 –	5	4	1 –	6	5
2 –	6	5	2 –	1	6
3 –	1	6	3 –	2	1
4 –	2	1	4 –	3	2
5 –	3	2	5 –	4	3
6 –	4	3	6 –	5	4

In the second system, which is best suited to nine or more numbered units, the defect of the first system is eliminated.

Round I			Round II		
Aff – Neg		J	Aff – Neg		J
1 –	3	2	1 –	5	3
2 –	4	3	2 –	6	4
3 –	5	4	3 –	7	5
4 –	6	5	4 –	8	6
5 –	7	6	5 –	9	7
6 –	8	7	6 –	1	8
7 –	9	8	7 –	2	9
8 –	1	9	8 –	3	1
9 –	2	1	9 –	4	2

Round III			Round IV		
Aff – Neg		J	Aff – Neg		J
1 –	7	4	1 –	9	5
2 –	8	5	2 –	1	6
3 –	9	6	3 –	2	7
4 –	1	7	4 –	3	8
5 –	2	8	5 –	4	9
6 –	3	9	6 –	5	1
7 –	4	1	7 –	6	2
8 –	5	2	8 –	7	3
9 –	6	3	9 –	8	4

This basic pattern can be adapted to more rounds and more school units. It has been used in five rounds for forty schools and in four rounds for seventy schools competing at Northwestern University. In case a school enters more than one unit, then numbers at least ten points apart should be assigned to those units before other schools draw numbers.

The foregoing arrangement does not apply to an elimination tournament. The determination of a championship is based upon the percentage of victories or upon high-point totals of quality ratings. If an elimination tournament is desired, and if one defeat is sufficient to eliminate a school, a bracket such as the following can be used:

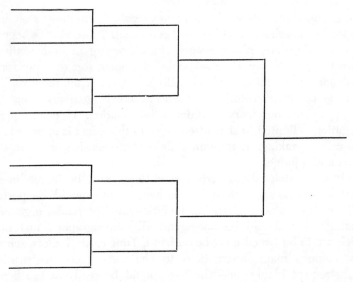

These two schemes can be combined to form a third. Some tournaments have several non-elimination rounds, after which some of the highest-ranking teams are placed into elimination brackets as in the illustration above.

There are several additional matters of tournament administration which often make the difference between a successful event and a hopeless confusion. These details require advance planning and several good workers to carry out the plans. Emotional stability is useful, too. The first decision which needs to be made concerns the kind of tournament, its size in relation to available class-room, hotel, and restaurant space, and the date. The dates of other campus events and those of near-by tournaments should be checked to avoid embarrassing conflicts. Concerning the kind of tournament, the director and his assistants should determine whether to have only debate or to add events in discussion, oratory, extempore speaking, etc. Although one may wish to have something more unique than "just another debate tournament," he need not adopt the extreme to which some tournaments have gone. Even a large circus has only three rings. The maximum size of the tournament should be established by a survey of the local facilities. After all, size is less important than the quality of the competition and the availability of competent criticism.

Following these steps, the announcements or invitations should be sent to the schools which have been listed. These notices should announce the date, place, events, rules, housing accommodations and rates, fees if any, time schedule, etc. Some sort of reply form or advance registration card is usually enclosed. When these replies are received, the director should send acknowledgements of entries and give any necessary additional information. If each school delegation is limited in size, a reminder to this effect is appropriate. Generally speaking, a minimum delegation consists of four debaters and a judge.

Before the delegations arrive, everything must be in readiness. Chairman-timekeepers must be on hand, signs should be posted to direct the traffic, registration facilities must be ready, a general meeting room should be open, and all mimeographed materials which are to be issued must be on hand. Time cards, ballots, schedules, campus maps, instructions to chairmen-timers, registration forms, receipt blanks, and the like should be ready at the head-quarters.

Each four-man unit and the accompanying judge should be assigned a serial number in the registration process, if the flexible numbering system as described in this chapter is used. If the expected number of participants does not appear, the mimeographed schedule for round one must be revised and perhaps be written on a large board in the general meeting room. During the first round the schedule of all rounds can be duplicated and be ready for distribution between the first and second rounds.

If the proper planning has been done, the management should be able to issue results and the evaluation sheets or rating scales within approximately thirty minutes after the final round ends. In the meantime, some diversionary entertainment might well be provided. If a more detailed tabulation of results is to be issued, it can be made, duplicated, and mailed within a few days after the tournament.

VIII. THE ROLE OF THE DIRECTOR

A. Attitude toward the job. One who directs debating should consider it his job to teach argumentation and debating. Obviously he should have been selected because of his ability to do so. There ought, of course, to be an academic offering as well as co-curricular work in this field in a college or a university. These remarks lead us to our distinction between teaching and coaching. One is teaching debating when his efforts enable students to become competent debaters of any proposition in the future, but he is coaching when he strives merely to enable his students to win a given contest.

This distinction means that the director or teacher should direct or lead but not drive or "spoon feed" his students. He will direct the reading, lead some discussions, criticize practice debates, and help in other ways short of compiling reference cards, drawing case outlines, and writing speeches.

B. Promotional activities. Often the most difficult of the promotional activities consists in the inauguration of a program where none has existed. Some who have met this problem have started with a nucleus of former high-school debaters or a small group of interested students in speech classes. Others have announced propositions of interest to some students in political science, history, or economics. In some cases an intramural event has been developed among classes, fraternities, or societies, using a proposition of campus interest. Still others have presented entertaining demonstration debates featuring visiting teams of recognized ability.

These and other devices have more prospect of success if the administrative officers provide moral and financial support. This important support may be obtained if the case for forensics is convincingly presented. We have suggested some arguments in our treatment of the educational objectives and the criticisms of the activity.

After the activity has been started with official sanction and support, there remains the problem of motivating the participants. They are typical human beings in their desire for recognition and interesting experiences. These may be provided by means of interesting propositions, attractive schedules, academic credit, school awards, membership in honorary societies, and publicity.

News stories of forensic activities are of interest not only to the town and campus papers but also to the papers of the participants' home towns. Appropriate news stories and editorials tend to interest other students in participating, stimulate attendance at debates, and show the community that the activity is making progress. The publicity should continue from the announcement of try-outs to the publication of the awards which are made at the close of the season. Newspaper publicity may be supplemented by pictures, posters, oral announcements, yearbook features, and off-campus appearances before community audiences. The peculiarities of the local situation will govern the relative emphasis which is given to each of these media of publicity.

C. Selecting the squad. If the prospective debaters exceed the number that can be taught properly, the personnel of the squad may be determined by means of try-outs. These are held in the fall, usually a month or six weeks before the first intercollegiate engagements. The time intervals between the first meeting and the try-outs, and between the try-outs and the first contests, vary because of local conditions, such as the experience of the students, the difficulty of the propositions, the available meeting time, and the standard of achievement which the director holds.

There is much difference of opinion among directors concerning the number of debaters who should be retained on the squad through the season. Some believe that the squad should be reduced from time to time until a first team remains to enter the principal contests. Others use the squad system, which means that different teams from the squad are chosen to represent the school in each contest. These alternatives are said to constitute the dilemma between winning and training, because only a few schools are able to use many debaters and still maintain superior records. The use of several teams during a season is educationally sound, but novices ought not to be foisted upon public audiences. Their first experiences are obtainable in intrasquad practices, intramural programs, and novice tournaments.

D. Practice experiences. These practice experiences are essential but not of such importance that regular class work may be disrupted for a considerable period. It is advisable to establish a regular meeting time so that the debaters may budget their time. If regular squad meetings are not desired, one can schedule practice debates and small group meetings. Sometimes there are separate meetings for affirmatives and negatives, and at other times there are separate squad meetings for men and women, or for varsity men, varsity women, and freshmen.

In order to make the most of the intrasquad practices, several procedures may be used.[16] One is the unvarying practice of criticizing each oral presentation. Another is the insistence upon the use of extemporaneous delivery. A third is the use of various types of debate. Fourth, an occasional shifting of sides and team personnel has much to recommend it. Occasional changes in cases or methods of handling specific arguments constitute a fifth suggestion. Finally, a short version of the direct-clash debate form may be used with profit as a rebuttal practice device. We have discussed the basic skills and the principal methods of preparation in previous chapters.

Intercollegiate competition is the next stage in the series of practice experiences. It is available in many invitational practice tournaments which provide a maximum of experience at a minimum cost. Some of these tournaments are divided into novice and experienced sections. They are scheduled between late November and April. Typically the visiting teachers serve as judges without fee. Each entrant usually receives a quality rating and perhaps an oral critique. If only a decision is rendered, the educational value of the

[16] Week-by-week training schedules may be found in C. P. Lahman's *Debate Coaching*, New York, H. W. Wilson Company, 1936, pp. 140–142. See also Kenneth Hance, "Adapting 'the Teaching Cycle' to Debate," *Quarterly Journal of Speech*, December, 1944, pp. 444–450.

experience is less than it might be. Individual debates between schools are quite common also. They may be held before assemblies, classes, campus organizations, or off-campus audiences.

Exercises

1. If circumstances permit, have some demonstration debates in class. It is usually more interesting to use a variety of types, such as a modified English debate, a problem-solving debate, a cross-question debate, a direct-clash debate, a mock trial, etc.
2. Use the shift-of-opinion ballot in an audience situation, and apply the formula in measuring the shifts.
3. Advanced students who are preparing to direct forensics may be asked to prepare study outlines, briefs, cases, discussion outlines, bibliographies, evidence files, or rebuttal charts on a question or a proposition, as the case may be, which will be used in the following season.
4. Advanced students in a coaching course should have supervised practice in giving critic decisions. The demonstration debates or intercollegiate debates on campus may be used for this purpose.
5. Prepare lesson plans, a training schedule, or a syllabus for use in a debate class, a debate squad, or a social studies class in which debate is used as a teaching device.

APPENDIX A

Town Meeting

BULLETIN OF AMERICA'S TOWN MEETING OF THE AIR

GEORGE V. DENNY, JR., MODERATOR

MARCH 21, 1950   VOL. 15, No. 47

WHAT SHOULD WE DO ABOUT FEDERAL AID TO EDUCATION?

Announcer: Tonight, Town Meeting is the guest of Illinois Wesleyan University in Bloomington, Illinois, celebrating the 100th anniversary of its founding by contemporaries of Lincoln. Also hosts are the nationally known 104-year-old newspaper, *The Daily Pantagraph,* which for more than three years has sponsored Town Meeting in central Illinois, and Radio Station WJBC, whose ABC facilities we are using tonight.

A typical grass-roots college, Illinois Wesleyan is independent and non-tax-supported. It boasts a nationally recognized school of music. It trains 1,200 students for responsible American citizenship with a strong religious and moral emphasis.

Coincidentally, Bloomington celebrates its Centennial this year. It's the center of one of the richest farming districts in the world, and is known as the hybrid corn capital of the Nation. Now to preside over our discussion, here is your Moderator, the president of Town Hall and founder of America's Town Meeting, George V. Denny, Jr. Mr. Denny. (*Applause*)

Moderator Denny: Good evening, neighbors. Tonight, we are happy to be the guests of Illinois Wesleyan University in Bloomington, celebrating the 100th anniversary of its founding, and of *The Daily Pantagraph,* now in its 104th year and the fourth year of its sponsorship of Town Meeting, and also of Station WJBC, our local ABC Station.

It is fitting that we discuss this highly controversial question of federal aid to education under these auspices, for tonight we are to see an excellent example of the need for the Town Meeting method in dealing with such questions as this one.

Both Senator Lucas and Dr. Gould are familiar with the facts in the case, but they are in complete disagreement as to the meaning of these facts and the action that should be taken.

The central controversial issues of this subject were and are: (1) can the Federal Government provide financial aid without exercising undesirable control; and, (2) should any federal aid whatever, such as free transportation, be extended to parochial and nonpublic schools.

We are informed that 46 states—all except Maine and North Carolina—forbid the use of public funds for nonpublic schools. Therefore, the only way for parochial and private schools to share in the federal aid is for it to be specified in legislation. The Senate bill, passed last May, did not cover this point and was rejected by the House Education and Labor Committee last Tuesday by a vote of 13 to 12. The next day, by the same vote, this Committee decided to take up what was described as a "mild substitute."

What should we do now?

We'll hear first from a distinguished alumnus of Illinois Wesleyan, who started life as a school teacher and who is now the Majority Leader in the United States Senate—the Honorable Scott W. Lucas, Democratic Senator of Illinois. Senator Lucas. (*Applause*)

Senator Lucas: I am happy to participate in this centennial celebration, especially so in view of the fact that I graduated from Illinois Wesleyan Law School in 1915.

Before entering college here I had some experience as a country school teacher. One year, believe it or not, I taught all eight grades to 56 children in a one-room schoolhouse. I was larger than most of the students; that solved one of the most difficult educational problems of that day and age.

But that was many years ago. Times are different. Tonight, many students in the most remote districts of the country are probably listening to this very program.

We live in a fast-moving mechanized age in which men and women should have at least a minimum education to the high school level, in order to earn a comfortable living. I am certain Dr. Gould will agree to that.

Local and state governments have made Herculean efforts to keep their standards of education up to the requirements of the times, but for many reasons certain sections of the country have fallen hopelessly behind.

There are some states in the South where the children are getting a quality of education often only about a third as good as the rest of the Nation. These states are trying to solve their problems, but they need a little help from their richer state sisters. Most of them, in relation to the income of their residents, are spending for schools at better than the average rate for the Nation as a whole, but the people of these states haven't enough wealth to finance the kind ot schools they need. Dr. Gould may challenge that statement.

I would not be for federal aid to education, Dr. Gould, if I could find any other logical solution to the problem. Because we are the leaders in an ideological war for freedom in the world, we have and will continue to have national and international problems which will require the best brains in the country for solution.

Young people are our greatest national asset. They will have to be competent in the world to come, and the vast majority of the people most qualified to judge—parents, teachers, and educational experts—tell me the only solution is for the Federal Government to join in aiding the states and local school districts in raising the educational level of the children in the most retarded sections of our country.

The problem has been to maintain our splendid tradition of keeping control of local schools in the hands of local people.

The fairness of the bill we worked out in the United States Senate is demonstrated by the fact that it passed the Senate by a vote of 58 to 15. Every possible point of intervention by federal officials has been blocked in that bill. We simply would divide up the money among states, with those states where the need is greatest getting the most assistance. Dr. Gould, I believe this is federal aid without federal control.

I believe that the need for federal action has been demonstrated beyond any real doubt. We cannot let our educational system continue to go downhill. We cannot continue to ignore our underpaid teachers and our overcrowded classrooms.

I think this bill will go far towards aiding states and localities to give millions of children a better chance for a better education. (*Applause*)

Moderator Denny: Thank you, Senator Scott Lucas. Our next speaker was also a school teacher before he became a college president. Dr. Gould's major in college was geology. He has assisted in a number of expeditions in this field, including the first Byrd Antarctic Expedition in 1928–1930. After teaching for a number of years at Carleton College in Northfield, Minnesota, he was made President of Carleton in 1945. We are happy to welcome to Town Meeting, Dr. Laurence Gould. Dr. Gould. (*Applause*)

Dr. Gould: The Senate Committee report, in my opinion, is not an objective study of our educational needs. On the contrary, the real facts of the situation are disguised by careless and misleading statements.

For instance, Senator Lucas, the report states that federal aid to education is not new. Whether by design or not, this is misleading. Federal aid for general school purposes, which this bill provides, is entirely new and without precedent and is revolutionary in our history.

The argument that many of the states are unable to provide adequate educational opportunities is fallacious. A state should not receive federal aid when it establishes its case by refusing to tax its people properly, or by neglecting its schools while it can afford to build great bridges and highways and things of that sort.

It does not follow that because Illinois is richer than Arkansas or Louisiana that the latter states cannot afford good schools. Individuals do not all need to have the same incomes to afford the basic necessities of life. The current proposals would grant aid, not on the basis of incapacity to support education, but on the failure to do so.

Department of Commerce figures show that from 1940 to 1948 the per capita income for the United States as a whole increased 145 per cent. During that time, however, in New England it increased only about 90 per cent, and in the Middle Atlantic States 107 per cent, and yet those are considered the richest states in the Union.

Mark you that on the other hand the increase for the 11 "poor" Southeastern states was 197 per cent. Here is the interesting thing: that this per capita increase is reflected in greater increased support for its schools in the Southeastern states than anywhere else in the Nation.

South Carolina led the Nation with an increase of 255 per cent in the last 10 years, and the other near-by states were not far behind. If time permits later on, I want to tell you about Arkansas.

Even so, Senator Lucas, no single state is making Herculean efforts. Not one of the 48 states is spending as high percentage of its income on education now as it did before the war.

That's true of all 48 states. Before the war, Mississippi spent 3.7 per cent of its income on education, and last year it spent 1.7 per cent. It has spent more money, but the more money is a reflection of the great economic increase. These trends are based upon sound economic factors, and there is no good reason to suppose they will not continue.

The gap between the rich and the poor states is closing faster than we realize. Even so, my friends, such inequalities as we have in education now are far less hazardous toward the preservation of our democratic institutions than would be centrally subsidized system of education.

My principal objection to federal aid, Senator Lucas, is that it means federal control, and, of course, that is what it should mean. Congress hasn't any business appropriating my tax monies and not exercising some supervision over them. To defend the idea that Congress should do so is to defend the principle of irresponsibility in government and, heaven knows, we've got enough of that without defending it as a principle. (*Applause*) Furthermore, Senator Lucas, in spite of what you say, there are strings attached to this bill. I want to read just a few lines from the bill itself. Here is what the state must do: It has to "provide for an annual audit and for the submission of a copy thereof to the Commissioner, of the expenditure of funds received under this Act, and for a system of reports from local public school jurisdictions and other state public-education agencies to the state educational authority; and provide that the state educational authority shall make such reports in such form and containing such information concerning the administration of this Act as the Commissioner may reasonably require and give him upon request access to the records on which such reports are based."

Now, good Great Caesar's ghost, if those are not strings attached to the bill, I'm a Mohammedan—and I'm not a Mohammedan. (*Laughter and applause*)

Right here, written into the bill, is all the machinery that's necessary for the Federal Government to control educational aid—and, of course, that's what it should do. Saying that no control is authorized in this bill is like giving a man a sock in the jaw and saying at the time, "I wouldn't hurt you for the world." (*Laughter and applause*)

Moderator Denny: Well, I'd say these two men have exchanged pretty tough blows. Senator Lucas, now will you step to the center of the ring for a moment and take a sock at this next speaker in the form of a question?

Senator Lucas: Mr. Denny, I was tremendously interested in the statement made by Dr. Gould with respect to the argument that he makes between the rich and the poor states.

Dr. Gould seems to think that the poorer states are just as qualified to carry on as the rich states. I challenge that statement, and I should like to have Dr. Gould tell me why he thinks so.

Dr. Gould: That isn't quite what I said, Senator Lucas. All I'm saying is that there is no state in the Union which has been spending an appreciable part of its income for education. I am saying that, until the states that are so-called poor tax themselves in the same proportion that we are taxing ourselves here, there is no basis for giving them federal aid.

When Mississippi only spends 1.7 per cent of its income for education, I think it is time that we say something else should be done before we give them any additional help.

That is what I mean. There is an old saying that the Lord helps those who help themselves. I think that applies to education as well as to everything else.

I thing it might be well while we're looking at this just to take a glance at what we really do spend on education. You might get the impression from the way we're talking that we're spending a great deal of money. We don't! That's the trouble!

Don't for heaven's sake—anyone who's listening to me tonight—get the idea that I think we're spending enough. We are not! None of us school teachers gets enough money! I hope the trustees of Carleton College are listening tonight. (*Laughter*)

Ten years ago, our public school expenditures were 3.1 per cent of our individual incomes. Today, that has been reduced to 2.4 per cent.

Public education today costs less than 2 per cent of the expenditure for personal consumption. We spend less on education than we do for radio and movies. We spend less on education than we do for tobacco. We spend less than half of what we spend on alcoholic beverages. I repeat, in all 48 states, the per cent of income spent on education is less now than it was in 1940, and the Southeastern states are not spending a higher per cent of their income than the Northern states. They're spending less. I'll get back to that in a moment. (*Laughter and applause*)

Mr. Denny: Thank you. Yes, Senator?

Senator Lucas: Well, I'm glad to hear Dr. Gould say that the teachers of this country are not getting enough pay. I want to say to Dr. Gould and to this distinguished audience that the only way that the teachers, not only in some of these poorer states, are going to get adequate pay, but in some of the richer states in certain districts—right here in Illinois—is to have some federal aid for education. Unless we get federal aid to education, teachers throughout the country are going to continue to leave the schools as they have done in the last four years.

Now, Dr. Gould talks about Mississippi. He said something about Arkansas. I'd like to call his attention to this fact: If you want to compare Arkansas and New York on the question of effort to finance its schools, you'll find that the balance is all in favor of Arkansas as to what they're doing at the present time.

Arkansas spends 1.97 per cent of the average annual income of its residents on public school education. New York spends 1.74. Arkansas is making an effort in relation to its resources above the average of 1.87. Yet Arkansas is able to spend only about one third as much per pupil as does New York.

The per capita income in New York is something like $1,980. The per capita income in Arkansas is $890, and that's the difference. That's why these areas in the South and other sections of the country cannot because of economic reasons take care of themselves. (*Applause*)

Mr. Denny: Thank you, Senator Lucas. One more word, very briefly, from Dr. Gould.

Dr. Gould: Here's what happened in Arkansas. In 1940, it was spending $31 per pupil; right now, $83; and next year it'll be spending $100 per pupil.

I'm talking about economic trends. In the last ten years, the per capita income in Arkansas has trebled. Its industrial production has quadrupled. You must take account of these tendencies.

Here, will you please remember this? In all of this talk, no state has asked for federal aid. The whole thing has been instituted by propaganda from above.

I have a letter from the Secretary of the Labor Committee in the House, saying that not yet had any state appeared before them asking for help. In 1946, the State of Mississippi Legislature went on record saying, "We don't want any federal aid." (*Applause*)[1]

[1] Used by permission of the Town Hall, Inc., New York.

Vital Speeches of the Day

New York, June 1, 1948   Vol. XIV, No. 16

SHOULD THE COMMUNIST PARTY IN THE UNITED STATES BE OUTLAWED?

Debate delivered over the radio from Portland, Oregon, May 17, 1948
(As transcribed in New York by the Mutual Broadcasting System)

Affirmative: HAROLD E. STASSEN
Former Governor of Minnesota

Negative: THOMAS E. DEWEY
Governor of New York

STASSEN'S AFFIRMATIVE

Chairman Van Buskirk, your excellency, Governor Dewey, and my fellow citizens: During the recent war I saw many young Americans killed, I watched ships explode and burn, planes crash in flames, men, our men, my friends, fall. I met thousands of prisoners of war as they were liberated from indescribable conditions of imprisonment and suffering. I viewed the devastation of cities and of farms.

In the midst of these experiences I thought more deeply than ever before of the way in which men should live, of the preciousness of freedom, of the future of America.

I made a quiet resolve to do everything within my power after V-J Day to keep America free and to prevent a third world war. Four principal objectives appear to be essential.

First, to maintain a sound and humanitarian, free American economy, which would include avoiding inflation booms with their out-of-reach prices, preventing depression crashes with unemployment, widely developing the superb natural resources of water, forests and minerals, constantly improving housing and health, establishing a fair balance between capital and labor, assuring to agriculture a fair share of the

314

national income, advancing in civil rights, decreasing discrimination and bigotry, and constantly endeavoring to win happier homes throughout America.

And second, to keep America and other free countries strong in a military sense, especially in the air.

And third, to safeguard against the undermining and overthrow of free governments, and to defend the freedom of men.

And fourth, to establish a strong organization of united nations for peace and economic progress, without a veto, and with a real system of justice.

With a firm conviction that a full and frank discussion would lead to better answers of the manner in which to make progress toward these objectives, I have talked directly to the people of my views and invited their questions and welcomed any opportunity to meet with others in a joint discussion.

This is the background for my Oregon campaign. I submitted to the people of Oregon my position on the building of the resources and the rapid development of the Columbia basin, the need for long-range programs in agriculture and forestry and the importance of that fair balance between management and labor, of progress in housing and health. I presented my view of a strong foreign policy for America, with an alert and trained military, the Marshall plan, leadership toward amending and strengthening the United Nations Charter, the stopping of machine tools and equipment supplies to Russia, the direct outlawing of the Communist organizations in America, and in the free countries, and positive action in ideals and moral standards and justice to a world-wide basis.

I have presented my optimism, my hope, that such policies would lead to a future of peace and of progress for ourselves and for others, without the tragedy of a third world war.

One part of my proposed program for America has been directly challenged. It has been challenged by a man for whom I have great respect, a man who is a fellow Republican, and who has joined in campaigns in Wisconsin and Nebraska and now in Oregon. Tonight we meet in a joint discussion of that one point. I will give you my position on this one point in detail and give the reasons why I have reached this conclusion.

When World War II ended I felt that the key question as to future peace would arise if bad policies were followed by the Soviet Union of Russia and by the world Communist party directed from Moscow, I therefore gave special study to their actions, to their methods, to their party intentions. I journeyed to many of the European countries and to Russia and questioned leaders of many nations for a first-hand look-and-listen trip. I followed closely the results of the peace conferences of Potsdam and Yalta and the developments in country after country.

I have reached the conclusion that the Communist organizations in the world are absolutely directed by the rulers of Russia in the Kremlin. I have reached the conclusion that the objectives of these Communist organizations in the world are to overthrow free governments, to destroy the liberties of men, and to bring other countries under the domination of the dictators of Russia. I have watched country after country in which these Communist organizations have taken every legal advantage but have recognized none of the corresponding obligations and moralities.

The most recent and extreme instance is Czechoslovakia. The Communists never had the support of a majority of the people of Czechoslovakia, but they were given full legal standing and Communists were appointed to some of the ministries of government. The people of the country were free, they were rebuilding from the war, there was no tyranny, there was no threat to Russia, there was a politeness and a friendliness toward the Communists, but the Communist organizations, directed from Moscow, took all of these legal blessings and at the same time moved underneath the surface, established Communistic committees in all the departments of government, in the big labor unions, in key industries, and in the universities and colleges. Then a few weeks ago, the overground and underground moving together, Czechoslovakia was betrayed, the liberties of the people were wiped out, and another country was brought under the domination of the Kremlin. These developments do give rise to a danger of war.

Analyzing what they mean, it seems clear to me that the free countries, including America, do not now have adequate laws to safeguard themselves in the face of this menace. I consider it to be clear that these Communist organizations are not really political parties, they are actually fifth columns, they are Quisling cliques. If we are to have the best chance of winning through for freedom without the horror of a third world war, the free countries must take action to protect themselves against this fifth column in this unsettled period which has been called a cold war.

I do not think it is generally realized in America that we do not now have any law to effectively oppose the actions of these Communist organizations, either overground or underground. There is now no law in America to prevent these Communist organizations from secretly developing organizations of hidden members, from carrying on secret conspiracies, to promote strikes, to establish hatred of religions and races in America.

Neither is there any present law to prevent the Communist organization from maintaining large offices of telephone switchboards and a network of communication to be used in reaching and co-ordinating these underground activities and in recruiting new members.

In facing up to the problem, we must maintain complete constitutional rights and liberties in America. The right of free speech, of free press, of freedom of conscience and freedom of religion must be kept inviolate. It must always be open to any individual in this country to protest, to object, to dissent. But there is no constitutional right to carry on organizations above ground or below ground directed by the rulers of the foreign power with the purpose of overthrowing the government of the United States and taking away the liberties of its people.

I, therefore, have urged for some months that we need a new law to directly outlaw these Communist organizations. Governor Dewey has insisted that our present laws are adequate. I submit that a new law is needed. It should directly make it illegal after its passage to carry on any organization, either above ground or below ground, which is directed by the rulers of a foreign power for the purpose of overthrowing the government of the United States, destroying the liberties of its people and bringing this country under the domination of the rulers of a foreign power. Such a law would not outlaw ideas, it would not outlaw thoughts, it would make illegal organized conspiracy of fifth columns. Such a law is constitutional under Article 4 Section 4 of the United States Constitution. A very eminent lawyer, the honorable William L. Ransom, past president of the American Bar Association, agrees on its constitutionality in an able article in "The American Law Journal" this month. The language of the Supreme Court in Ohio v. Akron indicates that the Supreme Court would uphold its constitutionality. In fact, the national Congress is right now moving to do this very thing.

A law has been introduced known as the Mundt-Nixon bill, which provides that it shall be unlawful to attempt in any manner to establish in the United States a totalitarian dictatorship, the direction and control of which is to be vested in or exercised by or under the domination or control of any foreign government, foreign organization or foreign individual or to attempt to perform any act toward those ends.

The report of the committee that investigated the Communist activities specifically found that the Communist organization was an organization whose basic aim, whether open or concealed, is the abolition of our present economic system and democratic form of government and the establishment of a Soviet dictatorship in its place.

Now, the chairman and secretary of the Communist Party of America have protested that this bill would outlaw their organization. I agree that it would and I say that it should. The United States Congress indicated in a preliminary way their approval of the bill when they voted on last Friday by a vote of 296 to 40 to bring it up for action on Tuesday. It might well be amended to some extent before it is finally passed by both Houses, because in some cases directed against individuals it goes even beyond what I have urged. But I do believe that it will pass in the near future in a form that will definitely outlaw these Communist organizations in both their underground and over-ground activities.

I further believe that this will be a precedent for similar action by the other free countries of the world and that effective means will be developed to safeguard against the fifth-column infiltration of the Communists.

Now, I recognize full well that there are some who have sincerely opposed my position in this matter. I am not certain of the reasons for Mr. Henry Wallace's opposition to my position, but I am confident that Governor Dewey's opposition is completely sincere. But I respectfully ask him to reconsider his opposition as I believe he is mistaken. His position in effect means a soft policy towards Communism and all the evidence around the world shows that a soft policy wins neither peace nor respect nor improvement from the Communists. We must not muddle Communism with legality. They grasp every concession made and continue their undermining action.

Consider these facts: There are now eleven countries of the world under the domination of the Communist leaders in Moscow. They are Russia, Poland, Czechoslovakia, Hungary, Yugoslavia, Romania, Bulgaria, Albania, Estonia, Latvia and Lithuania. In none of these eleven did the Communists ever receive majority support of the people in a free election. The last three were taken over by force during the war and held ever since. In every one of the remaining eight, the Communists used the legal recognition of Communist organizations as an underground nerve center and recruiting station for their underground movements, until they had seized power and brought the nation under the dictation of the Communist Politburo.

Russia was the first Communist-dominated nation. It came under this dictatorship through a combination of two main reasons: First, the bad government of the czar. Second, the organization developed by the legalized Bolshevik party, which formed throughout Russia and elected six members to the Russian Parliament in the last election held in that country before the Communists came to power.

There seems to have been some mistaken idea that the Communists were outlawed in Russia. This is not correct. The Bolshevik party was active in Russia right up to the first war with Germany. The Communists carried on a nation-wide election campaign in Russia in 1912 and elected six members to the Parliament or Duma.

They used this means of developing their revolutionary organization, and when they were caught in the attempted revolution and in various sabotage, in train wrecking and bombings, they were severely punished, but they were not outlawed as an organization. When this present Communist party did come into power in Russia, they promptly wiped out all other political parties and took the whole peoples under a firm and dictatorial grip. In each of the other countries—Poland, Hungary, Yugoslavia, Romania, Bulgaria, Albania and finally Czechoslovakia—the Communists used the blessing of legality as an aid to organizing an underground movement, and finally betrayed the liberties of the people and brought them under the domination of the Kremlin in Moscow.

These are the facts which today cause a menace to Scandinavia and western Europe. These are the facts which today present a danger of future world war.

Another mistaken impression is the claim that if we outlaw the Communist organization, we thereby endanger the liberties and civil rights of other people. This is not true. In Canada the party was outlawed for years and the people lost none of their liberties. In fact, the Communists were permitted to operate legally again under the name of the labor progressive party in 1943, and soon afterwards, in less than three years, it was found that the Communists were working directly with the Russian embassy at Ottawa in a spy ring.

In order that we might narrow down our discussion and find out just exactly what the differences are in our positions, I should like to ask Governor Dewey specifically these questions:

1. Do you agree that the Communist organizations throughout the world are directed from Moscow?

2. Do you agree that the objective of the Communist organizations throughout the world is to overthrow free governments, destroy liberties, and bring the countries under the domination of the Kremlin?

3. Do you agree that Communist organizations throughout the world are a menace to future peace?

4. Do you agree that because of this menace to world peace, it is necessary that we acquire American young men to serve in our armed forces and to take military training?

To make my position, then, clear, I say very definitely that it does not add up to me to say that loyal, patriotic young Americans must, of necessity, be drafted; that their liberties must be taken away in order to make America strong in the face of the menace to peace caused by Communist organizations, but that none of the privileges and blessings of legality should be taken away from the Communist organizations themselves, which in fact are causing the menace that makes the drafting necessary.

The fundamental principles of human liberty upon which this nation is founded are drawn from our basic religious concepts. Our founding fathers did believe that man has a spiritual value; that he is endowed by his creator with certain inalienable rights; that he should have a human dignity, a respect for the welfare of others; that there is a brotherhood of man.

The constitutional rights in America are based on that concept. When one speaks of the constitutional right of organizations that are seeking to destroy freedom there is a misconception of the deep basis of constitutional rights. There is no such thing as a constitutional right to destroy all constitutional rights. There is no such thing as a freedom to destroy freedom.

The right of man to liberty is inherent in the nature of man. To win it and to maintain it requires courage and sacrifice, and it also requires intelligence and realism and determination in the establishment of the laws and the systems of justice to serve mankind.

I submit that the Communist organization in America and in the freedom-loving countries of the world should be outlawed.

CHAIRMAN: Thank you, Governor Stassen.

And now, speaking for the negative, is the Honorable Thomas E. Dewey, Governor of New York.

DEWEY'S NEGATIVE

Mr. Chairman, Mr. Stassen, ladies and gentlemen: I am delighted to participate in this discussion with my distinguished confrere, and have listened with great interest to his eloquent discussion of the subject and of all the other matters which he brought up. He asked me four questions:

1. Do you agree that the Communist organizations in the world today are under the direction of the Kremlin in Moscow? Certainly.

2. Do you agree that the world Communist organization is a threat to world peace? Certainly.

3. Do you agree that the objective of these Communist organizations is to destroy the liberties of other men? Certainly.

Finally, fourthly, if you agree to these things, under what provisions of the Constitution—as I glance at my quick notes here—and what legal action, are you against outlawing them when we are drafting young men in time of peace to build up the defenses against Communist aggression?

The last question, of course, entirely begs the question. The question is not whether any one is interested in helping any Communist preserve his liberties. No one in America has the slightest interest in the Communists. My interest is in preserving this country from being destroyed by the development of an underground organization which would grow so closely in strength, were it outlawed, that it might easily destroy our country and cause us to draft all of the young men in the nation.

Now I find that the difficulty here tonight is that Mr. Stassen has not adhered to his subject or his statements. He says he is for the Mundt bill because, says Mr. Stassen, it outlaws the Communist party. But the fact of the matter is, he is in grievous error. The only authority he quotes is the head of the Communist party, which is not exactly a very good authority for seeking the truth. Usually, if a Communist says it does this, you know it does the opposite. So let's find out whether the Mundt bill does outlaw the Communist party. That is the first job. If the Mundt bill did outlaw the Communist party, then we would be able to debate here.

Here's what Mr. Mundt says on May 14, 1948: "This bill does not outlaw the Communist party."

On Feb. 5, 1948, Congressman Mundt said: "I have been one of those who have not looked with favor upon proposals to outlaw the Communist party or to declare its activities illegal because I fear such action on the part of Congress would only tend to drive further underground the forces which are already largely concealed from public view."

"What I want to do," said Mr. Mundt, "is to drive the Communist functionaries out of the ground, into the open, where patriotic Americans of every walk of life can come to learn their identity and understand their objectives."

Now, we have the head of the Communist party saying that it does outlaw it, and Mr. Stassen says so. Mr. Mundt, whose bill it is, says his bill does not outlaw the Communist party.

So, as between that debate, let us now see what the committee says. After all, here is a committee bill, and the committee presumably knows what its bill does. In short—I have studied the bill—what it says is that it shall be a crime to endeavor to teach, to advocate or to conspire to establish in the United States a dictatorship under the control of a foreign government.

Well, if that isn't a crime now, then I have greatly misread all the sections of the laws as they now are. But, before going to that—that's No. 1 in the Mundt bill. That certainly does not outlaw the Communist party. That simply says it is a crime to try to overthrow the government of the United States and establish a dictatorship under the control of a foreign power. And if that isn't good sound doctrine, I don't know good sound doctrine. But it doesn't outlaw the party. It says the Communists can't hold public office. Well, theoretically they are not supposed to hold them now. It says they can't get passports, and they can't get them now.

Does that outlaw the Communist party? Mr. Foster, the head of the Communist party, and Mr. Stassen say it does. Mr. Mundt says it doesn't. So, what does the committee say. The committee report—and this is the report of the congressional committee on un-American activities, whose bill this is—this committee has been widely criticized in our country because it has been called a red-baiting committee. As a matter of fact, it has been doing a fine, solid, good American job for a great many months. It has done a fine job of exposing Communists and bringing them out in the open, where they belong. Here is what the committee says about the Mundt bill, April 10, 1948: "Too often a cursory study on this problem leads one to believe that the answer is very simple, that all we have to do is outlaw the Communist party or pass a law requiring its members to register and the problem will solve itself. This is not the case. The Communist party in its operations presents a problem which is something new under the sun. It changes its spots, its tactics, its strategy without conscience." I am continuing to quote the report.

"Several bills before the committee attempt to approach this problem by outlawing the Communist movement as a political party. The subcommittee has found it necessary," and mark you, this, "to reject this approach." It seems perfectly clear that this bill does not outlaw the Communist party, and Mr. Mundt in the committee says it doesn't, but just to complete it, let me give you the rest of this point so there can be no possible misunderstanding that Mr. Stassen and Mr. Foster, the head of the Communist party, are wrong.

The report of the committee and the Mundt bill continues: "The committee gave serious consideration to the many well-intentioned proposals which attempted to meet the problem by outlawing the Communist party." Now I am skipping a little—no, I will read it. "Opponents of this approach differed as to what they desired. To bar the Communist party from the ballot, others would have made the Communist party illegal per se political. Several advanced an argument against compelling that approach." And then it gives them:

"No. 1. Illegalization of the party might drive the Communist movement further underground.

"2. Illegalization has not proved effective in Canada and other countries which tried it.

"3. We cannot consistently," and this is of the greatest importance, "we cannot consistently criticize the Communists of Europe for spreading opposition to political parties if we resort to this same totalitarian method here.

"4. If the present Communist party severs the puppet strings by which it is manipulated from abroad, if it gives up its undercover methods, there is no reason for denying it advocating its beliefs in the way other political parties advocate theirs."

It is absolutely clear that the Mundt bill does not outlaw the Communist party, was not intended to, and that is the exact opposite of what the Mundt bill has intended to accomplish and does accomplish. So let's get back to the debate.

Mr. Stassen, here in Oregon on April 27, said: "I hold that the Communist party organization should be promptly outlawed in America and in all freedom-loving countries of the world." And he repeated this in many states all the way from New Jersey to Oregon. That is the issue—not the Mundt bill. The issue is, shall we pass a law outlawing the Communist party. Now, I suppose, if you say, "Let's outlaw the Communist party and preserve our liberties," and if you say it fast enough and don't think, it seems to make sense. But, my friends, it makes no sense. You cannot do both, and no nation in all the history of the world ever succeeded in doing it.

The question before us is, shall the Communist party be outlawed? The only way I know that could be done is to declare by law that people calling themselves Communists would be denied a place on the ballot and that anyone who is a member of that party, after it, the passage of the law, should be tried, convicted, and sentenced to prison for a crime. I believe in keeping the Communist party everlastingly out in the open so we can defeat it and all it stands for.

Now, this outlawing idea is not new. It is as old as government. For thousands of years despots have shot, imprisoned, and exiled their people, and their governments have always fallen into the dust. This outlawing idea is as old as communism itself. It is the fact, and I might again refer, just to get our history straight, to the report of the House Committee on Un-American Activities. I quote from page eleven, no, page thirteen, of the report dated—well, I can't find the date. It is the report of the hearing before the subcommittee on legislation activities of the Eightieth Congress on H. R. 4422 and H. R. 4480. I quote from page thirteen:

"The Communist party was illegal and outlawed in Russia when it took over control of the Soviet Union."

The fact is that the czars of Russia were the first people in the world to follow this idea of outlawing the Communist party. They whipped them and they drove them to Siberia, they shot them, and they outlawed them. In the year 1917 Lenin and Trotsky were exiled. What was the result? This outlawing gave them such colossal following, such enormous popularity, such great loyalty on the part of the people that they were able to seize control of all Russia with its 180 million people, and the first nation to outlaw Communists became the first Communist nation.

That is what I do not want to happen to the United States of America. For twenty-five years Mussolini outlawed Communism, and they grew and flourished underground despite their punishment and their killing and their shooting. As a result, four weeks ago the Communists and their allies polled more than 30 per cent of the vote in the recent Italian election.

In all of Nazi Europe the Communists were underground and they emerged at the end of the war so strong that they were so popular the French Maquis and others almost seized power in the governments of Europe at the end of this war because of the enormous strength that came to them from the underground.

And Czechoslovakia is another example, and I am grateful to Mr. Stassen for bringing it up. For seven years in Czechoslovakia the Communists were forced underground by the Nazi tyranny, and in those seven years they developed such enormous strength that they were able shortly after the liberation of Czechoslovakia—which we could have done, but our troops were pulled back and the Russian troops were allowed to go into Prague—they were able, before long, to take over the whole nation because they had flourished in the dark, underground.

Here is an issue of the highest moral principle. In the present issue the people in this country are being asked to outlaw communism. That means this: shall we in America, in order to defeat the totalitarian system which we detest, voluntarily adopt the method of that system?

I want the people of the United States to know exactly where I stand on this proposal because it goes to the very heart of the qualification of any candidate for office, and to the inner nature of the kind of country we want to live in. I am unalterably, wholeheartedly, and unswervingly against any scheme to write laws outlawing people because of their religious, political, or social or economic ideas.

I am against it because it is a violation of the Constitution of the United States and of the Bill of Rights, and clearly so. I am against it because it is immoral and nothing but totalitarianism itself. I am against it because I know from a great many years' experience in the enforcement of the law that the proposal wouldn't work, and instead it would rapidly advance the cause of communism in the United States and all over the world.

Now, let's look at this thing. It is a war of ideas in the world, and we are in it. It is also a war of nerves. The conflict between two wholly different ways of life—system of human freedom and the brutal system of the police state. On one side of this great world struggle are ranged all those who believe in the most priceless right in the world—human freedom. We believe that every man and woman has a right to worship as he pleases, the freedom of speech, assembly and the press. We believe that every man and woman has an absolute right to belong to the political party of his choice. We believe, in short, that human beings are individuals and that they do and should differ among themselves. We know that each of us has within himself a portion of error and we believe that each of us has within himself a touch of God.

On the other side of this struggle are the advocates of the all-powerful totalitarian state. They believe human beings are cogs in a machine, God-less creatures, born to slave through life with every thought and every act directed by an overpowering, all-powerful government. Everywhere, these two conflicting schemes of life, the free system and the police state, are struggling for the soul of mankind. The free world looks to us for hope, for leadership, and most of all for a demonstration of our invincible faith. The free way of life will triumph so long as we keep it free.

Now, as in all the days of our past, let us hold the flag of freedom high. I have watched this proposal, this easy panacea of getting rid of ideas by passing laws, I have been increasingly shocked. To outlaw the Communist party would be recognized every place on earth as a surrender of the great United States to the methods of totalitarianism. Stripped to its naked essentials, this is nothing but the method of Hitler and Stalin. It is the control borrowed from the Japanese war leadership. It is an attempt to beat down ideas with a club, the surrender of everything we believe in.

There is an American way to do this job, a perfectly simple American way. We have now twenty-seven laws on the books, and I have the whole list of them in front of me, outlawing every conceivable act of subversion against the United States. I spent eleven years of my life as a prosecutor in New York. That was in the days when they said nobody could clean up the organized underworld. They said we had to use the methods of dictators, that we have to go out and string them up. I had judges and even men in high places tell me that. A group of young men took it on, and week after week, month after month, year after year, they worked and they delivered the City of New York from the control of organized crime, and they did it by constitutional means and under the Bill of Rights.

We can do that in this country. All we need is a government which believes in enforcing the law, a government which believes wholeheartedly in human freedom, and the administration of our government which will go ahead and do the job. I have no objection to the strengthening of the law. In fact, I have spent a good many years of my life endeavoring to strengthen the criminal laws of our country. And they should be strengthened. But let us remember for all time to come in these United States, we should prosecute men for the crimes they commit but never for the ideas that they have.

Now, times are too grave to try any expedients and fail. This expedient has failed, this expedient of outlawing has failed in Russia. It failed in Europe, it failed in Italy, it failed in Canada. And let me point out that in Canada they tried it once and the Communist party grew so powerful and dangerous that they repealed the law in 1936, and in 1940 they tried it again and the Communist party came right up with a dozen new false faces exactly as it would do if you passed the ludicrous law to outlaw them here. They would come up under forty new fronts. They would then say, "we are not Communists any more," exactly as they did in Canada—"we are just good Canadians working to support our government." And what happened. What happened in Canada is exactly what would happen here. They became so strong that during the war, in the face of a law which says it is illegal to belong to the Communist party, they developed the greatest atomic bomb spy ring in history, and Canada had to repeal the law.

Let us not make such a terrific blunder in the United States, that we build up these dangerous, venomous, subversive people with the power to overthrow our government. Let us never make the blunders that have been made throughout the history of the world. Let us go forward as Free Americans. Let us have the courage to be free.

CHAIRMAN—Thank you Governor Dewey. We pause now ten seconds for station identification . . . and now, to offer the rebuttal for the affirmative is Governor Stassen.

STASSEN'S REBUTTAL

Mr. Van Buskirk and your excellency, Governor Dewey; my fellow citizens:

Apparently we have narrowed this question down very much. It hinges now primarily on the Mundt-Nixon bill. The Mundt-Nixon bill says, "It shall be unlawful for any person to attempt in any manner to establish in the United States a totalitarian dictatorship, the direction and control of which is to be vested in or exercised by or under the domination or control of any foreign government, foreign organization or foreign individual, or to perform or attempt to perform any act with the intent to facilitate such end."

Now I hold that that directly fits and applies to the Communist party organization in the United States and in the world today.

The question then is: Does it so apply? Obviously you cannot and should not draft your law in such form that a mere name results in an outlawing. It is being directed by a foreign power, with the purpose of undermining the liberty of the American people and overthrowing our government, which is the key point. They are so doing. There should be no doubt of that.

Here is a quote from Louis Budenz who left the Communist party. He said: "We must understand then before we get to the meat of the matter that we are dealing with a conspiracy to establish Soviet dictatorship throughout the world."

Many such instances—Generalissimo Stalin himself said in the speech to the American delegation in 1928, and they are now reverting to that policy, the Communist party of America as a section of the Third Internationale must pay dues to the Comintern. All the decisions of the Congress of the Third Internationale are obligatorily carried out by all the parties affiliated.

In other words the decisions in Moscow by the Kremlin must be carried out in America, so that definitely and directly the Mundt-Nixon bill will outlaw the Communist party as it is now functioning in America and in the world.

In fact, perhaps we are coming down to a point where we can reach agreement. Although I heard the Governor say that he did not think the Mundt-Nixon bill would outlaw the Communist party, I did not hear him say whether he would support that bill. Now, if he will say that he approves of and will support the Mundt-Nixon bill, I will be satisfied that we have reached an agreement that we have thereby outlawed the Communist party as it actually operates and, therefore, we can go on to these other very important issues in this campaign.

I reiterate, if the Governor feels that he can support the Mundt-Nixon bill, I will agree that that is sufficient to outlaw the party as it is now constituted, and he can go on to other important issues in the development of Oregon and in America.

On the matter of the Communist party in Russia, the actual report, "The History of the Communist Party," which is an established work on what happened in Russia, states very positively that the Communists were not outlawed; the Bolshevik party, so to speak, were not outlawed in Russia, and elected six members to the last Duma in the last elections which were held. So, I of course realize that we cannot in these few minutes left in the debate check references, but I submit to the Governor that he should look up his references in the history of what happened to Russia.

Now then, the Governor says that we have effective laws now—seventeen of them—that all they need to do is use them. May I ask then why is it that the Communist party organization has been growing so strong in New York?

New York is the national headquarters of the Communist party of America. New York, with 9 per cent of America's population, has 40 per cent of the Communists in America. New York is the capital Communist center in America, and from that center, from the national headquarters in New York, they have been reaching out and infiltrating in the labor organizations of America, they have been prejudicing the sovereignty of this country and the harmonious relationships in labor.

Clearly, does the Governor not agree that they have been operating underground now?

It is not a matter of driving them underground by the passage of a law. They are underground and over-ground and they themselves pick out which one best serves their purposes in each instance.

Now, I submit so far as I have observed, there has only been one conviction of a Communist in New York in the last eight years and that was the publisher or editor of "The Daily Worker," and he was convicted for a libel against another editor that really had no connection with Communist activities.

If there are these laws now that are adequate, why have they not been used in New York?

Why have they not been used in the Federal government, and has the Governor of New York called upon the Federal government to use Federal law in cooperation with the state?

We found in a limited way in Minnesota, where we did have some Communist infiltration in 1938, which was causing strikes and violence and killings on the streets of Minneapolis, we found that we could make progress if we cooperated with the Federal government, the state government and the local government, moving together with the assistance of the loyal, patriotic American workmen; that we gradually weeded them out. We found we were greatly handicapped in completing the job because there was no law that directly related to the manner in which the Communists took their orders from a foreign power.

Let's be specific. If an underground order came from the Kremlin to the Communists in America, and they held a secret meeting at which it was agreed that they were going to seek strikes in certain essential industries and stir them up, we will say, industries that were going to develop some great dynamos or hydro-electric power, some great generators, or in another way interfere with the potential of this country, even though every fact of that secret move was discovered, there is no law under which we could act.

Or, suppose the underground word came and said that the Communists should move in around the Panama Canal and Alaska, and establish themselves in various jobs, and secret meetings were held where that was arranged. There is no law on the books of this country that would permit us to move directly against that conspiracy.

Under the present laws, you would have to wait until a move of force was made, or until they uncovered their hand in a very flagrant way.

What we need is a law that goes directly to the problem of the way in which the Communist organizations have been operating since the end of the war. They are the threat of war. We should not stumble along with laws that are out of date. We should bring our thinking up to date.

This is not a matter of outlawing any ideas. It is not a matter of any thought control.

What constitutional provision would prevent the kind of a law like the Mundt-Nixon bill? Which article of the Constitution would it violate? I know of none that says that an organization may carry on in the manner in which the Communist organization is carrying on now.

Therefore, it is open for legislative action. And I submit to the Governor that he earnestly reconsider his position and specifically, if he will say that he will now agree to support the Mundt-Nixon bill unequivocably.

Then I will agree that we have reached a point of union on this important issue, and we will go forward with a constructive campaign in Oregon on those other very important questions that are before the people of this great state and before our America in the wake of war.

CHAIRMAN: Thank you, Governor Stassen. And now in sur-rebuttal is Governor Dewey.

DEWEY'S REBUTTAL

Mr. Van Buskirk, Governor Stassen, ladies and gentlemen: I gather from Mr. Stassen's statement that he has completely surrendered. The Mundt bill obviously does not outlaw the Communist party. Mr. Stassen in these words has, from Oregon to New Jersey and back again, gone before audiences, the American people, demanding in these words that the Communist party be outlawed in the United States and in other free nations of the world.

The Mundt bill does not outlaw the Communist party. The only authorities Mr. Stassen cites for the fact that—for his claim that—it does, are the present head of the Communist party and a former Communist, whereas I point out very clearly that the author of the bill, Mr. Mundt, and the committee which sponsored it, both say in the official records of the Congress of the United States that the bill does not outlaw the Communist party.

Now, if Mr. Stassen says that that is all he wants, then he has completely surrendered, because he admits that he didn't mean it when he has been demanding from one end of this country to the other that the Communist party be outlawed, and he is willing to settle now when confronted with the facts for a law which the author and the committees say does not outlaw the party, which, of course, it doesn't.

As a matter of fact, there are—I made a mistake a while ago—there are not seventeen laws, there are twenty-seven laws in this United States on this subject. There is the 1938 act requiring all agents of foreign governments to register under penalty of five years imprisonment and $10,000 fine; the Voorhis act of 1940 requiring registration of all subversive political organizations; the Smith act, which makes it unlawful to teach or advise the desirability of overthrowing the government of the United States by force, or to publish any literature teaching, advising, suggesting, or to conspire to do so, all under penalty of ten years imprisonment and $10,000 fine—all of the things of which Mr. Stassen has spoken are covered by the Smith act, by the Treason bill, the misprision of treason, inciting rebellion, insurrection, correspondence with a foreign government—I am reading a few of the titles—criminal sedition, conspiracy, subversive activities, sabotage, broad conspiracy, inciting desertion, sabotage, non-mailable matter inciting mutiny, espionage, mutiny, sedition, conspire to commit espionage or sedition—that's about it—the list is endless.

The Mundt Bill is perfectly harmless, probably. I have some doubts about its Constitutionality. It supplements these bills in a very small way. It doesn't outlaw the Communist party. It may have the virtue of helping to keep them out in the open, because its main provisions are: that the Communists must register all their members and keep them everlastingly out in the open. That is a very good provision of law. The other parts of it, if they are constitutional, they are swell.

Now, let's get on to the rest of the subject. Mr. Stassen has surrendered. He is no longer in favor of outlawing the Communist party. He is now willing to be content with a bill which simply says what is practically already in the law and which all people in the Congress say does not outlaw the party. This is so dangerous, this idea. It is so fundamental to American liberties that I should like to enlarge upon it just a little.

Mr. Stassen has spoken of New York. He has spoken of our history. Let me give you just a bit of history. One hundred and fifty years ago the French were the Bolsheviks of the world. They had a violent revolution and they beheaded their nobility just as the Communists did in Russia. First, they had purges of the old government and then they had purges among themselves, and then they started rattling their swords for world conquest. It is just like the movie we have been through, and this is where we came in. We see the same thing now, 150 years later. Many people in the infant America were trembling in their boots just the same as Americans are now trembling in their boots. They were afraid for the cause of free government.

Let me quote from Chaffee, one of the great American historians. He writes: "In 1798 the impending war with the French, the threat of revolutionary doctrines by foreigners in our midst, and the spectacle of the disastrous operation of these doctrines abroad"—I am still quoting—"facts, all of which," says Mr. Chaffee, "have a familiar sound today, led to the enactment of the alien sedition laws."

These laws punished false and malicious writings, if they were intended to excite the heat of the people, or to aid any philosophic design of any foreign nation against the United States. The act created such a furor and opposition that the whole country was in turmoil. The only Federalist leader who dared speak out for the Bill of Rights was John Marshall, who later became the great Chief Justice of the Supreme Court.

Soon every person who was prosecuted, however violent the language he used, was treated as a martyr and a hero. Adopting what the historians Charles and Mary Beard described in their *Basic History of the United States* as underground political tactics, Thomas Jefferson wrote an indictment of the laws and persuaded the State of Kentucky to declare them null and void. At the next election Thomas Jefferson was elected President of the United States, and the Federalist party was utterly wrecked. Jefferson pardoned all the victims of these laws, Congress later refunded all the fines, and Thomas Jefferson's party held uninterrupted office in the United States for twenty years. That was the result of an early American attempt to shoot an idea with the law. You can't do it. And now that Mr. Stassen has surrendered in his outlawing idea, let's nail this thing down so hard no American will ever again seek to give the slightest impression to our people that it can be done. It can't. It is self-destructive. Even in the midst of the Civil War, General Burnside tried to suppress the newspapers that were hostile to our government. General Burnside put them out of business and Lincoln gave him orders to quit, saying in strong language: "It is better that the people hear what they have to say than fear what they might say if they were suppressed."

Now, we have a lot of Communists in New York; we have a great many of them, and they cause us great trouble. But we lick them. The number in the country is down from a hundred thousand two years ago to 70,000 last year, to 68,000 this year. In New York their influence is at the lowest ebb in their history. They ganged up with the Democrats, the American Labor party, the mis-called "Liberal party," and the PAC to beat us two years ago. The Communists labeled me as their public enemy Number One, and we licked them by the biggest majority in history. Why? Because we kept them out in the open; because we everlastingly believe in the Bill of Rights; because we know that if, in this country, we will always keep every idea that's bad out in the open, we will lick it. It will never get any place in the United States.[1]

[1] Used by permission of the City News Publishing Company, New York.

INDEX